EXPLORATIONS IN TYPING PSYCHOTICS

Explorations in Typing Psychotics

EDITED BY

MAURICE LORR

The Veterans Administration and
Catholic University of America,
Washington D.C.

PERGAMON PRESS

OXFORD · LONDON · EDINBURGH · NEW YORK
TORONTO · SYDNEY · PARIS · BRAUNSCHWEIG

Pergamon Press Ltd., Headington Hill Hall, Oxford
4 & 5 Fitzroy Square, London W.1

Pergamon Press (Scotland) Ltd., 2 & 3 Teviot Place, Edinburgh 1

Pergamon Press Inc., 44–01 21st Street, Long Island City, New York 11101

Pergamon of Canada, Ltd., 6 Adelaide Street East, Toronto, Ontario

Pergamon Press (Aust.) Pty. Ltd., 20–22 Margaret Street, Sydney, New South Wales

Pergamon Press S.A.R.L., 24 rue des Écoles, Paris 5ᵉ

Vieweg & Sohn GmbH, Burgplatz 1, Braunschweig

First edition 1966

Library of Congress Catalog Card No. 66-24021

PRINTED IN GREAT BRITAIN BY ADLARD AND SON LIMITED, DORKING
2850/66

CONTENTS

v

LIST OF CONTRIBUTORS

JONATHAN O. COLE
Psychopharmacology Service
Center
National Institute Mental
Health
Washington, D.C.

MARTIN M. KATZ
Psychopharmacology Service
Center
National Institute Mental
Health
Washington, D.C.

C. JAMES KLETT
Central NP Research
Laboratory
The Veterans Administration
Perry Point, Maryland

MAURICE LORR
Outpatient Psychiatric
Research Laboratory
The Veterans Administration
Washington, D.C.

HENRI A. LOWERY
Psychopharmacology Service
Center
National Institute Mental
Health
Washington, D.C.

NILS B. MATTSSON
Biometric Laboratory
George Washington University
Washington, D.C.

DOUGLAS M. MCNAIR
Psychopharmacology
Laboratory
Boston University Medical
School
Boston, Massachusetts

CHARLES E. RICE
Biometric Laboratory
George Washington University
Washington, D.C.

PREFACE

MUCH of this volume presents the findings from a large-scale study devoted to the identification of types among newly hospitalized psychotic men and women. However, the idea for the book grew out of a desire to offer a more extended series of investigations or explorations in discovering psychotic types. In many respects the present report represents a sequel to the *Syndromes of Psychosis*. The hope of developing an objective quantitative scheme for classifying the behavior disorders motivated the first effort and continues to represent the main goal of what is recorded here. Data from several chapters were collected within the framework of larger projects designed to assess the effectiveness of the newer drugs on hospitalized patients. The outcomes of these studies definitely suggest that eventually a specific drug will be found most effective with a specific patient type. This belief has also provided a stimulus to the type identification projects.

The book is written for students, teachers, research workers, and clinicians of any discipline in the mental health field. It is hoped that the university teacher and the researcher in psychopathology or abnormal behavior will find much that is provocative. The clinician may find the better established psychotic types a good basis for experiments with drugs. Psychiatric residents and students in clinical psychology may find here the beginnings of an objective taxonomy.

Chapters 4, 5 and 6 represent the outcome of a project entitled "An Approach to the Classification of Psychotics". This study, carried out in collaboration with C. James Klett and Douglas McNair, received partial support from a National Institute of Mental Health Research Grant (MH 06653–02). For this help we are most appreciative. For time, support, and freedom to follow our own bent we owe special thanks to the Research Service of the Department of Medicine & Surgery of the Veterans Administration. Acknowledgment is also due to members of the Psychiatry, Neurology and Psychology Service of the V.A. Central Office for their interest and endorsement. The Executive Committee on Cooperative Research in Psychiatry has followed our periodic reports. We are indebted to them for discussion and comment. It is also a pleasure to acknowledge the morale-building help of Eugene M. Caffey, Jr., M.D. From time to time, Thomas G. Andrews and Samuel B. Lyerly have given us critical but friendly advice. Finally I want to thank members of my unit for many hours of toil.

MAURICE LORR

PART I

PROBLEMS IN TYPING

CHAPTER 1

INTRODUCTION

THE major aim of the monograph is to present the findings from a series of explorations in typing psychotic patients. Because many of the procedures and approaches are relatively novel the first part of the book presents some of the theoretical concepts behind the classification process. The various problems encountered in designing and constructing a quantitative system of classification are described. A brief review and examination of most of the available methods for typing persons is also offered.

The typing investigations presented differ in four ways. First they differ as to the behavior situations they reflect. Descriptive data in the form of ratings came from the conventional psychiatric interview, the hospital ward, and the community. The studies also represent the evaluations of professional observers (psychiatrists and psychologists), nurses and aides, and relatives of the patient. A third difference is with respect to the kinds of patients studied. Both male and female samples were analyzed. Patients also differed in chronicity and duration of hospitalization. The fourth difference among the reports presented concerns the period of observation. One study is based on repeated measurements while the remainder are cross-sectional analyses. Fortunately all of the reports based on interview observations employ the same instrument, the Inpatient Multidimensional Psychiatric Scale (IMPS).

THE NEED FOR A NEW APPROACH

While the need for a fresh approach to the classification of the behavior disorders has been documented in detail in the preceding volume (Lorr, Klett and McNair, 1963) and elsewhere some discussion seems appropriate here also. Dissatisfaction with the present psychiatric nomenclature and diagnostic scheme is widespread. In much of American psychiatry formal diagnosis is actually ignored as relatively unimportant and outmoded, or

3

disparaged as undynamic and useless. What then are some of the main defects of the system?

An important complaint, well supported, is that diagnosticians disagree too much as to which class a patient belongs. Agreement among judges is best with respect to assignment to broad generic classes such as the brain disorders, the functional psychoses and the psychoneuroses. Agreement among judges for the more specific diagnostic categories, however, is far below acceptable levels.

Another defect of the system, frequently reported, is the high proportion of unclassifiable cases. Patients do not fit the available categories because the diagnostic classes are ill-defined or because the criteria of inclusion overlap too much. The diagnostic manual fails to indicate how many symptoms must be present or to what degree, before a patient can be regarded as a member of a category. The third and most important defect is the system's lack of validity. The diagnostic classes fail to indicate the treatment of choice. They are rarely useful for estimating the duration or course of a patient's illness, or length of hospitalization. The psychotherapist also would argue that a specific diagnosis is of little value to his treatment procedure. In short the system is unreliable, tends to be lacking in validity for ordinary uses, and is inapplicable to a great many cases.

From the viewpoint of measurement theory both symptoms and syndromes lack precise operational definition and determination. The length, scope and structure of the psychiatric interview is not specified. The role of the interviewer in eliciting behavior or reports from a disturbed individual is left open ended. Nor are the observer's evaluations characterized. Should they describe symptoms in terms of frequency, intensity or as qualitatively present or absent? In most instances no time reference is given for an observation. Should a symptom be evident in the interview, a week ago or sometime in the individual's history? The method of weighting signs and symptoms in arriving at a decision as to where a patient belongs is left undetermined. These are only a fraction of the measurement problems that are ignored in the present official scheme of classification.

By the 1920's Kraeplin's nomenclature had been widely adopted in the United States. Nevertheless, variations among teaching centers in the extent to which they adhered to the system was considerable. The American Psychiatric Association published a

Manual for use of hospitals for mental diseases in the 1920's. The *Manual* was revised several times but with few changes. A new nomenclature, published by the Army in 1945 emphasized Adolph Meyer's concepts of disorders as reaction patterns to life stresses and anxiety. In 1952 the *Diagnostic and Statistical Manual for Mental Disorders* (Mental Hospital Service, Washington) appeared. In all of these instances, changes were introduced by majority vote based on the modifications suggested by experts.

Even this brief sketch of some of the limitations of the present diagnostic system suggests the usefulness of launching a broad experimental, quantitative program to define the major behavior disorders. Such a program would first seek a set of uniform classificatory criteria. Since the measures should be objective, relatively independent and non-redundant, the statistical procedure of factor analysis might be tried. The factors identified would represent the behavior syndromes which are now established entirely through clinical observation. A factor analysis of behavior observations is a process not too different from what a good clinician does. When a psychiatrist identifies a syndrome on the basis of observations of a select sample of patients he notes that certain behaviors and signs go together and form a functional unity. He gives the complex of deviant behaviors a label such as "retarded depression". Factor analysis is simply a more systematic rigorous procedure. The same observations are recorded for all patients and the measured covariation among the variables on a standard patient sample are broken down into their several independent sources. A report of the present state of such an approach to data on psychotics may be found in a prior report by several of the present authors (Lorr, Klett and McNair, 1963).

Once the investigator solves the problem of selecting and measuring a set of characteristics (syndromes), on the basis of which individuals can be classified, he can go on to finding patient types or classes. The next chapter describes some of the methodological problems involved. The remainder of the book presents some of the findings.

THE BASIC CONCEPTS

Three concepts are used throughout the book and thus require definition. As ordinarily defined, a symptom refers to a sign of any change occurring during disease and serving to point out its nature and location. The term symptom will not be used here as a sign of a disease. As used here a *symptom will mean any deviant behavior, posture, attitude, or ideational process* accepted by experienced clinicians as an indicant of a behavior disorder or disturbance.

Another important concept is that of a syndrome. The term *syndrome will be used here to refer to a group or complex of symptoms that tend with high frequency to go together.* In medicine a syndrome means the sum of signs of any morbid state or disease. As used here, the term involves no such implication of a physical disturbance or disease. The disease concept carries with it the notion of an all-or-none characteristic. A disease like measles is something you either have or do not have. In the behavior disorders the concept of a syndrome is more like that of a personality trait or dimension. Here it is regarded as a continuous quantitative variable measurable in terms of degree. Another important difference between the disease and the behavioral concept is that the former is ordinarily something not possessed by everyone. Characteristics like anxiety, paranoid tendency, or depression are not only measurable magnitudes but are considered as being present in all individuals but in different degrees. It is assumed here that every individual can be measured and described in terms of all existing syndromes.

The third concept of importance in the investigations reported here, is the idea of a type. By a *type is meant a class or group of individuals who possess in common a set of characteristics that clearly set them apart from other groups.* Phrased somewhat differently, a type might be defined as a set of individuals each of whom is more like other members than he is like members of any other type. Consider, for example, the class of Hostile Paranoids. Each member is distinguished by high scores on measures of hostility and paranoid tendency and by relatively low scores on all other characteristics that define the psychotic disorders. Now it should be understood that members of a type can, of course, belong to types in other areas. Thus in each instance it is essential to define the domain of similarity, say, political opinion, psychotic behavior, religious belief, or morphological characteristics.

The next chapter will be devoted to a sketch of the steps required in developing a quantitative model for the classification of people into types. Later chapters will describe the psychotic types identified when objective typing procedures are applied to sets of systematically collected measurements of patient samples.

CHAPTER 2

TYPING AND TAXONOMY

Maurice Lorr

THIS chapter will present in broad outline the major problems involved in constructing a quantitative scheme for the classification of people into types or into hierarchically arranged classes. The problem of choosing and measuring a set of characteristics on the basis of which individuals can be classified is first considered. The estimation of similarity between individuals is reviewed. Next the problem of how to identify subgroups or hierarchies of subgroups in non-random populations is examined. Given K subgroups, recognizable and definable, another problem is to draw boundaries between groups so as to separate them optimally. The problem of specifying a decision function for assigning individuals to the types established is the final problem. The chapter ends with a sketch of some requisites for a valid and meaningful classification system.

TYPES AND THEIR VALUE

One of the most common steps in scientific investigation is the grouping of entities into classes on the basis of their similarity on one or more defining characteristics. The entities grouped may be objects, people or concepts. The type defining variables may be qualitative and categorical or quantitative and continuous. Of course entities may be classified in a great many different ways. A person, for example, may be classed as a Democrat with respect to his political views, as a Catholic in religion, and as a mesomorph with respect to body type characteristics. In general, people (entities) regarded as similar with regard to one set of classificatory variables are not necessarily more alike on another set than people in general. Members of a class or subset are necessarily similar

7

only with respect to a specified set of defining characteristics; similarity is not a general quality.

The nature of the types or classes will depend upon their purpose. If the purpose is special or restricted the type will convey less information and tend to be more transient and less general than a "natural" type. A natural class will have a great many predictive implications and be useful for many purposes. Gilmour (1937) has suggested that a system of classification is the more natural, the more propositions that can be made regarding its constituent categories. Natural, multipurpose types are more likely to provide a basis for advancing psychological theory and to relate to common processes, common structure and to antecedents of behavior patterns.

The single or special purpose classes are those derived for use in decision making. Should a patient be placed on chlorpromazine or given electroshock? How long will this patient remain in the hospital? Can the patient be safely released from the hospital? Each decision, each new treatment modality, and each separate prediction calls for the collection of data and the validation of new types and patterns tied to an external criterion. The basic difficulty is that such types or classes are narrow and lack scientific generality.

The scientific and practical uses of natural multi-purpose types are numerous. Members of a type are more easily remembered, understood and differentiated than people in general. Knowledge of type membership is also immediately useful in predicting behavior. A person properly classed as a Depressive can be expected to be dejected, pessimistic, withdrawn and slowed up. Another individual diagnosed as Paranoid is likely to be hostile, suspicious, and defensive. In general any subset of persons of identical or similar trait-profile will tend to be more homogeneous as to behavior than the parent population.

The integrity of the individual is preserved in types; whereas in trait measurement the individual is fractionated. When a set of K scores are viewed and treated jointly, higher order dependencies and interactions among the defining variates may be utilized if they exist in the data. As Meehl has shown (1950) two variables unrelated to an external criterion when considered singly may correlate highly with the criterion when scored for their joint presence or absence.

THE CLASSIFICATORY VARIABLES

The first problem in the development of a classificatory scheme is the selection of the criteria of classification in the domain of interest. The variables on which individuals are compared should be highly reliable, relevant to the domain of similarity and as independent as possible. As Cattell (1957) emphasizes, categorical variables are to be avoided if the attributes can possibly be measured as continuous-trait concepts, for they are inferior as measures. In general there is a loss of information in qualitative categorical scores where a graded variable is available and can be measured. But more important still, is the use of defining variables that measure independent dimensions or concepts. These criteria should be representative of, or a sample from, a specified domain and not a *ad hoc* collection of variables. Otherwise no stability can be achieved in the types that are isolated. For example, if interest is centered on the domain of psychotic behavior, the first task is to select a set of reliably measured and distinctly different psychotic syndromes. One method for the isolation of attribute dimensions is factor analysis.

THE EVALUATION OF SIMILARITY

The problem of assessing the degree of similarity between pairs of individuals on the basis of a set of classificatory elements or attributes is not a new one. Statisticians, psychologists, biologists and ecologists have contributed to their development. The type of coefficient of similarity (resemblance, association, agreement, connection) can be conveniently grouped into those based on dichotomous categories and those based on continuous variates.

As early as 1898 Heincke used a measure of distance to distinguish between races of herring. Pearson (1926) proposed the Coefficient of Racial Likeness for use in physical anthropology. Subsequently Mahalanobis developed from it a Generalized Distance measure. Since then an extensive literature on the measurement of resemblance has developed. A large number of simple indices used with binary data are described and reviewed by Sokal and Sneath (1963). Cronbach and Gleser (1953) have reviewed a wide range of indices used by psychologists. They show that most similarity indices may be subsumed under a general measure of distance between two profiles in K-dimensional space defined as

$$D_{ab} = \sum_{j}^{k} (x_{ja} - x_{jb})^2$$

Here j represents any of the K independent measures while a and b denote two persons. The set of scores for person a will be x_{1a}, $x_{2a} \ldots x_{ka}$, while those for person b will be x_{1b}, $x_{2b} \ldots x_{kb}$. Each score x_{ja} may be regarded as a coordinate of a point P_a in K-dimensional space, and each score x_{jb} will represent coordinates for a point P_b. The closer the scores of the two individuals, the closer the points P_a and P_b are in space.

It can be shown that each person's set of scores (his profile) can be differentiated into three components. His profile can be characterized in terms of its mean or level, the extent of scatter or dispersion of the scores, and the "shape" of the profile. By "shape" of the profile is usually meant those scores, either high or low, that distinguish it. Now D^2 or distance square takes all of these components into account. Most other indices proposed tend to lose information either about level or about level and scatter. For example, a correlation coefficient loses information about level and scatter. The correlation process involves subtracting out the means of each individual and equalizing the dispersion of scores. The effect is to increase the jaggedness of flat profiles and to decrease the score variation of jagged profiles.

While D^2 loses no information concerning level or scatter it fails to take other important conditions into account. It cannot recognize two profiles with opposite sets of scores. Nor does D^2 reflect whether the mean level of one profile is higher or lower than another. Cronbach and Gleser (1953) as well as Penrose (1954) suggest alternate formulas for separating out level ("size") and shape.

THE PROBLEM OF TYPING

The problem of typing is to determine whether a population of individuals may be regarded as comprised of a number of subgroups or whether it is homogeneous. Suppose, for example, a set of measures or observations are available on a sample of hospitalized psychiatric patients. The question is whether the sample might better be described as a mixture of fairly distinct types of psychotics. It should be noted that this is not the usual problem of discriminating between known groups, because neither the number nor the nature of the groups is known *a priori*.

As an aid to visualization let each of the individuals be represented as a point in three-dimensional space where each dimension represents a measure. Suppose now that there are several regions of this space with high densities of points separated by regions of thinner density. This separation of swarms of points into clusters or clumps would suggest that several different populations are represented. On the other hand, if the points form a single homogeneous mass and only one mode is visible, only one population may be represented. The problem then, given a set of measures, is to detect the existence of subgroups, their number and their boundaries.

The numerical techniques for defining or isolating natural types have been called "cluster analysis". Throughout the book the terms typing and clustering will be used as synonyms. It is important to observe that typing proceeds without resort to *a priori* notions as to the nature of the classes or as to their number. Instead, the analysis tests the possibility that the sample analyzed is not homogeneous but a mixture of several distinct and more basic types.

The clustering process begins with a basic data matrix consisting of K scores for N persons. The data matrix is then converted into a symmetric derived matrix consisting of indices of similarity among the N persons with respect to the K measures. The problem is to recover information about the grouping of persons given such a matrix. What properties must the groups have? Clearly the results will depend on the definitions of type employed. Each of the procedures described in the next chapter differs a little with respect to the definitions of type used. McQuitty (1961) defines a type as a subset of persons such that each member is more like each of the others in the set than he is like any person not in the type. Using distance measures, Gengerelli (1963) defines a type as an aggregate of points (persons) in the test space such that the distance between any two points in the set is less than the distance between any point in the set and any point outside of it. These two definitions illustrate that the subgroups identified can differ depending on how they are conceived.

THE DISCRIMINATION AND CLASSIFICATION PROBLEMS

The discrimination problem is one of differentiating between two or more groups of individuals. Fisher (1936) proposed the discriminant function as a suitable technique for this purpose. The method determines the best system of weights to apply to the various independent variables in order to produce a maximum separation between the groups.

Classification (also called assignment) deals with the problem of assigning one or more individual to one and only one of several possible groups or populations on the basis of a set of measured characteristics. It can be considered as a type of statistical decision procedure. The problem is to reach a decision, on the basis of the measurements, as to which population each individual belongs. The solution can be done according to various criteria: minimizing the number of misclassifications, minimizing the costs of misclassifications, and so on. The statistical procedures involved are known as discriminating function techniques (Lubin, 1950). It is important to note that discriminant functions can be applied only *after* groups or types have been identified. They presuppose the existence of known groups.

REQUISITES FOR A TYPING ANALYSIS

Typing or cluster analysis has as its goal the identification of homogeneous subgroups in a non-random population. No assumptions are made regarding the nature, size or number of subgroups present. However, there are a number of prerequisites for a sound and meaningful result. Some of the criteria for such an analysis are as follows:

1. The classes generated should be replicable under any arbitrary change in the scales of measurement (Saunders and Schucman, 1962). Whatever classification may be established, it should not be a function of a particular set of scales or items. This requirement suggests a corollary need for the widest possible input of information. All major sources of behavior variations in the domain of similarity analyzed should be represented. For example, should a dimension, such as anxious depression, not be represented in the defining measures, then certain types of depressive subgroups will not emerge from the analysis.

2. The classes generated should be replicable under changes in the sample of persons studied. Any type identified should emerge when analyzed within another representative sample. If, for example, a Hostile Paranoid is a psychotic type, then regardless of the sample, a Hostile Paranoid class should be identified providing members are present in sufficient numbers.

3. Nearly all subgroups in a given population should be present for a definitive analysis. A comparable requirement in factor analysis is that all known dimensions of variation should be represented by several marked variables. It is not possible to establish that a particular type is distinguishable and differentiable from other types unless related patient subgroups are included in the analysis. Suppose, for example, an Anxious patient group were identified. Is it separable from Anxious–Retarded patients? Unless members of both groups are included in the analysis, it will not be possible to determine their separate existences.

4. Each type identified should be definable in terms of relatively few of the classification variates. This criterion suggested by Saunders resembles the simple structure principle, enunciated by Thurstone, used in factor analysis. It is a principle of parsimony as applied to subgroups and implies that surely not all descriptive variables should be needed to define a type. Rather, it can be expected, that most types can be sufficiently defined as functions of a relatively small number.

CHAPTER 3

APPROACHES TO TYPING: A CRITIQUE

MAURICE LORR

THE chapter will be devoted mainly to a critical examination of the available procedures for sorting people into groups on the basis of qualitative or quantitative data. Methods like factor analysis, multiple scalogram analysis and latent profile analysis are examined first. Following this a variety of clustering procedures proposed by psychologists, statisticians and taxonomists are reviewed. Finally, a clustering procedure employed in many of the studies reported in the book is described.

STRUCTURAL MODELS

Before examining specific proposed procedures for grouping people into homogeneous classes the question of structural models should be considered. The most basic step in classification may be simply the grouping together of entities into classes on the basis of "similarity", "relationship" or "overlap". The classes emerging can be mutually exclusive or overlapping. If different levels of generality or inclusiveness are recognized, then some classes will be regarded as subordinate to others. Classification by subordination may go on to several levels. Such an arrangement is a hierarchy, or sequence of classes (or sets) at different levels in which each class except the lowest includes one or more subordinate class.

The method of grouping may involve a scaling or rank ordering operation of persons, with respect to a set of measures, on a single dimension or continuum. For example, a group of Senators can be ranked or scaled with respect to the extent of their agreement in voting behavior on a set of political issues. The Guttman scale and multiple scalogram analysis (Lingoes, 1963) represent such a structural model. Another structural model is latent structure analysis. Manifest data are analyzed to determine a number of mutually exclusive and exhaustive latent or underlying classes. The manifest-latent distinction is also central in factor analysis as well. There the persons and their intercorrelations are manifest and the factors and the factor correlations derived are latent. Whatever the structural model chosen it is important that it be consistent with the nature of the data. The structural relations of the objects and of the classes derived should parallel the structural relations basic to the model. Hierarchical models, for instance, should not be imposed on mutually exclusive classes. Dimensional models like factor analysis should not be applied to discrete subgroups. Preferably structure should be discovered rather than imposed in grouping objects. In brief, the structural model hypothesized should be appropriate to the objects being classified and to the relations among the attributes that characterize them.

THE METHOD OF FACTOR ANALYSIS

Factor analysis has often been suggested as a procedure for identifying subgroups within a heterogeneous population (Stephenson, 1952; Broverman, 1961; Nunnally, 1962). The method has a number of important limitations that can only be sketched here. The procedure is fundamentally inappropriate as it is designed to isolate dimensions and not "clusters". There is no logical reason why clusters of persons defined by one or more dimension may not be much more numerous than dimensions. The rotational process, for the same reason, is inappropriate for the task of isolating groups. The usual rotational processes tend to miss groups altogether or dismember them. If a cluster should happen to fall between two factors, each type-factor will be defined by persons on the margins of the cluster. Also, factoring tends to yield a multiple classification of persons rather than mutually exclusive classes. Unless a unifactor solution is obtained, and this is most unlikely, most persons will correlate significantly with several type-factors. Only a few persons will correlate substantially with one and only one type-factor.

When correlations or covariances between persons are factored, then all unrotated factors are bipolar and such bipolarity cannot be completely removed (Ross, 1963). One consequence is that groups with opposite score profiles (mirror images) will emerge on the same bipolar type-factor. For example, manics and depressives will tend to appear on the same type-factor. Thus each bipolar type-factor based on correlations is actually defining not one but two groups. In brief, the number of dimensions defined by factoring correlations among persons will not be the same as the actual number of groups.

The most cogent general argument advanced against use of factor analysis of measures of similarity between persons is that it does not yield unique information. The number and nature of factors resulting from a direct "R" analysis of tests and an obverse "Q" analysis of persons will be the same (Burt, 1937; Cattell, 1952; Harris, 1955; Slater, 1958; Ross, 1963; Ryder, 1964). It has also been contended that there are three types of profile factor analysis: correlational, covariance and raw score sums of crossproducts. However, if variables have been standardized over subjects, factor analysis of raw sums of profile crossproducts yields exactly the same results as factor analysis of correlations among variables (Ryder, 1964).

LATENT STRUCTURE ANALYSIS

Lazarsfeld's latent class model (1950) has been proposed as a method for isolating homogeneous subgroups. The technique analyzes the interrelations of dichotomous attributes or continuous variables. Manifest joint frequencies are accounted for by a set of q mutually exclusive and exhaustive subgroups (latent classes). The model assumes that each subgroup or latent class is homogeneous in whatever underlying dimensions are necessary to account for the observed interrelations. Stated otherwise, there is within-class independence between pairs of tests. The number of latent classes and the class sizes are determined by a factor analysis of the lower order joint occurrence matrix.

One question raised is how configural information from higher order joint occurrences can affect this solution. Lunnenborg (1959) has argued that the independence of items effectively precludes the possibility of configural information unless the latter is present in the sets of items prior to the determination of latent classes. Another limitation to the method is that it appears to be confined to variates of relatively small dimensionality—nearly always one. Most typing problems in psychology involve at least six or more dimensions. There is nothing in the development of the model equations that restricts the number of dimensions, and yet empirical examples involving more seem not to have been published. Another obstacle is that detailed descriptions as to how to conduct the analysis are not readily available.

MULTIPLE SCALOGRAM ANALYSIS

Guttman (1944) developed a scaling procedure for simultaneously rank ordering dichotomous items and persons responding to the items. However, the specification of item content was unclear. Recently Lingoes (1963) developed an objective and empirical procedure for selecting dichotomous items that meet Guttman's scaling criteria. The method, called Multiple Scalogram Analysis (MSA), yields a scale as well as an index of how well the model requirements are met.

The initial step in the scaling process involves the formation of a subject by item matrix of responses. Positive responses are denoted by a "1" and negative responses by "0". The investigator selects the number of errors he will accept between any pair of items in a given scale, thus limiting the minimum reproducibility of any scale. Next the persons are ordered from the one with the greatest number of positive responses to that person with the smallest number. If a person "responds" negatively to an earlier item but "responds" positively to a subsequent item, an error is said to occur. The investigator first reflects (changes 0's to 1's and 1's to 0's) all persons who have marginal sums of less than 0.5. The person with the highest marginal sum is selected as pivot. Then the computer searches for the person who has the highest agreement with the initially selected person and the fewest errors. If this person does not produce more errors than the criterion and passes a test of statistical fit, he is added to the scale. The process continues as described above until the person set is exhausted.

The advantages of MSA are that it yields a rank order among individuals on the scale and an index of how well the model requirements are met. Limitations of the method relate to the variates and to the nature of the classes that emerge. Most variates of interest in psychology are continuous rather than discrete. If the investigator regards it important to use cluster scores, conversion of such a score to a dichotomous form would represent a considerable loss of information. A more crucial limitation of the method is that the rank ordering of individuals is unidimensional. The same criticisms directed at latent structure analysis apply here. Types of interest are likely to be multivariate rather than univariate.

THE B-COEFFICIENT

Holzinger and Harman's (1941) coefficient B (belonging) has been frequently used for grouping variables. This coefficient is defined as 100 times the ratio of the average of the intercorrelations of a subset of variables to their average correlation with all the remaining variables. A group is begun by selecting the two variables which have the highest correlation. To these is added the variable for which the sum of the correlations with the preceding is highest. This process is continued, always adding a variable which correlates highest with those already in the argument of B until a sharp drop appears in the value of B. Another variable may then be inserted in its place, but if the drop in B is still large, it is withdrawn. Then excluding the variables already assigned, two others which have the highest remaining correlation in the matrix are selected to start another group. As an arbitrary standard for "belonging" a group of variables is required to have a minimum B-coefficient of 130. The B-coefficient procedure has many desirable properties but it fails to take into account correlations between clusters. The ratio assumes only that variables identifying a group have higher intercorrelations than with other members of the total set. Thus the method does not prevent clusters from overlapping. In factor analysis of tests this lack is unimportant; in typing for mutually exclusive sets additional limits must ordinarily be set. Another serious limitation of the method is that the point for ending a cluster is not objectively defined. Although the B-coefficient is still above 130, the addition of persons to the cluster is discontinued because there has been "a sharp drop in B". It would be difficult to computerize such a vague limit.

THORNDIKE'S CLUSTER METHOD

One of the earliest efforts to develop a systematic procedure for identifying homogeneous subgroups was reported by Thorndike (1953). The method is designed to subdivide the N specimens of a sample into K subsets under the restriction that the average of all distances between specimens within a subset be a minimum. The square of the distance between persons (D^2) is the index of similarity. The procedure begins by assuming that the two profiles which are the greatest distance apart fall into different subgroups. A third subgroup is established with a profile which is furthest away from either of the other two. Each cluster is built up by adding that profile nearest the pivot defining the cluster. A profile is added to each cluster in turn until all specimens are assigned. This yields sets of clusters of equal size. Profiles found closer to members of another cluster than to their own are re-assigned until further shifts do not reduce within-cluster distances. Increases in the number of clusters are made in the same manner until the average within-cluster distances relative to the number of clusters stabilize. While the procedure is comparatively objective it has some limitations, a few of which will be mentioned. For instance the goal of assigning specimens so that the average within-cluster distances are at a minimum involves a fair degree of trial and error and no criterion for optimal termination. There are no limits set in assigning profiles close to two clusters; every profile is allocated to a cluster. A process for determining within-cluster profile homogeneity is lacking; close profiles are not necessarily similar in shape. There also appears to be no justification for assigning every profile to a cluster, nor for seeking subgroups of equal size.

THE SAWREY–KELLER–CONGER METHOD

Sawrey, Keller, and Conger (1960) also have designed a procedure for grouping profiles on the basis of the distances (D^2's) between each and every profile. First an arbitrary maximum D^2 is set as a definition of "similarity". Then with each profile are listed all other profiles in the D^2 matrix whose D^2 is less than the maximum. The profile with the largest number of other profiles similar to it is selected to form a potential nucleus group. The profile selected and all those similar to it are crossed out from the table. The profile with the next highest number of similar profiles is then selected to become the second potential nucleus group. Again the associated list of profiles is crossed out from the table. The process is repeated until only profiles having no similar profiles remain. Next a minimum D^2 value is set for the definition of "dissimilarity" and a matrix of the selected profile D^2 is prepared. The columns of the matrix are summed and dissimilar pivot profiles are selected. Selection proceeds from the profile having the largest sum to the profile having the smallest sum. As a profile is selected all other profiles which are not dissimilar to it (i.e. whose D^2 from the selected profile is less than the minimum) are eliminated from the matrix. The selected profiles are all at least the minimum D^2 from each other. The centroid of each nucleus group (the selected profile and associated list) is determined. Each remaining profile is added to a nucleus group if its D^2 is less than the limit of dissimilarity from any member of the nucleus group. Several maximum limits may be set for adding in additional profiles to existing groups. There are other details, but the above steps describe the main process.

Consider now some of the limitations of the procedure. Only the maximum D^2 is used to form the nucleus groups. Distances among members similar to a pivot profile are ignored although they may vary greatly. Also the maximum limit as well as the minimum D^2 has no clear justification. Several maxima would appear needed to define similarity as otherwise a group whose members are widely separated from each other as well as from other groups will remain unrecognized.

THE ZUBIN–FLEISS–BURDOCK METHOD

Zubin, Fleiss, and Burdock (1963) have recently described a procedure, resembling Thorndike's, for fractionating a population into homogeneous subgroups. First the matrix of D^2's is scanned and the largest entry identified. The two profiles involved, say X and Y, then form the foci of two subgroups. About each of these foci separately is clustered each profile whose D^2 from the focus is less than the fifth centile of all the squared distances. About each of these nuclei are clustered profiles whose average D^2 from members of the nucleus is less than the tenth centile of all distances. The criterion of inclusion may be relaxed still further until every profile in the sample has been assigned to one of the subgroups. A profile that satisfies a criterion for both clusters is assigned to the group to which it is closer. The subgroups are then tested for homogeneity. If the clusters are not yet homogeneous, the next step is to identify that trio of profiles mutually furthest apart from one another or any other triplet. Profiles are again clustered about each of these foci and the homogeneity of the resulting subgroups is tested. This procedure is continued either until all groups are homogeneous or the number of groups to be found is so great as to be meaningless.

The method assumes normality of score distributions, and mutually orthogonal variates in each of the sub groups. Additionally it assumes equality of covariance matrices among the subgroups. Suppose the defining variates were mutually orthogonal and multinormal, then as Horst (1964) points out, configural nonlinear elements would have been eliminated. Yet it is with the hope of capturing nonlinear effects that typing procedures are pursued.

SAUNDERS' SYNDROME ANALYSIS

Saunders and Schucman (1962) have developed a procedure, called syndrome analysis, for the clustering profiles that is also based on distances between persons. It begins by regarding every individual in the sample as a cluster of order one. First, all pairs that are mutually closest to each other are identified. Then all triplets whose members are closest to each other are found. Clusters of higher order are identified by the same process until no more clusters appear by this process. The list of "closed" clusters is examined to eliminate those which are contained in larger closed clusters that came to light later in the process. The resulting list of non-overlapping closed clusters are regarded as "nodes" for the given D^2 matrix. The third step is to characterize the nodes. This may involve finding the mean profile of members of each node, or it may involve construction of the within-node–variance–covariance matrix of test scores. The latent roots and vectors of the matrix may provide the necessary coefficients for partialing out intra-node variability preparatory to iteration of the procedure. Once membership has been established the resulting aggregate is called a "syndrome".

The method appears to be effective as judged by the results reported. Studies are needed to compare the groups it evolves with those evolved through use of other methods. An unpublished preliminary comparison with the Lorr–McNair procedure (to be described, on the same data indicates certain differences. Saunders's method tended to carve up the D^2 matrix into smaller regions.

MCQUITTY'S TYPING METHODS

Since 1954 McQuitty has proposed and modified a considerable array of specific procedures for defining categories of people (McQuitty, 1954, 1957, 1960, 1961, 1963, and 1964). No review of all of these methods can be made here. This section will be confined to a brief description of several of his methods of "typal analysis".

1. The method of Linkage Analysis (McQuitty, 1957, 1964) classifies people into clusters such that every person in a cluster is more like some other person in that cluster than he is like any person in any other cluster. The analysis starts with a matrix of interassociations between persons. First the highest entry in each column (a linkage) is found and then the highest index in the matrix, say r_{ij}. Then if person i has the highest index in column j and person j has the highest index in column i, i and j are reciprocal. Pair ij constitutes the beginning of the first cluster.

Person j may also be the highest entry in some other columns, such as k and l. Then by definition of a cluster, persons k and l must be classified with j and consequently with i. Furthermore person k may be highest in another column m. Then by definition again, person m must be classified with person k and consequently with persons i, j, k and l. If none of the persons i, j, k, l and m is highest in any other column, the first cluster is completed. The highest remaining entry in the matrix is used to build the second cluster. In an analogous fashion, other clusters are evolved until all persons have been classified.

2. The method of Typal Analysis applies a more comprehensive definition of clusters. It is based on all of the relationships between persons as distinct from Linkage Analysis which is based on the highest interrelationships only. A type is defined as a category of n people such that everyone in the category is more like each of the

other $n-1$ persons than he is like any other person in any other category. The method starts with a table of interassociations between people. The next step is to arrange all of the indices of association in rank order. A modification of the method, called Rank Order Typal Analysis, arranges the indices of every column, separately in rank order. Then submatrices are built that satisfy the definition of type.

If a submatrix satisfies the definition of a type then it will contain no rank larger than the number of persons in the type. Suppose a type is composed of persons A and B, A being most like A and second most like B, and B in turn being most like B and second most like A. Then the submatrix constitutes a type if it contains no rank larger than the number of cases. These procedures continue until all persons of the original matrix have been chosen in order of their similarity to A. The problem is to select from the full matrix of indices all of the submatrices which fulfil the definition of a type. The advantages claimed for the method are that (a) it can reject an hypothesis of types; (b) it reports exceptions to a type. If typal analysis fails to yield types it is possible to relax the definition and permit inclusion of persons with slightly higher ranks than are permitted by the usual definition.

Whether or not types are found to exist, as McQuitty points out, depends in part on how they are defined. In fact the strength of McQuitty's approach is his explicit use of clear definitions. As with Saunders's method which presupposes a logic similar to typal analysis, the procedure yields relatively small initial groups. Since the classes pivot on a few fallible profiles it would seem that less stringent definitions would yield more useful and larger groups.

THE GENGERELLI METHOD

Like McQuitty's typal analysis, the procedure proposed by Gengerelli (1963) is based on a definition of a subgroup. Consider a population of N persons each measured on K variates. Let each person be represented as a point in K-dimensional space where K is the number of variates considered as relatively independent dimensions. Then a subgroup is defined as an aggregate of points in the test space such that the distance between any two points in the set is less than the distance between any point in the set and any point outside of it. Suppose N persons as points are distributed in three-dimensional space as two spheres, A and B. Two subsets will exist only if the two spheres are separated by a distance greater than the diameter of the larger sphere. The method begins with an N by N matrix of D^2's. A frequency distribution is made of distances between all possible pairs. The existence of one or more discontinuities in the distribution of distances indicates that a population consists of two or more subsets. The first point of discontinuity in the distributions, D_c, provides a criterion for determining the point of separation between two subsets. A subset is then defined as the aggregate of points (persons) who are mutually no farther apart one from another than D_c. The existence of subsets in a population is thus associated with multimodality in the distribution of inter-point distances.

The details of the proposed procedure are too lengthy to be given here. While the publication presents only a synthetic problem, the approach is provocative and appears promising.

THE LOEVINGER–GLESER–DUBOIS METHOD

This method (Loevinger, Gleser and DuBois, 1953) proceeds by maximizing the homogeneity of each subgroup and minimizing the correlations between subgroups. One condition is that the inter-correlation among the persons not be too high. Under certain restrictions the saturation, defined as the ratio of inter-person covariance to total covariance, is maximized for each subgroup. The method also assumes that the test variables are either given as dichotomous or can be reduced to dichotomous form.

The process is begun with a nucleus of three persons with high covariances among them. All persons who will lower the saturation are rejected. The one person is added who will maximize the saturation of the resulting group. The process is repeated until all persons are included or rejected for the subgroup. If the correlation between any subgroups approaches the geometric mean of their saturations, the members form a new pool for one or more subgroups.

One of the limitations of the method is that it assumes that the test variables are dichotomous or can be reduced to dichotomous form with a consequent loss of information. The method also assumes that a large number of profile elements will be available. If these measures are factors there is likely to be only ten to fifteen and there will be consequent loss in reliability. The denominator of the saturation coefficient for a single profile is the variance of the profile elements. Thus a flat profile with small variance is added too easily to a cluster.

THE ROGERS–TANIMOTO PROCEDURE

Rogers and Tanimoto (1960) have reported a computer program for the classification of plants. As in the Loevinger procedure the variables are binary and a simple similarity coefficient is used. After a matrix of similarity coefficients has been obtained a value R_j is computed as a measure of the number of nonzero similarity coefficients possessed by a given individual. Next computed is a quantity H_j which is the product of all the similarity coefficients of j with others. All persons are then grouped in a table in order of descending value of R_j. The person having the highest R_j and the highest H_j is considered the prime node. The problem is to find a criterion to determine the number of persons who go into a cluster. To do this a second node is found. The radius around the first node must be such as not to include the second node. At this point the similarity coefficients are converted into distances defined as $D_{ij} = -\log_2 S_{ij}$. These distances permit visualization of taxonomic similarity. Finally a measure of cluster inhomogeneity is computed. The method has proved to be fairly effective in isolating subsets when the variables are truly qualitative categories.

THE LORR–MCNAIR PROCEDURE

The procedure that follows is useful primarily for isolating clusters of profiles with a minimum of overlap when the indices of profile similarity are correlations or congruency coefficients (Harman, 1960). The distance measure (D^2) was not chosen as the preferred index of similarity between individuals for a number of reasons. No D^2 value has a unique meaning. A D^2 can represent a large difference between two individuals on only one dimension, or the sum of many small differences on all of the dimensions involved. Furthermore, in a matrix of D_5^2's pairs of individuals will be found who are (a) close to each other (low D^2) and similar in profile; (b) far apart (high D^2) but alike as to profile; (c) close to each other but very dissimilar in profiles; (d) far apart and with very dissimilar profiles. The D^2 measure also fails to take the direction of differences into account. Although two profiles may be mirror images of each other, i.e. represent opposite patterns of scores, the distance measure does not reflect this difference. In general D^2 blurs the distinction between profile and level. It is always possible to consider level at a later stage, if further differentiation of a group defined by the procedure seems needed. Also, level is not lost since it can be brought in by defining a group by the highest and lowest score on each classificatory variable.

The method implicitly is based on a type defined as a class of persons in which each person in the class is, on the average, more like every other person in the class than he is (on the average) like any other person in any other group.

Let it be assumed that each of the test variates have been standardized. Then given a matrix of coefficients the clustering steps are as follows:

1. For each profile in the matrix list all other profiles having r above the cutting point C_l.

2. Find the pivot—the profile having the largest number of associated profiles above C_l.

3. Find a pair by adding to the pivot the profile that on the average correlates highest with all members in the pivot list.

4. Find a triad by adding to the pair that profile with the highest mean r with members of the two lists belonging to the pair.

5. Search the entire matrix (exclusive of the profiles already assigned to the triad) and add successively to the cluster the profiles with the highest mean r with members already in the cluster.

6. Stop when there are no other profiles whose mean r with the cluster exceeds C_l.

7. If the number in the cluster exceeds 5 and this cycle is not the first, eliminate all profiles in clusters formed in preceding cycles that have a mean r greater than C_u with the cluster of this cycle.

8. Eliminate from the residual matrix all profiles with a mean r of C_u or higher with the members of each of the clusters already formed.

9. If the members in the last cluster are more than four, go to step (10); otherwise repeat steps (1) to (8).

10. List code numbers of profiles defining each cluster, the mean r within and between each cluster, and the mean r of each profile with each cluster.

Each cluster or type identified may be characterized (a) by the mean score on each of the profile elements, and (b) by the highest and lowest scores on each of the profile elements. A member of the cluster (type) is then one whose standard scores fall within each and every bound on the classificatory variables.

The choice of the upper and lower cutting points C_l and C_u is based on a determination as to when a correlation coefficient is significantly different from zero. For example, in the studies presented in Chapter 4 the profile was based on ten relatively independent variates. A coefficient of 0.55, based on ten variates, is significant at $p < 0.050$ while a coefficient of 0.40 is significant at $p < 0.10$. These values, introduced into the computer cluster program, proved to be effective in differentiating each sample into mutually exclusive subgroups.

EXPERIMENTAL AND THEORETICAL INNOVATIONS

A group at the Cambridge Language Research Unit has begun a theoretical and experimental extension of multiple classification based on Boolean algebra. Their approach is called a Theory of Clumps and seeks to find subsets of objects with the property that there be a stronger "connection" between members of a group than between a member and a nonmember. The person–attribute data matrix is replaced by a connection matrix consisting of indices of similarity between objects. A series of definitions have been proposed (Parker-Rhodes and Needham, 1960; Needham, 1961) and a number of clump finding linear programs developed. An experiment in medical classification is reported in which the grouping of patients suffering from diseases of the blood such as leukemia and Hodgkins disease was undertaken. The clumps or subsets selected were found to correspond to recognized diseases.

Another novel approach has been initiated by Forgy (1963). The problem posed was: Given a set of variables descriptive of individuals, how can "natural" clusters in the data be detected?

By a natural cluster is meant two or more regions in test space with high densities of points separated by regions of thinner density. The concept is seen to be the same as that suggested by Gengerelli. Forgy's proposal was to give the points physical properties so that they would actually group themselves. The points could be regarded as in a viscous medium, then the sequence in which individual points combined would provide information about the clusters. This "gravity-grouping" process and a picture-drawing process has been programmed and trials made on experimental data. On the computer trials with eighty cases and eight variates, none of five methods studied offered a dependable way to see clusters in sample data.

AN OVERVIEW

Any review of clustering procedures would be incomplete without some reference to Zubin's (1938) "technique of like-mindedness". Tryon's (1939) method of grouping variables with similar correlation profiles also should be mentioned. In one of the earliest reviews of cluster search methods Cattell (1944) classified these as (a) the Ramifying Linkage Method, (b) the Matrix Diagonal Method, (c) the Correlation Profile Method, and (d) the Approximate Delimitation Method. As Cattell indicates, all methods reviewed require, directly or indirectly, that some lower limit to the index of similarity be set as qualification for entry to a cluster. After some minimum is set the search is a matter of looking for linkages, the latter being defined as one above the established minimum.

A reading of the procedures described in this chapter reveals that other principles have evolved since that time. One technique is the imposition of a lower limit (Lorr–McNair) to establish subgroups that are mutually exclusive. Gengerelli's requirement that subsets be separated by a distance greater than the diameter of the largest is similar in purpose.

Another important approach is to generate clusters on the basis of sets that are mutually or reciprocally closest. McQuitty and Saunders both employ this technique to build up clusters. The requirement that the average of all distances between profiles within a cluster be a minimum involves a related principle.

Procedures that take into account within-cluster correlations represent related approaches.

The cluster method selected by an investigator will depend upon such matters as (a) the kind of variables used (binary or quantitative continuous), (b) the nature of the coefficient of similarity employed, (c) how much time it requires and the size of sample it can handle, and (d) his definition of a subgroup.

In the chapter to follow the Lorr–McNair clustering procedure was used to generate a set of subgroups within a sample of acute and newly admitted psychotic men and women.

PART II

INTERVIEW-BASED TYPES

CHAPTER 4

ACUTE PSYCHOTIC TYPES

MAURICE LORR, C. JAMES KLETT

AND DOUGLAS M. MCNAIR

THEORETICAL and methodological problems related to classification and typing were discussed in the preceding chapters. Some of the available approaches to identification of homogeneous groups of entities were critically examined. The present chapter will be devoted to a report on the evolution of a scheme for classifying newly admitted psychotic men and women.

THE RESEARCH PLAN

The study reported here had as its goal the evolution of a scheme for the classification of functional psychotics. Specifically the investigation sought to isolate some of the more frequently occurring psychotic types among patients newly admitted to psychiatric wards in state and university hospitals. Another aim was to evaluate the stability of such classes of patients as were identified.

Sixteen state and university hospitals and clinics contributed data on 374 men and 448 women. The interview-observer teams were located in Arixona, Arkansas, California, Colorado, Kansas, Kentucky, Illinois, Michigan, Minnesota, Nebraska, New York, Oregon, Texas and Washington. About a fourth of the teams consisted of psychiatrists, while the remainder were clinical psychologists. Each team attempted to examine a random sample of the local clinic or hospital intake.

Interviewers were asked to select only those patients who (1) manifested a functional psychosis; (2) were of at least dull normal intelligence; (3) were between 18 and 55 years of age; (4) had been hospitalized for psychiatric reasons either for the first or second time; (5) were without a central nervous system or other neurological disorder; (6) did not exhibit evidence of an organic or toxic psychosis; (7) had not been hospitalized primarily for alcohol or drug addiction; (8) were on a minimum drug dosage schedule when interviewed and for at least 3 days preceding. A "hospitalization" was defined as 14 or more days in length. If more than 30 days had elapsed since the previous admission, the new admission was regarded as the beginning of another hospitalization. Since manics are rare and depressives seldom appear in state hospitals, rule 4 was occasionally relaxed. If a manic or a depressive was encountered, he could be included even though he had been hospitalized several times for a recurring disorder.

The tranquilizer drugs are known to be effective. They reduce symptom patterns and thus obscure characteristic symptom profiles. Therefore it was deemed important to minimize their effects at the time of interview. Interviewers sought to keep patients off of tranquilizers until the interview was completed, or to arrange to have the dosage minimized for 3 or more days prior to and on the day of the interview.

Patients included in the study were all interviewed within 10 days of admission. The interview, which was from 30 to 60 minutes in length, was conducted during regular office hours (8 a.m. to 5 p.m.). The focus of the interview was on observable behavior and on patient self-reports of current feelings, attitudes and beliefs. The raters were asked to disregard social history data, as well as prior interview observations and ward reports.

An independent observer was included as part of the procedure to assure adequate levels of scale reliability and to provide checks on agreement levels. Ordinarily the observer remained silent throughout the interview. At the discretion of the interviewer, the observer could ask questions concerning topics neglected or overlooked. The observer was always present in the same room with the interviewer.

While the rating schedule was designed for use by experienced clinicians familiar with psychotic behavior and symptoms, some familiarity with its form and contents was necessary. For this reason, the interviewer–observer teams were encouraged to interview several different types of patients and to rate them independently thereafter. Differences were then discussed with a view to determining and rectifying the basis for the discrepancies. However, once the study was begun differences between observers and interviewers could be noted and discussed following the rating but no modifications were to be made in their recorded ratings.

THE MEASURING INSTRUMENT

The Inpatient Multidimensional Psychiatric Scale (IMPS) is designed to measure ten psychotic syndromes established by repeated factor analyses (Lorr, Klett and McNair, 1963). The schedule consists of 75 brief, unlabeled rating scales and dichotomous items. Completion of the form requires from 10 to 12 minutes and consists in recording each judgment on a separate answer sheet, the interviews preceding the ratings typically are from 30 to 45 minutes in length. The raters, be they interviewers or observers, are assumed to be trained clinicians reasonably experienced in interviewing psychiatric patients and familiar with their behavior and symptoms.

Each syndrome is defined by a set of scales, from five to eleven in number, that measure a unitary pattern of behavior. The labels given the syndromes are designed to describe the underlying response tendency. For convenience in referral each syndrome is also identified by three letters. The ten syndromes are briefly characterized below:

1. Excitement (EXC): The patient's speech is hurried, loud and difficult to stop. His mood level and self-esteem are elevated and his emotional expression tends to be unrestrained or histrionic. He is also likely to exhibit controlling or dominant behavior.

2. Hostile Belligerence (HOS): The patient's attitude towards others is one of disdain and moroseness. He is likely to manifest much hostility, resentment and a complaining bitterness. His difficulties and failures tend to be blamed on others.

3. Paranoid Projection (PAR): The patient gives evidence of fixed beliefs that attribute a hostile, persecuting and controlling intent to others around him.

4. Grandiose Expansiveness (GRN): The patient's attitude towards others is one of superiority. He exhibits fixed beliefs that he possesses unusual powers. He reports divine missions and may identify himself with well-known or historical personalities.

5. Perceptual Distortions (PCP): The patient reports hallucinations (voices and visions) that threaten, accuse, or demand.

6. Anxious Intropunitiveness (INP): The patient reports vague apprehension as well as specific anxieties. His attitudes towards himself are disparaging. He is also prone to report feelings of guilt and remorse for real and imagined faults. The patient's underlying mood is typically dysphoric.

7. Retardation and Apathy (RTD): The patient's speech, ideation, and motor activity are delayed, slowed or blocked. In addition he is likely to manifest apathy and disinterest in the future.

8. Disorientation (DIS): The patient's orientation with respect to time, place and season is defective. He may show failure to recognize others around him.

9. Motor Disturbances (MTR): The patient assumes and maintains bizarre postures and he makes repetitive facial and body movements.

10. Conceptual Disorganization (CNP): Disturbances in the patient's stream of thought are manifested in irrelevant, incoherent and rambling speech. Repetition of stereotyped phrases and coining of new words are also common.

IMPS (Lorr, Klett, McNair, Lasky, 1962) consists of 45 nine-point scales, 13 five-point scales, and 17 two-point scales. In order to equalize score ranges for the ten scores, simple weights are applied to each of the scales when combined. These weights are 1, 2 and 8 respectively for the two-point, the five-point, and the nine-point scales. A raw score for an individual is thus a weighted combination of the ratings received on the scales that define the syndrome. Finally each syndrome raw score is converted into a standard score.

In the present study each patient was rated by an interviewer and observer. The two raw syndrome scores received by an individual were combined and transformed into standard scores. The male patients were scored relative to the total male sample norms and the female patients were scored relative to the total female sample norms.

THE CONSTANCY OF PSYCHOTIC SYNDROMES

Are the same psychotic syndromes found both in men and women? The problem is important because any comparison of the sexes assumes the existence of comparable dimensions of behavior. The search for common patient profiles also presupposes similar psychotic syndromes. To this end an effort was made to ascertain whether the syndromes evidenced in the interview behavior of men were equally descriptive of women (Lorr and Klett, 1965).

The basic data analyzed consisted of the correlations among the 75 variables of IMPS. The two samples analyzed consisted of those male and female patients described earlier in this report. A hypothesis testing procedure (Horst, 1956) was utilized in the factor analysis. Of the 12 factors postulated, 10 were those previously isolated. In addition an Obsessive–Compulsive and an Apathy syndrome were presupposed. Each matrix was factored by the method of principal components. Next, a least squares solution of the *a priori* hypothesis matrix was obtained separately for men and for women. Tests of the degree of congruency between hypothesized and actual factor weights indicated a highly satisfactory solution. The indices of similarity indicated that men and women were very much alike with regard to the syndromes generated. Although the data indicated the presence of a small but separate Obsessive–Compulsive syndrome, and evidence for a distinguishable Apathy syndrome, neither was used in subsequent analyses. The Apathy factor scores were too highly correlated with Retardation to warrant separation at this time. The Obsessive–Compulsive syndrome was not scored separately because of its narrow variance and the desire to keep the present analyses comparable to previous investigations.

SAMPLE CHARACTERISTICS

The patient sample, drawn from 16 hospitals, consisted of 374 men and 448 women. The median age of the total group was 32 but the women were on the average slightly younger. Eighty-two per cent of each sample were Caucasian while the remainder were spread over several other ethnic groups. As far as religious affiliation was concerned, 69 per cent were Protestant, 22 per cent were Catholic and the remainder were Jewish or without any known affiliation. Sixty-three per cent of the men and 52 per cent of the women were single. High school graduates constituted 76 per cent of the sample while 24 per cent received 8th grade education or less. Of the men, 75 per cent came from a city or town, as compared to 85 per cent of the women.

Commitment to the hospital was voluntary for 37 per cent of the men and for 40 per cent of the women; the remainder were involuntary. The requirement that patients have not experienced more than one previous hospitalization was adhered to closely. Fifty-four per cent of patients had never been hospitalized before, 41 per cent had been hospitalized once before, and 4 per cent had been admitted 2 or more times. The distribution of patient psychiatric diagnoses at the time of admission is shown on Table 4.1. These are the diagnoses made by the interviewer–observer teams following the initial interview. Of the men 81 per cent were classified as schizophrenic while only 73 per cent of women were so classified. Depressives constituted respectively 14 and 21 per cent of the male and female samples. As may be seen from the table, virtually all diagnostic classes are represented. Most infrequent were the simple and hebephrenic types of schizophrenia.

Patient characteristics are described in further detail in the chapter on the validity of the types. Each of the actuarial variables is related there to the patient types evolved.

METHOD OF ANALYSIS

The computer program developed for clustering or typing is capable of handling simultaneously only 150 profiles. For this reason the male and female samples were partitioned into 3 randomized subsamples. Randomization was needed because data as coded did not arrive at equal rates from the 16 participating hospitals. The male sample of 374 was divided into 2 subsamples of 125 cases and one of 124. The 448 female sample was divided into 2 subsamples of 150 cases and one of 148. The typing program described in Chapter 3 was then applied to the correlations (Q) and congruency coefficients (C) among all members of each subsample.

Two measures of similarity, Q and C, were applied to investigate the advantages and disadvantages of each and to study the relative replicability of types based on each. The correlation coefficient is primarily a measure of the similarity in shape between the 2 profiles. The congruency coefficient takes into account not only shape but differences in profile level as well. The limitations of the distance measure have been discussed and will not be repeated here.

The results of the typing analysis posed several problems. The

TABLE 4.1

DISTRIBUTION OF PATIENTS

INITIAL DIAGNOSES

DIAGNOSIS	FEMALE		MALE	
	NO. PATIENTS	%	NO. PATIENTS	%
SCHIZOPHRENIC REACTION				
PARANOID TYPE	146	32.6	153	40.9
CATATONIC TYPE	28	6.2	14	3.7
HEBEPHRENIC TYPE	8	1.8	4	1.0
SIMPLE TYPE	9	2.0	15	4.0
SCHIZO-AFFECTIVE TYPE	32	7.1	21	5.6
ACUTE UNDIFF. TYPE	74	16.5	60	16.0
CHRONIC UNDIFF. TYPE	30	6.7	35	9.4
AFFECTIVE REACTION				
POOLED DEPRESSED TYPES	94	21.0	54	14.4
MANIC TYPE	23	5.1	16	4.3
OTHER DISORDERS				
PSYCHONEUROTIC	3	0.7	0	0
PERSONALITY	1	0.2	2	0.5

first problem was to determine cluster profile consistency. In the clustering program a profile was included if it correlated (on the average) 0.55 or higher with other cluster members. Yet it is possible, by raising the limit for inclusion in a cluster, that the consistency or uniformity of profiles could be increased. To determine the need for a new limit of inclusion, each of the ten syndrome scores of each member of a cluster was listed. The order or sequence of listing was in terms of the size of the average correlation of the cluster member with other cluster members. The profiles were then inspected for uniformity of shape and level. Whenever needed, a new limit for inclusion was set at that point where profiles became distinctly different from those preceding. Profiles below the new limit or cutoff were then excluded. The percentage thus excluded was typically quite small.

The second problem was to determine whether analysis of the correlations and congruency coefficients within and between subsamples yielded the same or different patient classes. It was necessary to match clusters across similarity indices and across subsamples. The clusters were first matched within each subsample across the two indices of similarity. Next the clusters were matched across the three subsamples. Finally a stratified sample was selected as a further check on the cross-sample and cross-index matching. Each clearly defined type found in at least two subsamples was represented in the stratified sample in proportion to its relative frequency. Analysis of the stratified sample provided not only a check on the accuracy of the matching but provided a test of cluster invariance. Any type or class evolved should be replicable under changes in the sample of persons examined providing it is represented in sufficient numbers.

Matching within a subsample across similarity indices involved several steps. Two clusters defined by a high proportion of identical cases were judged identical. In addition the ten standard scores of cluster members were averaged. Then congruency coefficients between the mean syndrome profiles of the two sets of clusters being compared were computed. Clusters were considered identical if the congruency coefficient between their profiles was at least 0.75.

Type matching across subsamples was also achieved by comparing the congruency coefficients between the mean syndrome profiles of the various clusters. Two clusters were judged identical if the congruency coefficient between their profiles was 0.75 or greater and all other indices of similarity were negative or close to zero. Such matching was checked by resort to the clusters identified in the stratified sample. When subsample clusters had been correctly matched their representatives in the stratified sample were nearly all found in the same cluster evolved. Thus the matching by congruency coefficient could readily be confirmed or rejected.

METHOD OF LABELING TYPES

The profile of a type can be characterized in terms of those mean syndrome scores that lie at some point above or below the general mean on the standard score scale. Since the syndromes are descriptive of behavior deviation, the higher the score the greater the deviation from the norm. Thus the most critical syndromes are those in which all members score above the mean. Syndromes on which all members of a type score below the mean are also important; they indicate the relative absence of pathology. On the other hand, syndromes on which members of a type score as frequently above as below the mean are simply undifferentiating and can be ignored.

For convenience and brevity let each syndrome be identified by a number as follows:

1. Excitement
2. Hostile Belligerence
3. Paranoid Projection
4. Grandiose Expansiveness
5. Perceptual Distortion

6. Anxious Intropunitiveness
7. Retardation and Apathy
8. Disorientation
9. Motor Disturbances
10. Conceptual Disorganization

Each type profile can be designated by a numerical label to indicate which mean syndrome scores are elevated 0.15 or more above the general mean. Thus a 1–10 profile means elevated Excitement (1) and Conceptual Disorganization (10) scores. Similarly a 2–3 type profile implies that Hostile Belligerence (2) and Paranoid Projection (3) are elevated above the mean. This notation will be used hereafter as a shorthand but objective way to identify each type.

THE RESULTS OF MATCHING

An initial question of interest concerns the number of types or clusters identified and the numbers of cases classified. Tables 4.2 and 4.3 indicate the number of men and women included in each cluster by index of similarity. The clustering process yields classes of decreasing size, the largest constituting 23 per cent (35 cases) of the subsample. The smallest cluster consists of 4 cases, a limit set by the program. Between 45 and 59 per cent of each subsample were classified into one of the clusters. Application of the typing process to the stratified sample yielded a substantially higher proportion of classified cases. Inspection of the tables reveals that the kind of similarity index employed is not important with regard to the size or number of clusters isolated.

4

TABLE 4.2

NUMBER OF CASES DEFINING EACH CLUSTER WITHIN

THE MALE SUBSAMPLES AND STRATIFIED SAMPLE

| | SUBSAMPLE | | | | | | STRATIFIED | |
| | .1 | | 2 | | 3 | | | |
INDEX	Q	C	Q	C	Q	C	Q	C
CLUSTER 1	23	22	9	19	16	21	22	21
2	15	14	17	9	13	13	23	24
3	14	7	8	8	6	10	18	11
4	7	8	6	7	11	7	5	9
5	7	5	6	6	6	7	6	12
6	4		5	6	5	5	6	6
7	4		6	5	5	5	6	7
8			6	4			5	4
No. CLASSIFIED	74	56	63	64	62	68	91	94
SAMPLE TOTAL	125	125	125	125	124	124	150	150
o/o CLASSIFIED	59	45	50	51	50	55	61	63

The results of matching clusters across subsamples and across indices are shown on Tables 4.4 and 4.5. The columns of these tables give the identifying numbers of the clusters as they emerged and the type each defined. For example, in subsample 1Q, cluster 5 defines type 1–10 while in subsample 2Q, cluster 6 defines type 1–10. It is apparent that neither similarity index yielded all of the types in every subsample. Nor did either index appear to be more useful than the other. Only in the stratified sample analysis was it clearly evident that a few different clusters were generated by use of the two similarity measures. One or two of the clusters in each sample are listed as "miscellaneous". These clusters were dropped because they were not matched in other subsamples, their members were

TABLE 4.3

NUMBER OF CASES DEFINING EACH CLUSTER WITHIN
THE FEMALE SUBSAMPLES AND STRATIFIED SAMPLE

	SUBSAMPLE						STRATIFIED	
	1		2		3			
INDEX	Q	C	Q	C	Q	C	Q	C
CLUSTER 1	22	35	20	32	22	24	23	29
2	15	13	13	7	16	12	22	17
3	15	12	10	10	15	13	16	14
4	11	8	9	7	9	7	11	10
5	5	5	10	9	9	6	12	9
6	6	5	7	7	5	7	9	10
7	5	5	4	6	4	5		6
8		4			5	4		
No. CLASSIFIED	79	87	73	78	85	78	93	95
SAMPLE TOTAL	150	150	150	150	148	148	150	150
o/o CLASSIFIED	53	58	49	52	57	53	62	63

inconsistent as to shape, or they were comprised of "flat" profiles. By a flat profile is meant one defined by syndrome scores all of which fall below the general mean. The last column in Tables 4.4 and 4.5 lists the number of cases included within each type after matching. These values do not necessarily agree with those of Tables 4.6 and 4.7 because the latter are based on a scoring procedure to be described.

TYPES AMONG MEN

The mean syndrome scores of each of the types identified in the male sample are given in Table 4.6. The figures serve to show the

TABLE 4.4

MATCHING Q AND C CLUSTERS THAT DEFINE

THE 9 MALE PATIENT TYPES

MALES: INITIAL

| TYPE | SUBSAMPLE | | | | | | NUMBER INCLUDED |
| | 1 | | 2 | | 3 | | |
	Q	C	Q	C	Q	C	
1-10	5	5	6	8			14
1-2-3-10	2	2	1	2	1	2	32
2-3			7	6	6	5	19
3-5					7	7	6
3-4-5			4	4	4	3	15
3-5-6-7-8-9-10	6	3	5	3		6	17
6	1	1	2	1	2	1	46
7-9	3	4	3	7	5		25
7-8-9-10			8	5	3	4	11
MISCELL.	4, 7						

shapes of the profiles and indicate as well the range of variation on each syndrome.

The 9 male psychotic types will now be described. The labels given each type are tentative and designed to be descriptive primarily. Conventional nomenclature was deliberately avoided since correspondence between types and official diagnostic classes has not been established. The 9 patient classes are as follows:

Excited (1–10) Type

The members of this group are characterized mainly by elevated Excitement scores. While high scores on Conceptual Disorganization are frequent, not all are above the mean. Occasionally patients

TABLE 4.5

MATCHING Q AND C CLUSTERS THAT DEFINE

THE 9 FEMALE PATIENT TYPES

FEMALES: INITIAL

| | SUBSAMPLE | | | | | | |
| | 1 | | 2 | | 3 | | NUMBER |
TYPE	Q	C	Q	C	Q	C	INCLUDED
1-10		7	5				13
1-2-3-10	2	2		2	2	2	32
1-2-3-4-5-9-10	5	3			(5)	(4)	11
2-3			2	6	4	7	16
2-3-5	4	6	3	4			10
3-4-5	6	8	6	7	5	4	13
2-3-5-6-7-9		5		3	8	6	17
6	1	1	1	1	1	1	49
7-8-9-10	3	4	4		3	3	33
MISCELL.	7		7	5	6, 7	5, 8	

in the group also manifest above-average scores on Motor Disturbances and Grandiosity. All other syndromes average well below the general mean. The Excited type corresponds most closely to the conventional manic type.

Excited–Hostile (1–2–3–10) Type

The scores of all members are above the scale mean with respect to Excitement and Hostility. Elevated scores on Paranoid Projection are also common. While the group as a whole is above average on Conceptual Disorganization, a fair proportion of members score below the mean. Thus the syndrome is only slightly differentiating.

TABLE 4.6

MEAN SYNDROME SCORES OF 9 PSYCHOTIC TYPES AMONG MALE PATIENTS

TYPE	SYNDROME									
	EXC	HOS	PAR	GRN	PCP	INP	RTD	DIS	MTR	CNP
Excited	1.29	-.65	-.80	-.32	-.53	-.68	-.48	-.28	-.03	.47
Excited-Hostile	1.42	1.39	.33	.05	-.51	-.75	-.74	-.46	-.29	.34
Hostile Paranoid	-.52	.80	.17	-.42	-.55	-.43	-.55	-.24	-.40	-.61
Hallucinated Paranoid	-.53	.04	1.24	-.23	1.32	-.05	-.24	.22	-.52	-.12
Grandiose Paranoid	.12	-.41	.20	2.02	.51	-.46	-.45	-.14	-.61	-.13
Intropunitive	-.46	-.63	-.80	-.54	-.43	1.15	-.45	-.45	-.44	-.62
Retarded-Motor Disturbed	-.70	-.83	-.68	-.56	-.55	-.30	1.43	.06	.52	-.26
Disoriented	-.43	-.84	-.93	-.60	-.38	-.88	.87	3.29	.39	.18
Anxious-Disorganized	-.50	.10	1.28	-.44	2.20	1.19	1.61	.62	1.18	.48

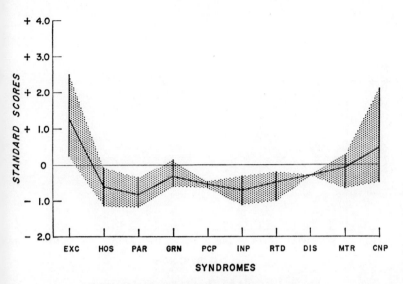

FIG. 4.1. Profile for Excited male type.

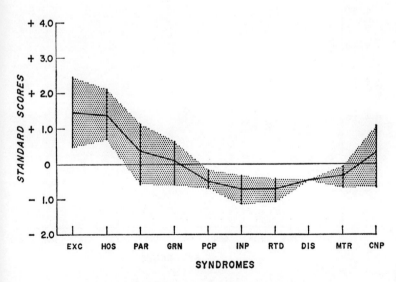

FIG. 4.2. Profile for Excited–Hostile male type.

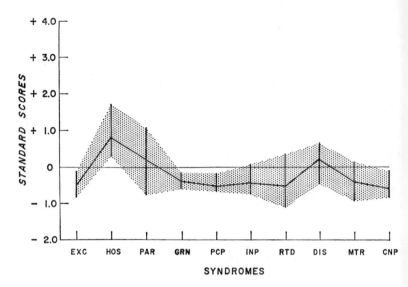

FIG. 4.3. Profile for Hostile Paranoid male type.

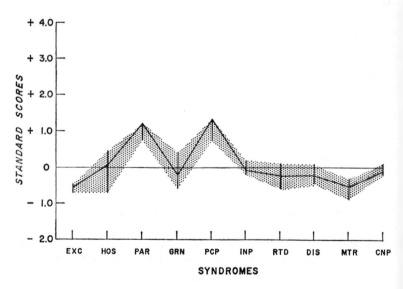

FIG. 4.4. Profile for Hallucinated Paranoid male type.

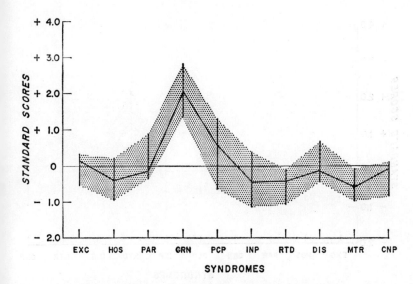

FIG. 4.5. Profile for Grandiose Paranoid male type.

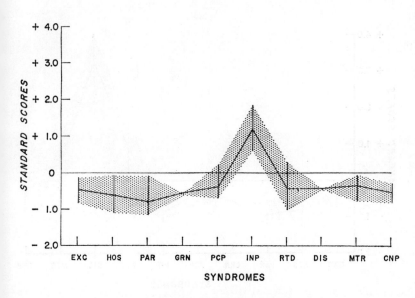

FIG. 4.6. Profile for Intropunitive male type.

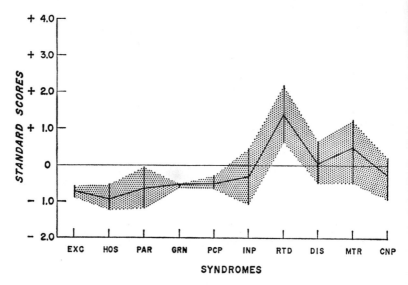

FIG. 4.7. Profile for Retarded-Motor Disturbed male type.

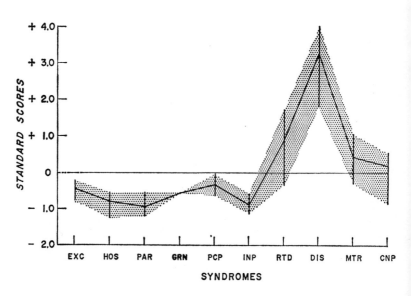

FIG. 4.8. Profile for Disoriented male type.

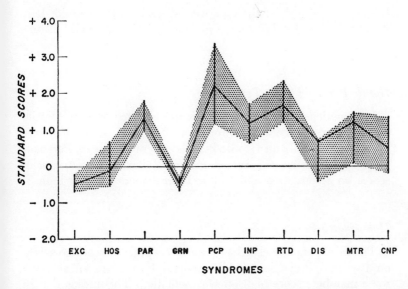

Fig. 4.9. Profile for Anxious–Disorganized male type.

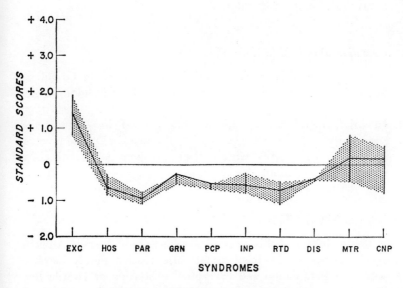

Fig. 4.10. Profile for Excited female type.

Roughly two-thirds of the type were diagnosed as paranoid. It is thus likely that the class represents one variety of paranoid disturbance.

Hostile Paranoid (2–3) Type

Most patients in this class have scores elevated on both Hostile Belligerence and Paranoid Projection. However, some members are elevated mainly on Hostile Belligerence or mainly on Paranoid Projection. Excitement is conspicuously low and occasionally scores on Retardation and Motor Disturbances are also high.

Hallucinated Paranoid (3–5–8) Type

The third paranoid class has as members patients scoring well up on Paranoid Projection and Perceptual Distortion. In addition some members score high on Disorientation. This means that in addition to delusional misinterpretation of the action of others as persecutory or conspiratory, the type members also hear voices that accuse, threaten or order. Diagnostically the group is nearly always categorized as paranoid.

Grandiose Paranoid (3–4–5) Type

All type members have extremely high scores on Grandiose Expansiveness. Most members, but not all, have in addition elevated scores on Paranoid Projection and Perceptual Distortion. In brief, members exhibit attitudes of self importance and superiority, and report the possession of unusual gifts and powers. At times they identify with well-known personalities or claim special divine missions.

Intropunitive (6) Type

The members of this class all manifest above-average Anxious Intropunitiveness. A few patients also receive mildly elevated scores on Retardation and Perceptual Distortion or Hostile Belligerence. However, the Intropunitive score is always highest.

Roughly 50 per cent of the group is diagnosed as Depressed (Psychotic or Involutional) while the remainder are seen as Schizo-Affective, Acute Undifferentiated or Paranoid. The Intropunitives are the most frequent of the types identified.

Retarded With Motor Disturbances (7–9) Type

Members of this class all have scores elevated on Retardation and Apathy. In brief, they are seen as slowed in speech and movement. Or they may also whisper, block, or fail to answer at all. Many of the class members also manifest high Motor Disturbances scores. This means they may posture, manifest bizarre or manneristic movements, talk to themselves and show muscular tension. The diagnoses for this group varied widely, the most common being Acute Undifferentiated, while others were labeled Depressed, Catatonic and Chronic Undifferentiated.

Disoriented (7–8–9–10) Type

This patient type is relatively small. Its members all have extreme Disorientation scores. In addition some members have high scores on Retardation, Motor Disturbances and Conceptual Disorganization. The most frequent psychiatric diagnoses were Simple, Catatonic, and Chronic Undifferentiated Schizophrenia.

Anxious–Disorganized (3–5–6–7–8–9–10) Type

The most striking feature of this class is the presence of anxiety in conjunction with behaviors indicative of disorganization or disintegration. All members of the type show elevated scores on Anxious Intropunitiveness, Perceptual Distortion and Retardation. Some members also are given high scores on Paranoid Projection, Disorientation, Motor Disturbances and Conceptual Disorganization. Patient members are typically diagnosed as Paranoid or as Acute Undifferentiated. It has been suggested that the type be labeled Anxious–Disorganizing in order to emphasize that members may be in process of becoming disorganized.

Thus the acute male psychotic sample can be viewed as including four kinds of patient classes. There is one Excited type and there are four Paranoid types, that is to say, Excited–Hostile, Hostile Grandiose and Hallucinated groups. The Intropunitives represent the anxious–depressive disorders. On the side of disorganization there are the Anxious–Disorganized who may represent transitional states, the Disoriented, and the Retarded–Motor Disturbed.

TYPES AMONG WOMEN

Seven of the nine types isolated in the sample of women are essentially the same as those found among men. The Excited (1–9–10) type closely resembles the male patient type except for a more elevated score on Motor Disturbances. As can be seen in Table 4.7 and from the figures, the four female paranoid classes differ little from the corresponding groups identified in the male sample. There is an Excited–Hostile (1–2–3–10), a Hostile Paranoid (2–3), an Hallucinated Paranoid (2–3–5), and a Grandiose Paranoid (3–4–5). The Hostile–Paranoid among women is somewhat more paranoid than the male variety. The Hallucinated Paranoid more frequently manifests hostile behavior, while the Grandiose type is less prone to exhibit excitement than corresponding male type members.

The Intropunitives (6) manifest a syndrome profile that is almost a duplicate of the corresponding male variety. The Anxious–Disorganized (3–5–6–7–9) resembles the correlative male class very closely with regard to Paranoid Projection, Perceptual Distortion, Intropunitiveness and Retardation; the female type, on the other hand, is distinctly less Disoriented and less Motor Disturbed.

The types that appear to be different from those found among men may now be described.

Excited–Disorganized (1–2–3–4–5–9–10)

All members of this class have much elevated scores on Excitement, Paranoid Projection, Grandiosity and Conceptual Disorganization. In addition, many score high on Hostile Belligerence, Perceptual Distortion (hallucinations), and Motor Disturbances. However, none of the group are disoriented. Evidently the Excited–Disorganized represented an acutely disturbed group. Members

TABLE 4.7

MEAN SYNDROME SCORES OF 9 PSYCHOTIC TYPES AMONG FEMALE PATIENTS

TYPE	SYNDROME									
	EXC	HOS	PAR	GRN	PCP	INP	RTD	DIS	MTR	CNP
EXCITED	1.49	-.62	-.89	-.25	-.55	-.58	-.70	-.39	.21	.17
EXCITED-HOSTILE	1.32	1.39	.49	-.04	-.57	-.49	-.65	-.39	-.28	.48
EXCITED-DISORGANIZED	2.13	.54	1.40	2.28	1.16	-.04	.13	-.20	1.51	1.81
HOSTILE PARANOID	-.63	.70	.41	-.42	-.53	-.58	-.59	-.27	-.43	-.55
HALLUCINATED PARANOID	-.51	.59	1.56	.04	1.73	-.44	-.42	-.24	-.52	-.56
GRANDIOSE PARANOID	-.15	-.07	.33	2.56	.36	-.79	-.47	-.05	-.46	.00
INTROPUNITIVE	-.46	-.51	-.67	-.52	-.45	1.13	-.33	-.35	-.47	-.63
ANXIOUS-DISORGANIZED	-.62	.13	.73	-.38	1.74	1.20	1.23	-.30	.38	-.33
RETARDED-DISORGANIZED	-.73	-.92	-.83	-.51	-.41	-.25	1.50	1.13	.38	-.19

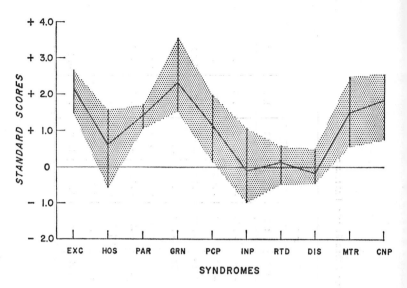

FIG. 4.11. Profile for Excited–Disorganized female type.

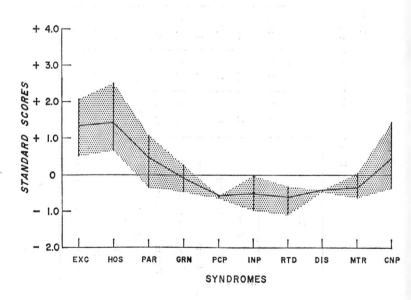

FIG. 4.12. Profile for Hostile–Excited female type.

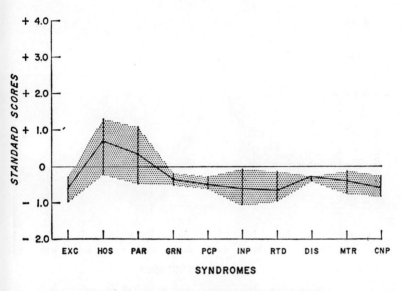

FIG. 4.13. Profile for Hostile Paranoid female type.

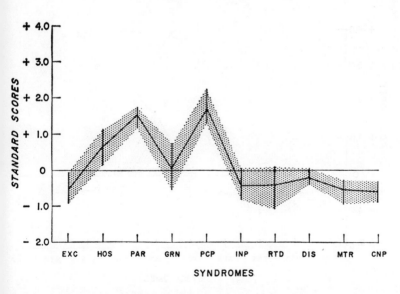

FIG. 4.14. Profile for Hallucinated Paranoid female type.

5

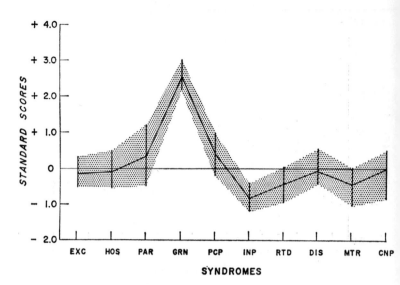

Fig. 4.15. Profile for Grandiose Paranoid female type.

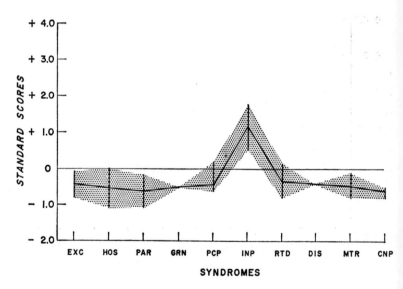

Fig. 4.16. Profile for Intropunitive female type.

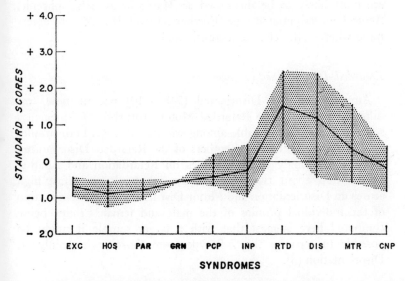

FIG. 4.17. Profile for Retarded–Disorganized female type.

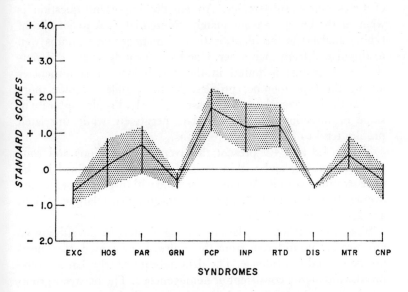

FIG. 4.18. Profile for Anxious–Disorganized female type.

are most likely to be diagnosed as Manic or as Schizophrenic, Acute Undifferentiated type. Further research is needed to determine whether the class is a transitional one.

Retarded–Disorganized (7–8–9)

Among men the Disoriented (7–8–9–10) patient type was differentiated from the Retarded-Motor Disturbed (7–9). Such a separation was not possible among women although both profiles appear among them. All members of the Retarded–Disorganized type have strongly elevated scores on Retardation and Apathy. In addition about two-thirds of the group also manifest high scores on Disorientation and Motor Disturbances. An examination of the individual profiles of the male and female groups being compared here suggest that with a larger sample it might be possible to separate the 7–9 type from those high mainly on Disorientation (8).

Differentiation of the Types

Thus far evidence has been presented for the relative constancy of types across subsamples. An equally important question is whether the groups are adequately differentiated. A major aim of typing analysis is the identification of homogeneous groups well distinguished from each other. One basis for judging the differentiation of groups is found in the correlations or congruencies among the type member profiles. As the profiles become more similar the intercorrelations increase positively. Profiles opposite in slope or direction tend to correlate negatively while unrelated profiles tend to have zero correlations.

Tables 4.8 and 4.9 present the average correlations and congruencies among and within each of the clusters defined in the male stratified sample. As may be seen the within-group coefficients average from 0.66 to 0.79. The between-group correlations seldom average higher than 0.25.

Since the average correlations among clusters in the subsample analyses are no different from those already presented, they need not be offered in evidence. The data indicate clearly that the type profiles are highly consistent or homogeneous. The between-group relations, on the other hand, are satisfactorily low or negative.

TABLE 4.8

AVERAGE CORRELATIONS AMONG CLUSTERS

OF STRATIFIED MALE SAMPLE

CLUSTER	1	2	3	4	5	6	7	8
1	.79							
2	-.33	.69						
3	-.44	.04	.72					
4	-.02	-.18	-.34	.70				
5	.01	-.24	-.21	.10	.77			
6	.22	-.07	00	-.42	00	.72		
7	.27	-.29	-.21	.34	00	.40	.72	
8	.32	-.12	.03	-.07	-.29	.27	.28	.70

TABLE 4.9

AVERAGE CONGRUENCIES AMONG CLUSTERS

OF STRATIFIED MALE SAMPLE

CLUSTER	1	2	3	4	5	6	7	8
1	.76							
2	-.42	.72						
3	-.28	-.27	.73					
4	.17	.11	-.43	.78				
5	-.42	.09	.15	.18	.71			
6	.04	-.09	-.31	.13	-.11	.74		
7	.18	.25	-.48	.01	-.01	.01	.66	
8	-.40	.24	.26	.07	.01	-.18	-.20	.69

TABLE 4.10

CONGRUENCY COEFFICIENTS AMONG MEAN SYNDROME SCORES OF 9 MALE TYPES

TYPE		A	B	C	D	E	F	G	H
EXCITED	A								
EXCITED-HOSTILE	B	.43							
HOSTILE-PARANOID	C	-.17	.33						
HALLUCINATED-PARANOID	D	-.56	-.15	.09					
GRANDIOSE-PARANOID	E	-.03	.16	-.19	.17				
INTROPUNITIVE	F	.03	-.41	.15	-.24	-.25			
RETARDED-MOTOR DISTURBED	G	.00	-.61	-.17	-.38	-.41	.19		
DISORIENTED	H	.06	-.37	-.21	-.13	-.23	-.16	.48	
ANXIOUS-DISORGANIZED	I	-.59	-.44	-.49	.54	-.21	-.28	.11	.09

TABLE 4.11

CONGRUENCY COEFFICIENTS AMONG MEAN SYNDROME SCORES OF 9 FEMALE TYPES

TYPE		A	B	C	D	E	F	G	H
EXCITED	A								
EXCITED–HOSTILE	B	.38							
EXCITED–DISORGANIZED	C	.11	.39						
HOSTILE–PARANOID	D	–.18	.34	–.50					
HALLUCINATED–PARANOID	E	–.52	.06	.15	.35				
GRANDIOSE–PARANOID	F	–.10	.06	.46	–.03	.28			
INTROPUNITIVE	G	.03	–.40	–.71	.10	–.32	–.40		
ANXIOUS–DISORGANIZED	H	–.66	–.44	.09	–.29	.49	–.22	.04	
RETARDED–DISORGANIZED	I	–.13	–.67	–.43	–.29	–.45	–.33	.12	.09

The entire sample of men and women was "scored" on each of the types on the basis of a computerized multiple cutting score program (see below). It was not feasible to determine the mean correlations within and between members of the types as in Tables 4.8 and 4.9. Instead the mean syndrome profile of each type was computed. Then, the similarity among profiles was determined by resort to the congruency coefficient. Tables 4.10 and 4.11 present the inter-congruency coefficients among the male and the female mean syndrome profiles of each of the types.

Among the male types the Hallucinated Paranoid (3–5) and the Anxious–Disorganized types resemble each other slightly in mean profile. The Disoriented (7–8–9) and the Retarded–Motor Disturbed types also show somewhat similar profiles. Among the female types the Excited–Disorganized (1–2–3–4–5–9–10) and the Grandiose Paranoid (3–4–5) show the greatest resemblances. However, in none of these instances does the congruency coefficient rise to the point where there would be doubt as to the difference between the groups involved. Further, it should be stated that the multiple cutting score procedure results in groups that are mutually exclusive for the present sample. Thus it can be concluded that differentiation of the groups is relatively satisfactory.

NUMBER OF CLASSIFIABLE CASES

One source of dissatisfaction with the current psychiatric diagnostic classes is the comparatively high proportion of unclassifiable cases. A useful typing scheme should account for a substantial proportion of all patients being considered. Earlier in the chapter it was stated that the types evolved included 55 per cent of the male sample and 53 per cent of the female sample. However, the typing program was designed to identify the major existing classes and not to establish decision rules for classifying patients. The question here is: what proportion of cases are classified within the limits set by the members of a type?

To answer this question a system of "scoring" was developed based on multiple cutting scores (MCS) for each type. The first step was to list the ten syndrome means and the highest and lowest scores on each syndrome for the type. Next a cutting score or bound was set for each and every differentiating syndrome. The nondiscriminating syndromes were ignored. The process was guided by two restraints. The cutting scores established should provide inclusion of nearly all cases defining the type and at the same time minimize the number of members held in common with other types.

The cutting scores or classification rules established for each type were applied sequentially by a computer to all cases in the sample. Finally, all cases satisfying the MCS for a type were listed by the computer. The nature of the cutting scores can be illustrated by the set constructed for the Intropunitive type. The rules, which are applied sequentially to a profile, are as follows:

(1) $Z_6 > 0.20$ (4) $Z_4 < 0.20$

(2) $Z_6 > Z_1, Z_2 \ldots Z_5, Z_7 \ldots Z_{10}$ (5) $Z_3, Z_8, Z_9, Z_{10} < 0.55$

(3) $Z_1 < 1.00$ (6) $Z_2, Z_5 < 0.80$

Expressed in words, $Z_6 > 0.20$, means that the sixth syndrome score must be greater than 0.20. The remaining five rules are self-evident.

It was possible to set common multiple cutting scores for both men and women for six of the types. Three of the male types and three of the female types required separate MCS. Furthermore, application of the MCS's revealed that the procedure kept the types mutually exclusive; no patient was assigned to more than one type by the rules. The scoring criteria are given in Table 4.16.

The number of cases assigned to each type by the multiple cutting score procedure are given in Tables 4.12 and 4.13. In all, 61 per cent of the men and 59 per cent of the women were classified. Thus, simply allowing the type members to define the limits on each syndrome, roughly 60 per cent of cases can be classified.

The MCS procedure is, of course, not the optimum method for assigning N patients, scored on Q syndromes, to a set of mutually exclusive categories. Theoretically the optimum solution is to develop and apply a set of discriminating functions with the aim of minimizing the number of misclassifications. Such functions were developed but will not be reported here. Instead each case unassigned by MCS was correlated with the mean syndrome profile of each type. If a case correlated 0.55 or higher with one or more of the type profiles, it was allocated to the class with which it correlated highest. The value of 0.55 was selected because a

TABLE 4.12

NUMBER AND PER CENT MALES CLASSIFIED BY
MULTIPLE CUTTING SCORES (MCS) AND BY R

TYPE	MCS	R	TOTAL	% CLASSIFIED
1-10	18	7	25	8.1
1-2-3-10	39	8	47	15.3
3-5	9	6	15	4.9
3-4-5	21	11	32	10.4
6	51	12	63	20.5
2-3	28	8	36	11.7
7-9	30	7	37	12.1
7-8-9	11	11	22	7.2
3-5-6-7-8-9	19	10	30	9.8
TOTAL	226	81	307	
% OF CLASSIFIED	73.6	26.4	100	

correlation based on a sample of ten is significant at $p < 0.05$ at this point. Using the correlation procedure another 21 per cent of the men and 19 per cent of the women could be assigned to one of the types. Thus these fairly simple methods show that the types account for about 80 per cent of all cases.

COMPARISONS WITH PRIOR ANALYSES

Two prior analyses of IMPS profiles have been published. The initial study described six syndrome-based types found among relatively more chronic male patients (Lorr, Klett and McNair, 1963). The second study (McNair, Lorr and Hemingway, 1964) identified nine patient types among a sample of newly admitted acute schizophrenics.

Data concerning the second schizophrenic sample came from a Phenothyiazine study by the Psychopharmacology Service Center of the National Institute of Mental Health (NIMH–PSC, 1964).

TABLE 4.13

NUMBER AND PER CENT FEMALES CLASSIFIED BY

MULTIPLE CUTTING SCORES (MCS) AND BY R

TYPE	MCS	R	TOTAL	% CLASSIFIED
1–10	19	10	29	8.3
1–2–3–10	37	11	48	13.7
3–5	12	8	20	5.7
3–4–5	17	9	26	7.4
6	66	7	73	20.8
2–3	34	8	42	12.0
7–8–9	54	8	62	17.6
1–3–4–5–9–10	12	9	21	6.0
3–5–6–7–9	13	17	30	8.5
TOTAL	264	87	351	
% OF CLASSIFIED	75.2	24.8	100	

From a total sample of 425 patients a subsample of 150 men and two subsamples of 108 women were randomly selected for the analysis. The NIMH sample ranged in age from 16 to 40 with a mean of 28 years. The IMPS profiles were based on two independent ratings of each patient interviewed just prior to assignment to a drug treatment group. The ratings followed a psychiatric interview of approximately 1 hour's duration. Since the NIMH sample was similar to the normative sample, the combined raw scores were converted into standard scores by reference to the tabled norms in the Manual (Lorr, Klett, McNair and Lasky, 1962).

The ten standard score profiles within each of the three subsamples were intercorrelated. The clustering process described in the previous chapter was applied to the two female subsamples. The procedures for typing the male subsample were somewhat different. The multiple cutting score procedure, similar to the one just described, was used to classify the male profiles into one of the six psychotic types found in the initial study (Lorr, Klett and McNair, 1963). In addition, a search was made for new patient types.

All six types identified in earlier work were confirmed in at least one NIMH subsample. Most types were replicated in two or three subsamples. Three new types were also identified and replicated. Table 4.14 presents the mean standard scores of the nine patient types isolated. Of this set all except two types were found among both men and women. The Excited–Hostile (1–2) and the Retarded–Intropunitive (6–7) were found only among women.

TABLE 4.14

MEAN STANDARD SCORES OF 9 NIMH PATIENT TYPES

	SYNDROMES									
TYPE	EXC	HOS	PAR	GRN	PCP	INP	RTD	DIS	MTR	CNP
1-4-10	1.4	.0	.0	2.0	.0	-.7	-.7	-.2	.0	.2
1-2	1.8	.7	-.3	-.3	-.7	-.7	-.9	-.4	-.1	-.2
1-2-3-4-10	1.4	1.4	1.1	2.0	.0	-.9	-.9	-.3	-.1	.6
2-3	.0	1.2	.9	-.4	-.4	-.5	-.7	-.3	-.4	-.2
3-5-6	-.6	-.2	1.2	-.4	1.2	.3	-.6	.0	-.4	-.6
6	-.2	-.1	-.7	-.4	-.6	1.2	-.5	-.3	-.4	-.4
6-7	-.8	-.8	-.4	-.6	-.5	.7	.4	-.3	-.7	-.4
7	-.6	-.2	-.8	-.5	-.4	-.5	1.2	-.1	.0	-.4
7-8-9	.0	-.4	-.8	-.4	-.4	-.6	.7	3.6	1.3	.1

The degree of similarity between seven of the NIMH types and the comparable acute psychotic male types reported here was evaluated by means of the congruency coefficient. The results are presented in Table 4.15. As may be seen five of the types in the two studies agreed quite closely. In addition, the Excited (1–10) type correlated 0.40 with NIMH Excited Grandiose type (1–4–10). The Grandiose Paranoid (3–4–5) resembled NIMH Excited–Hostile–Paranoid–Grandiose (1–2–3–4) to the extent of 0.60. However, there is some doubt concerning the differentiation of the NIMH type 1–2–3–4 from other patient classes. Its mean profile congruency coefficients with the mean profiles of the NIMH Hostile Paranoid, Excited–Hostile, and Excited–Grandiose are 0.57, 0.61 and 0.83. These coefficients are large enough to suggest that type 1–2–3–4 is insufficiently separated from the other types.

TABLE 4.15

CONGRUENCY COEFFICIENTS BETWEEN NIMH

AND NON-NIMH TYPES

TYPE	NON-NIMH PROFILE ·	NIMH PROFILE	C
EXCITED-HOSTILE	1-2-3-10	1-2	0.89
HOSTILE PARANOID	2-3	2-3	0.82
HALLUCINATED PARANOID	3-5	3-5-6	0.92
INTROPUNITIVE	6	6	0.94
RETARDED-DISORGANIZED	7-8-9	7-8-9	0.95

At this point it is pertinent to point out that the scoring keys for the norm sample of the *Manual* and for the present study differ slightly. Item No. 15 (Attitude of superiority) was dropped from the Excitement syndrome. Item No. 30 (Slovenly appearance) was eliminated from Motor Disturbances and added to Retardation. Thus the syndrome profiles compared do have slightly different meanings.

Comparisons with the six types found in the original study will not be made. The data in which the six types were identified have been re-scored, using the new keys, and re-analyzed by computer. The findings from the re-analysis will be presented in a later chapter on more chronic psychiatric patients.

TABLE 4.16

LIMITS FOR THE ACUTE PATIENT TYPES

TYPE	LIMITS COMMON TO MEN AND WOMEN
EXCITED	$z_1 > z_2,\ z_3,\ z_5\ \cdots\ z_8$
	$z_1 > .17$
	$z_2,\ z_3,\ < .12$
	$z_4 < 1.00$
	$z_5,\ z_6 < .35$
	$z_7,\ z_8 < .70$
EXCITED-HOSTILE	$z_1,\ z_2 > .20$
	$z_1,\ z_2 > z_4\ \cdots\ z_9$
	$z_4 < 1.40$
	$z_5,\ z_6,\ z_8 < .51$
	$z_7 < .10$
	$z_9 < .70$
HOSTILE PARANOID	z_2 OR $z_3 > .30$
	$z_2 > z_4\ \cdots\ z_7,\ z_9;$ IF LESS, THEN
	$z_3 > z_4\ \cdots\ z_7,\ z_9$
	$z_1 < .00$
	$z_4,\ z_5,\ z_{10} < .30$
	$z_6 < .45$
	$z_7,\ z_9 < .92$

TABLE 4.16 (*continued*)

TYPE	LIMITS COMMON TO MEN AND WOMEN (CONTINUED)
HALLUCINATED PARANOID	$Z_3, Z_5 > .37$
	$Z_3, Z_5 > Z_1, Z_2, Z_4, Z_6, Z_7$
	$Z_1, Z_6, Z_7, Z_9, Z_{10} < .56$
	$Z_4 < 1.00$
INTROPUNITIVE	$Z_6 > .20$
	$Z_6 > Z_1, Z_2 \ldots Z_5, Z_7 \ldots Z_{10}$
	$Z_1 < 1.10$
	$Z_4 < .20$
	$Z_3, Z_8, Z_9, Z_{10} < .55$
	$Z_2, Z_5 < .80$
GRANDIOSE PARANOID	$Z_4 > 1.10$
	$Z_4 > Z_1, Z_2, Z_3, Z_7, Z_8$
	$Z_1, Z_2 < 1.00$
	$Z_3 < 1.75$
	$Z_6 < .85$
	$Z_9 < .55$

TABLE 4.16 *(continued)*

TYPE	LIMITS COMMON TO MEN
RETARDED-MOTOR DISTURBED	$Z_7 > .20$
	$Z_7 > Z_3, Z_6, Z_8, Z_{10}$
	$Z_1, Z_2, Z_4 < .05$
	$Z_3, Z_6 < .95$
	$Z_5 < .20$
ANXIOUS-DISORGANIZED	$Z_3, Z_6 > .20$
	$Z_5 > .60$
	$Z_7 > .40$
	$Z_1 < .20$
	$Z_4 < .50$
DISORIENTED	$Z_8 > Z_1, Z_7, Z_9, Z_{10}$
	$Z_8 > 1.50$
	$Z_2, Z_3, Z_4, Z_6 < 00$
	$Z_5 < .50$

TABLE 4.16 *(continued)*

Type	Limits Common to Women
Excited–Disorganized	$z_1 > 1.00$
	$z_1 > z_2, z_6, z_7$
	$z_3, z_4 > .60$
	$z_5, z_9 > -.20$
	$z_8 < .55$
	$z_{10} > .00$
Retarded–Disorganized	$z_7 > .20$
	$z_7 > z_3, z_5, z_6$
	$z_1, z_2, z_4 < .10$
	$z_3, z_5 < 1.15$
Anxious–Disorganized	$z_5, z_7 > .19$
	$z_6 > .03$
	$z_1, z_4 < .20$
	$z_3 > -.35$
	$z_8, z_{10} < .51$

APPENDIX

Multiple Cutoff Criteria for Typing

The multiple cutoff procedure for classifying a patient to one of the types involves the following steps:

1. Record the patients ten raw syndrome scores on IMPS. By resort to the norm tables (available from the Editor), record the corresponding standard scores.

2. Inspect the profile and select a type most similar to that of the patient's.

3. Apply the limits successively to the patient's standard syndrome scores. If the profile satisfies every limit then it is assigned to the type.

Suppose a patient resembles two types but does not satisfy all of the criteria of either. Then count the number of instances that the patient's scores satisfy the limits established for the two types. Assign the patient to the group where the number of errors is least.

6

SUMMARY

The Typing Process

The procedures in identifying and characterizing the patient types have been fairly involved. Thus, a review of the steps followed would be useful:

1. The correlations and congruencies among each of the sub-samples was subjected to a cluster analysis as described in Chapter 3;

2. To increase consistency in profile shape among type members new limits for inclusion were set if deemed necessary;

3. The clusters were matched across similarity indices on the basis of agreement in membership and similarity in mean syndrome profile;

4. The clusters were matched across subsamples on the basis of similarity in mean syndrome profile and by means of a cluster analysis of a stratified sample of representatives from each;

5. Members of matched clusters were pooled and their mean syndrome score profile was determined. Each type was then characterized by the syndromes on which all members scored above the sample mean;

6. Finally the criteria for type membership were defined on the basis of the score range on each syndrome. Upper or lower bounds (cutoffs) were set for each differentiating syndrome.

The Patient Types

The clustering or typing process yielded nine male and nine female psychotic types. All except one male type, the Hallucinated Paranoid (3–5), appeared in at least two subsamples. In the female sample all except the Excited–Disorganized type (1–2–3–4–5–9–10) emerged in several subsamples. Evidence was offered that the types were well differentiated. The proportion of all cases satisfying the limits of each type was shown to be in the neighborhood of 60 per cent. When unassigned cases were allocated on the basis of correlations of at least 0.55 with the mean syndrome profile of a type, an additional 20 per cent of cases were classified.

Seven of the patient types are essentially the same for men and women. These are the Excited, the Excited–Hostile, the Hostile Paranoid, the Hallucinated Paranoid, the Intropunitive, the Grandiose Paranoid and the Anxious–Disorganized types. The

Retarded–Disorganized group among women appears to be differentiated into a Disoriented and a Retarded–Motor Disturbed class among men. The Excited–Disorganized group appeared only among women.

Comparison of the types with standard psychiatric diagnostic classes suggests that there may be four types of paranoids: Excited–Hostile, Hostile, Hallucinated and Grandiose. Three of the acute psychotic types can be characterized as "disorganized". The bases for this designation are high scores on Disorientation, Motor Disturbances and Conceptual Disorganization. Among women there are Excited–, Anxious–, and Retarded–Disorganized types. Corresponding male types are labeled Disoriented, Retarded–Motor Disturbed and Anxious–Disorganized. The Excited patient class probably corresponds to the conventional Manic type while the Intropunitives appear to encompass the depressed psychotics. Further research is needed to ascertain whether the Intropunitives can be further differentiated.

Many of the types identified in the acute psychotic sample also appeared in an all-schizophrenic NIH sample and in the original study of relatively more chronic patients. The findings look promising but the patient classes must now be shown to be of value for predicting treatment response, length of hospitalization, and course of the disturbance. Also needed are observations of the types over time to determine profile changes with and without treatment.

The reliability and the validity of the types will be examined in the next two chapters. Preliminary data will be presented concerning differences between the types as to background, length of hospitalization and outcome.

CHAPTER 5

RELIABILITY OF THE
ACUTE PSYCHOTIC TYPES

C. James Klett and Douglas M. McNair

The scientific and clinical importance of the nine acute psychotic types identified in this study depends entirely on their reliability and validity. Evidence for the reliability of the types is presented in this chapter. Validity data will be presented in the next chapter.

IMPORTANCE OF RELIABILITY

The scientific validity, the theoretical importance, and the practical utility of the nine established acute psychotic types depend strongly upon the degree of their reliability. To be meaningful, identification of class membership or type obviously must be determined by something other than a random configuration of syndrome scores. The types were generated by operations on the profile numbers without any specific assumptions about the reliability of the underlying measurement. However, in the development of the types it was required that a type appear in more than one of the six original randomly drawn samples and that it occur with at least minimum frequency in a given sample. Both of these ground rules decreased the probability that a type emerged simply because of a fortuitous combination of numbers.

The fact that nine naturally occurring groups of profile types emerged with sufficient frequency in at least two of the six independent sub-samples implies that the types, as well as the observations upon which the types are based, possess at least minimum reliability. Types would not be expected to emerge from a set of randomly constructed profiles or profiles based upon random syndrome scores. If no stable types had been identified it might have been concluded either that types did not exist or that the

76

observations were so unreliable that the existence of types was obscured.

Reliability of a rating scale is usually estimated by correlating the judgments of two or more individuals based on common observations of a number of subjects. The coefficients yielded by whatever correlation technique is used are interpreted in much the same manner as reliability coefficients of achievement tests or aptitude tests even though the situation that produces the rating scale scores is quite different. Some of these differences will be reviewed before presenting the reliability figures from the present data.

If two laboratory technicians were asked to record the per cent of eosinophiles in each of 200 blood smears, their responses could be correlated and interpreted as a sort of reliability. If the coefficient were high, say 0.95, it could be concluded that the counting of eosinophiles from blood smears could be done quite accurately. Or, if the same technician performed the same task on two occasions and his responses correlated at a similar level, it could be concluded that he was a reliable counter. However, neither of these approaches provides all that needs to be known about the reliability of estimating blood level eosinophiles from blood smears. A blood smear is made from a sample of the circulating blood. If two samples were drawn from each of 100 individuals, another kind of reliability could be computed which would depend upon the accuracy of counting but would also reflect the variability due to blood sampling. Other forms of reliability are also possible for the same problem. Since confidence limits for percentages are a function of sample size, simply enlarging the blood sample will give more precise, stable estimates of cell counts (Rumke, 1960).

A behavior sample can be thought of in similar terms. If a child is confronted with standard stimuli, e.g. toys, in a standard situation, the occurrence of defined behaviors can be counted by one or more observers from behind a one-way vision screen. The reliability of observations and counting can be estimated by comparing judges' scores. If the behavior sample is filmed or taped, a single rater could produce more than one set of ratings for the same stimuli. The behavior sample could be varied in length or could be obtained on successive days. In general, the larger the behavior sample the more stable or more reliable the estimates will be.

The psychiatric interview is the behavior sample for the IMPS ratings. The IMPS interview is different in some important respects from the sampling units discussed above where the technicians or raters are independent of the material they are observing. In using the IMPS, raters are not simply quantifying their observations but one or more of them are actually eliciting the behavior sample by means of the interview. Thus, they help produce the behavior that they then rate. The skill or the style of the interviewer therefore affects the sampling of behavior just as noise level, fatigue, or emotional distress might affect the sampling of a pupil's behavior on an achievement test. A skilled interviewer may elicit a rich sample of ratable patient behavior while an inexperienced interviewer may find little to rate in his observations of the same patient.

Unlike more standardized situations the IMPS interview tends to be of indeterminate length. Its length depends in part upon the patient's response and other variables. Other things being equal, longer interviews should produce more reliable ratings. Two shorter interviews on succeeding days might be even more desirable. The main point is that if one wishes to quantify behavior, there must be an opportunity for the behavior to occur. It may occur either spontaneously or in response to skilled interviewing techniques. In a sense, then, the reliability of the IMPS is affected by the reliability of the interview as a way of obtaining adequate behavior samples.

There is another sampling problem which also affects the reliability of IMPS. The problem concerns the number of items comprising each syndrome score. The behavioral items in the IMPS can be considered as random samples of behavior from the domain of psychopathology just as an achievement test can be considered a random sample of items from the achievement domain. This is an oversimplification of the construction of both behavior rating scales and achievement tests, but it is important to note because a common criticism of both kinds of instrument is that they do not measure everything they should measure. Although this criticism may seem to be more properly directed at the validity of the instrument than the reliability, the reliability of a test depends upon its length just as the stability of any sampling estimate depends upon sample size. Also validity presupposes reliability. Whether you are estimating the number of black marbles in an urn or the amount of paranoid projection, the larger the sample that is drawn the more stable the estimate will be. (This is one of several arguments against the use of so-called brief scales.) Thus, it should be recognized that within the IMPS, reliability of syndrome scores is partly a function of the number of items in the subscales.

RELIABILITY OF THE UNDERLYING SCALES AND SYNDROMES

Agreement between raters on the individual items making up the IMPS was investigated during the development of the scale. The median intraclass correlation was 0.77 and the range was from 0.61 to 0.92 (Lorr, Klett, McNair, and Lasky, 1963). Inter-rater agreement of the syndrome scores for the normative sample also can be found in the same source or in Lorr, Klett, and McNair (1963). Inter-rater agreement at both the scale and syndrome level was high considering the type of task.

In the present study all patients were rated by an interviewer and a non-participating observer. Table 5.1 presents several ways of assessing the degree of their agreement using ratings made at the time of admission. Intraclass correlation coefficients are shown separately by the sex of the patient for individual and combined raters. There was no pronounced tendency for one sex to be rated more reliably than the other. Also, as expected, the reliability of ratings by the individual rater was somewhat lower than the reliability of the ratings of the combined raters. However, since with few exceptions all the obtained coefficients are 0.90 or greater adequate inter-rater agreement is represented in the ratings of the syndrome scores for both individual or combined raters. Most of the obtained reliabilities are extremely high for rating scales and are probably attributable to the planning and training sessions at the beginning of the project.

The remaining columns in Table 5.1 give the median reliability of the 16 hospitals for each syndrome. Inter-rater agreement was calculated by hospital and by sex within hospitals to monitor the quality of the data being received. This generated 20 intraclass correlations for individual raters per hospital or a total of 320 intraclass correlations. The same number of intraclass correlations were computed for combined raters. As might be expected some coefficients were lower than is usually considered desirable, but these were the exception and in most instances they were based

Table 5.1

Intraclass Correlations Between Interviewers and
Observers on the Syndrome Scores
(Decimals Omitted)

	INDIVIDUAL RATERS				COMBINED RATERS			
	Male	Female	Total	Median*	Male	Female	Total	Media
EXC	90	90	90	85	94	95	95	94
HOS	91	91	91	87	95	96	96	95
PAR	92	94	93	90	96	97	97	95
GRN	93	91	92	91	96	95	96	96
PCP	92	94	93	89	96	97	96	95
INP	92	91	91	88	96	95	96	94
RTD	90	90	90	86	94	95	95	94
DIS	98	95	96	100	99	97	98	100
MTR	81	82	82	72	90	90	90	86
CNP	89	90	89	81	94	95	94	91

* Median intraclass correlation over 16 hospitals by sex.

upon small samples. There was no evidence that the reliability of
the data from any single hospital was consistently less than that
of any other hospital.

OVERALL INTERVIEWER–OBSERVER AGREEMENT

Since the 822 patients had been rated independently by interviewer and silent observer, it was possible to compute product-
moment correlations between these two sets of syndrome scores.
It was thought that canonical correlation might provide an estimate
of the overall degree of agreement between the two sets as well as
providing additional data about the independence of IMPS
syndrome scores. To the best of our knowledge, canonical correlation has not previously been used for this purpose.

In canonical correlation vectors of weights for the predictor
variables (interviewer ratings) and for the criterion variable
(observer ratings) are computed that maximize the correlation
between the resulting canonical variates. Additional pairs of linear

functions can be computed, each being independent of the others. In the present data, as many as ten canonical correlations and pairs of multipliers could be computed. Tests for the significance of the canonical correlations are available (Cooley and Lohnes, 1962). Often the intercorrelation of two sets of data can be expressed by a single canonical correlation or perhaps two or three. In these instances it may be more parsimonious to use canonical correlation, particularly if the vectors of weights can be interpreted in some meaningful manner.

The canonical correlations are given in Table 5.2. The associated linear functions for males, females, and total sample and the correlation matrices upon which these analyses are based appear in Tables 5.9, 5.10 and 5.11.

Table 5.2

Canonical Correlation Between Interviewer and Observer Ratings
(Decimals Omitted)

Canonical Variates	Male	Female	Total
I	985	963	966
II	957	957	956
III	946	937	941
IV	929	922	917
V	893	891	895
VI	891	873	875
VII	846	859	851
VIII	839	854	847
IX	785	782	800
X	754	734	739

In each of these three analyses, ten significant canonical correlations were obtained. This means that there are ten independent ways in which the interviewer set of ratings is related to the observer set of ratings. It would be desirable to be able to identify or describe these dimensions in meaningful terms but the successive pairs of linear functions become increasingly complex after the first set of canonical variates. In the sample of males, for example, the first canonical variate for both interviewer and observer is defined almost exlusively by Disorientation which has weights of —0.92 and —0.91. The next highest weights are —0.16 and —0.15 on Perceptual Distortion. The second pair of linear functions, independent of the first pair, has coefficients over 0.30 on only one variable—grandiosity—but there are other pairs of coefficients of almost equal magnitude. The third set of canonical variates is defined primarily by PAR and PCP and the remaining ones become even more complex. In the female sample, the first set is defined by PAR and PCP, the second by DIS, and the remaining ones again are complex.

Perhaps the most important information to be gained from this analysis is that a high degree of agreement is present between raters and that there is evidence of ten independent dimensions in the data.

RELIABILITY OF THE TYPES

Nine acute psychotic types were established through application of the typing procedure to the combined rater syndrome scores. The types were then enlarged by adding members to each type if they fell within the bounds set by the *multiple cutting scores* given in Chapter 12. The principal test of the reliability of the types was to determine the extent to which the interviewer and observer separately classified the same patients into each type.

It seems reasonable to demand as one essential of an adequate typing system that independent raters produce comparable results with the system. Observations of the interviewer and observer were made at the same point in time and, if the typology is to be useful, separate analysis of interviewer and observer ratings should show high interrater agreement in the type classification.

Another important feature of a patient typing scheme concerns its reliability over time. Although there should be stability of types over time, it is conceivable that types may be reliably classified at one point in time but be relatively unstable over a longer period. Thus, patients may be sufficiently variable over time that different type classifications result on different occasions. The resulting typologies may still be of value unless patients are so highly variable over such a brief span of time that typing becomes an artifact of the time selected. It is well known that patients are variable in the manifestation of symptoms from day to day or even from morning to evening, but the essential features of a type must survive this kind of variability. It is also conceivable that independent raters describe the same patient consistently on more than one occasion but show low interrater agreement. This suggests that patients are stable enough to rate accurately and that reliability of measurement over time is adequate but different raters have different sets or biases in their rating behavior. Training of raters in the use of the scale might be required.

SINGLE RATER VERSUS DOUBLE RATER TYPES

In the present context, greatest interest is in the degree to which the description of patients by independent raters resulted in the same type classification. Accordingly, the syndrome scores of the

Table 5.3

Interviewer - Observer Agreement in Typing 374 Male Psychotics

terviewer assification	Observer Classification										Total
	A	B	C	D	E	F	G	H	I	U	
) Type 1-10	9	2								3	14
) Type 1-2-3-10		24	2							8	34
) Type 2-3		1	17			1	1			3	23
) Type 3-5			1	3		1				1	6
) Type 1-3-4-5					15					5	20
) Type 6						38				7	45
) Type 7-9						1	19			7	27
) Type 7-8-9-10								8		2	10
) Type 3-5-6-7-8-9-10				1					11	3	15
) Unclassified	6	8	9	1	4	10	7	1	5	129	180
Total	15	35	29	5	19	51	27	9	16	168	374

73.0% Agreement

374 males were standardized separately for the interviewer and the observer. Next, the standard score profiles for the interview were machine sorted into nine types using the multiple cutting score boundaries. The process was repeated for the set of observer scores, and the resulting classifications compared.

Table 5.3 presents the results of the comparisons. The diagonal cells indicate persons whom the two raters classified as the same type. Altogether the interviewer and observer agreed in their rating of 273 or 73 per cent of the 374 males. They jointly assigned 144 or 38 per cent of the males to the same type category. The two raters agreed that another 129 cases or 34 per cent of the males were unclassifiable. Most of the disagreement between interviewer and observer consists of one rater classifying the patient when he could not be classified by the other rater's scores. Rarely did the two raters assign the same patient to different types. The overall agreement in "diagnosing" subtypes is highly promising although

Table 5.4

Interviewer – Combined Rater Agreement in Typing 374 Male Psychotics

Interviewer Classification	Combined Rater Classification										Total
	A	B	C	D	E	F	G	H	I	U	
(A) Type 1-10	13	1									14
(B) Type 1-2-3-10		29								5	34
(C) Type 2-3			21				1			1	23
(D) Type 3-5				5				1			6
(E) Type 1-3-4-5				1	17					2	20
(F) Type 6						43				2	45
(G) Type 7-9						1	23			3	27
(H) Type 7-8-9-10								10			10
(I) Type 3-5-6-7-8-9-10									14	1	15
(U) Unclassified	5	9	7	3	4	6	6	1	4	135	180
Total	18	39	28	9	21	50	30	11	19	149	374

82.9% Agreement

there remains the rather imposing problem that almost 60 per cent of the sample of males were not classified by one of the raters or by the combined raters.

A somewhat related problem is how closely the final combined rater classification could be approximated using the observations of only one rater. In some research situations it might not be feasible for various reasons to have more than one rater. Tables 5.4 and 5.5 present the extent of agreement in the present study between the interviewer and the observer separately with the combined rater types. Naturally the agreement shown in Tables 5.4 and 5.5 is higher than agreement between the two single raters as the combined rater includes the individual raters. These data are presented simply to illustrate that about 85 per cent of the typing decisions would be the same regardless of whether the classification is based on one or two raters.

Table 5.5

Observer-Combined Rater Agreement in Typing 374 Male Psychotics

server assification	Combined Rater Classification										Total
	A	B	C	D	E	F	G	H	I	U	
A) Type 1-10	14	1									15
B) Type 1-2-3-10	1	32	1							1	35
C) Type 2-3			21	2						6	29
D) Type 3-5				4							4
E) Type 1-3-4-5					18					1	19
F) Type 6			1			46			1	3	51
G) Type 7-9							26			1	27
H) Type 7-8-9-10								9			9
I) Type 3-5-6-7-8 9-1									15	1	16
U) Unclassified	3	5	5	3	3	5	4	2	2	137	169
Total	18	38	28	9	21	51	30	11	18	150	374

86.1% Agreement

SUMMARY

Some of the issues involved in the reliability of rating scale data have been discussed. At both the item level and at the syndrome level of the IMPS there is a high degree of interrater agreement. Using the combined scores of interviewer and observer 226 of the 374 male patients were classified; 144 were classified into the same type by both raters.

TABLE 5.6

Intercorrelation of Syndrome Scores for Interviewer and Observer

Males

(Decimals Omitted)

	Syndrome	Interviewer Ratings										Observer Ratings									
		EXC	HOS	PAR	GRN	PCP	INP	RTD	DIS	MTR	CNP	EXC	HOS	PAR	GRN	PCP	INP	RTD	DIS	MTR	CNP
I N T E R V I E W E R	EXC		43	16	39	00	-22	-34	-09	10	32	90	40	12	38	-01	-22	-33	-09	04	33
	HOS			42	19	-01	-14	-20	-12	03	16	34	91	42	21	-00	-15	-24	-12	-10	09
	PAR				24	43	02	07	04	18	25	11	41	92	25	44	02	04	06	09	20
	GRN					29	-17	-10	-02	05	23	29	18	24	93	27	-19	-09	-01	07	20
	PCP						22	28	19	32	27	-05	01	43	26	92	18	30	21	27	19
	INP							19	-09	09	-11	-23	-14	04	-21	24	92	10	-08	04	-15
	RTD								34	40	22	-32	-19	09	-13	32	19	90	33	40	18
	DIS									23	18	-07	-15	04	-03	23	-09	35	98	26	17
	MTR										38	07	02	16	03	32	10	40	22	82	26
	CNP											32	15	23	23	26	-10	26	18	27	89
O B S E R V E R	EXC												33	07	30	-04	-23	-32	-08	07	37
	HOS													42	21	02	-17	-23	-16	-09	09
	PAR														25	43	04	06	06	09	18
	GRN															28	-22	-10	-03	03	22
	PCP																23	33	24	27	20
	INP																	13	-08	07	-14
	RTD																		34	45	27
	DIS																			25	17
	MTR																				27
	CNP																				

TABLE 5.7

Intercorrelation of Syndrome Scores for Interviewer and Observer

Females

(Decimals Omitted)

Syndrome	Interviewer Ratings										Observer Ratings									
	EXC	HOS	PAR	GRN	PCP	INP	RTD	DIS	MTR	CNP	EXC	HOS	PAR	GRN	PCP	INP	RTD	DIS	MTR	CNP
EXC		42	21	33	03	-13	-25	-12	23	47	90	36	19	32	03	-13	-26	-12	20	45
HOS			50	21	10	-14	-19	-13	07	15	36	91	47	17	11	-13	-22	-13	02	12
PAR				36	44	-05	01	-08	18	26	20	49	94	30	48	-02	-01	-08	16	26
GRN					33	-17	-04	-04	18	33	34	20	35	91	34	-17	-05	-03	17	35
PCP						13	20	01	26	22	05	12	44	30	94	08	18	02	25	23
INP							20	-13	09	-17	-12	-13	-09	-18	11	91	17	-11	08	-19
RTD								40	40	14	-23	-20	02	-06	21	20	90	40	40	12
DIS									20	11	-09	-12	-06	-03	00	-12	39	95	19	09
MTR										41	22	06	21	16	25	10	34	19	82	36
CNP											49	14	27	31	22	-17	11	12	39	90
EXC												35	20	34	05	-11	-26	-09	22	48
HOS													50	17	13	-13	-24	-12	03	11
PAR														31	50	-05	00	06	20	27
GRN															31	-20	-08	-03	15	32
PCP																08	19	01	25	22
INP																	20	-11	11	-19
RTD																		40	37	12
DIS																			20	09
MTR																				40
CNP																				

(Rows EXC–CNP in the lower block are labelled OBSERVER.)

TABLE 5.8

Intercorrelation of Syndrome Scores for Interviewer and Observer

Total Sample

(Decimals Omitted)

Upper panel

Syndrome	EXC	HOS	PAR	GRN	PCP	INP	RTD	DIS	MTR	CNP	EXC	HOS	PAR	GRN	PCP	INP	RTD	DIS	MTR	CNP
EXC		43	18	35	02	-17	-30	-10	17	40	90	38	16	35	01	-17	-30	-10	13	39
HOS			46	20	05	-14	-19	-13	05	15	35	91	45	19	06	-14	-23	-12	-03	11
PAR				31	43	-01	05	-03	18	25	16	45	93	28	46	00	02	-03	12	23
GRN					31	-17	-07	-03	12	28	31	19	30	92	31	-18	-06	-02	12	28
PCP						17	24	08	29	24	01	07	43	28	93	13	23	10	12	21
INP							20	-11	09	-14	-17	-14	-03	-19	17	91	14	-10	26	-17
RTD								37	40	18	-28	-20	05	-09	26	20	90	36	06	15
DIS									21	14	-08	-13	-02	-03	10	-11	37	96	39	12
MTR										40	15	04	19	10	28	10	37	20	82	31
CNP											41	14	25	27	23	-14	18	14	34	89

Lower panel

Syndrome	EXC	HOS	PAR	GRN	PCP	INP	RTD	DIS	MTR	CNP
EXC		34	14	32	01	-16	-29	-08	16	42
HOS			46	19	08	-15	-24	-13	-02	10
PAR				28	47	-01	03	-02	15	23
GRN					29	-21	-09	-03	10	27
PCP						14	25	10	26	21
INP							17	-10	09	-17
RTD								37	40	20
DIS									22	12
MTR										34
CNP										

TABLE 5.9

Vectors of Weights Between Interviewer & Observer Ratings

Males

(Decimals Omitted)

Syndrome	Interviewer Canonical Variates										Observer Canonical Variates									
	I	II	III	IV	V	VI	VII	VIII	IX	X	I	II	III	IV	V	VI	VII	VIII	IX	X
EXC	04	26	-17	25	30	-01	-64	-67	-40	-71	04	26	-16	21	19	-03	-63	-61	-45	-75
HOS	01	23	22	41	-55	-16	-44	45	70	24	00	22	20	44	-44	-13	-56	43	64	30
PAR	-03	27	55	06	-10	17	51	01	-93	-16	-01	27	55	03	-16	20	47	03	-95	-17
GRN	02	38	-19	-65	19	-55	06	66	-03	03	03	41	-23	-61	23	-55	00	63	-02	-08
PCP	-16	-05	41	-34	-10	05	-07	-75	87	-14	-15	-06	44	-34	00	03	-04	-80	84	-06
INP	02	-29	33	40	57	-66	-10	28	-09	-03	03	-28	30	38	57	-64	-21	38	-14	-04
RTD	-05	-19	07	-24	-11	45	-68	45	-14	-80	-06	-20	02	25	-15	46	-70	50	-16	-87
DIS	-92	13	-24	36	-02	-37	16	03	-04	-01	-91	14	-24	40	-03	-37	14	12	-03	-02
MTR	-03	-11	-02	-29	-16	-16	-41	-18	-43	94	-03	-07	-02	-29	-10	-13	-35	-19	-39	97
CNP	02	17	05	28	77	57	29	33	33	35	01	15	07	28	75	53	34	27	34	49

TABLE 5.10

Vectors of Weights Between Interviewer & Observer Ratings

Females

(Decimals Omitted)

Syndrome	Interviewer Canonical Variates										Observer Canonical Variates									
	I	II	III	IV	V	VI	VII	VIII	IX	X	I	II	III	IV	V	VI	VII	VIII	IX	X
EXC	07	-08	41	35	27	20	31	08	-106	49	08	-09	42	29	29	22	30	05	-102	47
HOS	10	-08	-05	-61	26	69	-40	-63	39	-05	14	-07	-06	-55	29	69	-37	-65	36	-03
PAR	42	-07	-19	-40	23	-98	35	38	-32	13	39	-08	-12	-45	18	-108	30	34	-32	10
GRN	22	06	20	41	-04	-29	-100	-10	17	04	21	05	18	39	-03	-31	-99	-11	15	04
PCP	39	29	-45	18	-40	84	14	29	-15	02	39	29	-50	24	-36	85	12	31	-13	02
INP	12	-11	-33	29	90	04	-22	25	29	07	-08	-11	-35	30	89	03	-19	25	31	07
RTD	05	28	-18	18	-11	-19	14	-89	27	78	-04	25	-15	13	-10	-18	09	-91	-26	80
DIS	17	73	23	-36	41	12	-25	54	-08	-06	-17	73	22	-35	39	10	-22	55	-04	-08
MTR	00	00	-06	09	05	-14	03	-29	-24	-116	-02	04	-04	14	02	-09	05	-34	-25	-112
CNP	22	11	34	13	17	06	47	03	111	06	24	10	31	14	16	05	45	05	113	09

TABLE 5.11

Vectors of Weights Between Interviewer & Observer Ratings

Total Sample

(Decimals Omitted)

Syndrome	Interviewer Canonical Variates										Observer Canonical Variates									
	I	II	III	IV	V	VI	VII	VIII	IX	X	I	II	III	IV	V	VI	VII	VIII	IX	X
EXC	-10	09	35	10	45	22	16	-39	-89	65	-10	10	34	06	41	20	11	-38	-88	-66
HOS	-08	17	-02	-65	-12	-29	-36	-72	60	13	-08	18	-01	-61	-05	-23	-39	-76	56	15
PAR	-02	46	-28	-32	-04	14	-13	93	-61	12	-03	46	-24	-32	-11	13	-19	94	-63	-11
GRN	-02	26	22	60	01	-79	-39	18	27	00	-03	26	24	59	03	-79	-39	15	24	-05
PCP	22	30	-43	19	-18	09	81	-66	15	-11	22	29	-47	23	-11	09	83	-63	15	-09
INP	-06	-16	-37	-12	92	-36	-12	12	17	-02	-07	-15	-38	-09	91	-34	-19	13	17	-02
RTD	18	-06	-18	23	-21	33	-77	-33	-14	82	18	-06	-16	21	-24	30	-80	-33	-14	-84
DIS	81	-02	32	-40	27	-40	22	13	-04	02	81	-02	32	-41	28	-39	20	14	-01	03
MTR	02	-04	-09	16	-06	-05	-24	-19	-46	106	04	-03	-06	20	-06	-01	-22	-21	-41	104
CNP	03	21	21	03	42	63	-01	30	87	19	03	21	19	02	41	61	02	32	88	26

CHAPTER 6

VALIDITY OF THE
ACUTE PSYCHOTIC TYPES

C. JAMES KLETT AND MAURICE LORR

IN the previous chapter a variety of evidence was presented in support of the reliability of the psychotic types. It was recognized that some problems still exist, particularly in respect to the patients who failed to be classified by one or both of the raters but it is encouraging that active disagreement between raters in their classification was minimal. Ratings by independent observers rarely led to different type classifications.

Finding natural occurring patient types that are stable, reliable, and that appear repeatedly in independent random samples of patients is an essential first step in classification. However, even if there were no errors of classification, the types would be of only academic interest until some correlates of the types are established. In this chapter, the available data on the types are presented in a preliminary attempt to discover how the types are similar or different outside the context of the rating scale profile. This effort is considered preliminary because of limitations on the data available and because the search for discriminators is never really complete. The main effort of the study was to identify patient types. The data reported here were thus collected incidental to this goal. The tables are roughly organized in terms of background variables, status at time of hospitalization, and outcome variables.

BACKGROUND VARIABLES

Table 6.1 contains information on age, ethnic origin, and religious background of the male and female types. For each variable in this and subsequent tables, the percentage breakdowns of the entire male and female samples are also presented. These percentages provide the only base rate information that is available. All tabled percentages for the types should be compared with the base rates as well as with each other. It should also be remembered that percentages based upon small samples are extremely unstable estimates of the parameters. The larger patient classes are more stable and can be expected to show less deviation from the base rate figures. The Intropunitive type which constitutes almost 15 per cent of the total sample illustrates what is meant here.

Although the sample is fairly large, membership in most types is small. When these groups are further divided into categories, cell frequencies become even smaller. Thus tests of significance were not made. To a large extent, then the following description of the types is not as rigorous as might be desired but hopefully provides some insight into the nature of the types as well as some hypotheses that can be tested in future samples.

AGE AND ETHNIC ORIGIN

Almost half of the male sample were born before 1930. With this expectation, the Retarded–Motor Disturbed (7–9) and Anxious–Disorganized (3–5–6–7–8–9–10) types appear to be drawn from the younger age groups. In the latter group 32 per cent were born in the 1940's. The two Excited types (1–10 and 1–2–3–10), on the other hand, may be from an earlier generation. These trends receive partial support from the female sample which on the whole was slightly older. The Anxious–Disorganized (3–5–6–7–9) type, like its counterpart in the male types, is a younger group and only 13 per cent of the Excited–Hostile (1–2–3–10) group were born after 1930.

In both the male and female samples, there were slightly over 80 per cent whites, about 15 per cent Negroes, and a small percentage of patients with other ethnic backgrounds. All of the types therefore are predominantly white but male Negroes appear in the greatest proportion in the Hallucinated Paranoid (3–5–8) and the Grandiose Paranoid (1–3–4–5) types. Negro females are proportionately greater in the Grandiose Paranoid (3–4–5) and in the Excited–Disorganized (1–2–3–4–5–9–10) type which is a highly disturbed group that is often paranoid. The other types in which paranoid projection is central do not show any pronounced

TABLE 6.1

Description of the Types in Percent

Type	N	Decade of Birth				Ethnic Origin		Religion	
		Before 1920	1920 1929	1930 1939	1940 1949	White	Negro	Protestant	Catholic
Males									
Excited	18	28	39	17	17	83	17	94	6
Excited-Hostile	39	17	54	15	13	92	8	82	10
Hostile Paranoid	28	28	32	21	18	71	18	71	18
Hallucinated Paranoid	9	22	33	44		67	33	56	11
Grandiose Paranoid	21	24	28	43	5	62	33	81	14
Intropunitive	51	18	30	37	16	94	4	63	25
Retarded-Motor Disturbed	30	13	13	57	17	83	10	60	27
Disoriented	11	27	18	18	36	64	27	73	27
Anxious Disorganized	19	10	16	42	32	68	21	63	26
All Males	374	19	29	33	19	83	14	70	20
Females									
Excited	19	31	21	26	21	76	16	58	26
Excited-Hostile	37	44	43	8	5	92	8	65	30
Excited Disorganized	12	59	8	33		67	33	58	25
Hostile Paranoid	34	26	29	29	15	76	24	79	15
Hallucinated Paranoid	12	41	25	35		83	17	67	33
Grandiose Paranoid	17	24	35	35	6	59	41	70	18
Intropunitive	66	21	26	42	11	92	5	68	24
Anxious Disorganized	13		23	31	46	69	23	69	31
Retarded Disorganized	54	31	20	31	17	85	15	69	22
All Females	448	27	29	28	15	82	16	69	23

tendency to be associated with ethnic origin although white males may be underrepresented in the Hostile Paranoid (2–3) group. There are several types that are disproportionately high in whites. In the Intropunitive (6) groups, 94 per cent of the men and 92 per cent of the women are white. In the Excited–Hostile (1–2–3–10) groups, 92 per cent of each sex sample is white. The two somewhat similar Anxious–Disorganized types in men (3–5–6–7–8–9–10) and women (3–5–6–7–9) may be underrepresented by white patients; Negroes and the small number of other ethnic groups tend to occur in both in somewhat larger proportions.

RELIGIOUS AFFILIATION

In the entire sample, 69 per cent are Protestants, 22 per cent are Catholics, 2 per cent are Jews, and 1 per cent represent other classes. Six per cent of the patients would not acknowledge religious background or membership. There are no apparent sex differences in these overall percentages. However, sex and religious background may interact in type membership. The male Excited and Excited–Hostile groups contain the largest percentage of Protestants. In the three female Excited types, Protestants appear to be underrepresented. Female Hostile–Paranoids are more likely to be Protestant and female Hallucinated–Paranoids more likely to be Catholic than is true of the entire sample.

EDUCATIONAL BACKGROUND

Table 6.2 contains similar information on educational background, marital status, and place of residence. About half of the sample had some high school or vocational school training, about a quarter had an 8th grade education or less, and another quarter had at least some college training. Smaller percentages had college degrees or graduate training. Most of the male types approximate these base rates fairly well. The Excited group contains more high school–vocational and fewer college trained patients than might be expected. The Hallucinated–Paranoid and the Disoriented types are made up primarily of the less educated males, and the Grandiose Paranoid group seems to be a mixture of poorly educated and the college trained. The female Excited–Hostile type has more college

TABLE 6.2

Description of the Types in Percent

Type	N	Education			Marital Status			Residence	
		8th Grade or less	H. S. Vocat.	College	Never Married	Previously Married	Married Remarried	City Town	Village Rural
Males									
Excited	18	28	66	6	33	17	50	78	16*
Excited-Hostile	39	23	54	23	36	23	41	79	18*
Hostile Paranoid	28	21	47	32	43	21	36	86	14
Hallucinated Paranoid	9	55	33	11	11	45	44	66	33
Grandiose Paranoid	21	38	19	43	28	24	48	71	29
Intropunitive	51	22	51	28	31	22	47	88	12
Retarded-Motor Disturbed	30	20	60	20	63	17	20	63	37
Disoriented	11	45	45	9	55	36	9	54	46
Anxious Disorganized	19	26	52	22	58	21	21	95	5
All Males	374	26	50	24	45	17	38	75	25
Females									
Excited	19	16	53	32	37	42	21	100	
Excited-Hostile	37	11	49	41	16	46	38	95	5
Excited Disorganized	12	42	34	25	8	33	59	83	17
Hostile	34	24	56	21	26	41	33	88	9*
Hallucinated Paranoid	12	41	59		17	58	25	83	17
Grandiose Paranoid	17	6	70	24	29	41	30	88	6*
Intropunitive	66	20	56	24	9	26	65	88	12
Anxious Disorganized	13	15	53	31	39	15	46	92	8
Retarded Disorganized	54	24	61	15	20	24	56	74	26
All Females	448	22	54	24	20	32	48	85	15

*Group includes one nomad or transient

and fewer less educated but the opposite trend is present in the Hallucinated–Paranoid group. The poorly educated are under-represented in the Grandiose Paranoid group but are proportionately greater in the Excited–Disorganized type.

MARITAL STATUS

There are fairly pronounced differences between the male and female samples in terms of marital status. Nearly half of the males had never been married, and only 38 per cent were married at the time of hospitalization. Eighty per cent of the women had been married and nearly half of them still were when hospitalized. Against these base rates, the two sexes show further differences. The male Excited group has fewer never-married and more still-married than the base rates for males while the female Excited type is more likely not to get married or, if married, not as likely to be currently married. In the Hostile Excited type the women appear to have gotten married at the expected rate but their current status was more likely unmarried or separated. Paradoxically, in the Excited Disorganized type, 92 per cent of the women had been married and 59 per cent still were, when hospitalized. In both sexes, the different paranoid types got married at about the expected rates or, particularly in the males, at an even higher than expected rate, but if they were hallucinated they now tend to be single. The Intropunitives of both sexes have been married and tend to remain so. The bulk of the never-married are associated with the Retarded–Motor Disturbed, the Disoriented, and the Anxious–Disorganized groups in the males. The Anxious–Disorganized female also tends to be unmarried. All of these are the disoriented, retarded, slowed up, and motorically disturbed patients.

PATIENT RESIDENCE

Most of the patients resided in non-rural areas which is here defined as any city or town over 5000 in population. The male Hostile Paranoid, the Intropunitive, and the Anxious Disorganized groups are less likely to come from rural areas while the Retarded–Motor Disturbed and the Disoriented are more likely to originate in rural areas than the sample as a whole. The Excited and the Excited–Hostile women are less likely to come from rural areas while the Disorganized female is more likely to than would be expected from the base rate for women.

SOCIAL CLASS

The most direct measures of social class available on this sample of patients are the occupations of the patient, his father, and his spouse. These occupations were classified according to socio-economic level and are presented in Table 6.3 as Upper, Middle, and Lower. Because occupation of the spouse was available only from married patients and was particularly incomplete for male patients it is not tabled and will be discussed only briefly. The base rates for men's occupational level are 23 per cent upper, 39 per cent middle and 38 per cent lower. There does not seem to be any tendency for patients of particular types to be drawn from the upper socio-economic level. However, the Disoriented group is predominantly lower class level and the Excited, the Hallucinated–Paranoid, the Retarded–Motor Disturbed, and the Anxious–Disorganized also tend to be overrepresented in this group. The Hostile Paranoids appear to be middle-class. In terms of the occupation of the father, the picture is somewhat different. All of the Hallucinated–Paranoid males are from the upper socio-economic level by this criterion. The Intropunitive type is also included in this column. The Disoriented, the Grandiose Paranoid, and the Anxious–Disorganized patients come from homes of lower socio-economic level. The females are even more difficult to evaluate because of the large percentage who reported themselves as housewives. This is the primary reason for the smaller percentage in the upper socio-economic level of this group. The Excited and the Excited–Hostile women have upper or middle class jobs. The Excited Disorganized group have middle or lower class jobs. The Hallucinated Paranoid is almost exclusively lower social class. The Anxious–Disorganized woman is somewhat more likely to have an upper level job. The fathers of the Excited and the Excited–Disorganized women were likely to have had upper level jobs. Information on the occupation of the husbands of female patients was fragmentary and of course the percentages are appropriate only for those that are married. Excited Hostile and

TABLE 6.3

Level of Occupational Status of the Types in Percent

Type	N	Patient's Occupation			N	Father's Occupation		
		Upper	Middle	Lower		Upper	Middle	Lower
Excited	17		47	53	17	29	35	35
Excited-Hostile	38	29	47	24	33	39	48	12
Hostile Paranoid	26	15	54	31	26	38	31	31
Hallucinated Paranoid	8	12	38	50	8	100		
Grandiose Paranoid	21	28	48	24	20	15	35	50
Intropunitive	49	31	45	24	47	53	34	13
Retarded-Motor Disturbed	26	12	35	54	29	38	28	34
Disoriented	10	10	20	70	8	13	25	62
Anxious Disorganized	17	12	35	52	18	39	22	39
All Males	351*	23	39	38	343*	41	34	25
Females								
Excited	18	22	39	39	14	64	21	14
Excited-Hostile	37	19	35	46	31	48	42	10
Excited Disorganized	11		27	73	10	70	20	10
Hostile Paranoid	33	6	27	67	26	38	38	23
Hallucinated Paranoid	12		8	92	11	36	36	27
Grandiose Paranoid	17	6	24	70	25	40	32	28
Intropunitive	63	11	17	71	59	46	31	24
Anxious Disorganized	11	27	18	55	11	36	36	27
Retarded Disorganized	50	4	22	74	44	39	45	16
All Females	429*	11	22	67	376*	47	35	18

*Occupation was unknown or unclassifiable for 23 males and 19 females

*Father's occupation was unknown or unclassifiable for 35 males and 72 females.

Intropunitive women have husbands with upper level jobs. Hallucinated Paranoid, Hostile Paranoid, and Anxious–Disorganized women have husbands with lower level jobs. Excited women come from middle class homes.

THE PATIENTS AT THE TIME OF ADMISSION

Five per cent of the sample of patients were on high dosages of tranquilizers at the time of admission to the hospital and another 4 per cent had been receiving drugs of some type in unknown amounts for undetermined amounts of time. According to instructions these patients were to have been taken off medication or to have the dosage reduced prior to their rating interview. These patients were classified into types at about the same proportion as those that had not been receiving drugs and there is no evidence that they were systematically classified into only certain types. A higher proportion of patients had been started on some kind of drugs by the time of the interview, however. Only 79 per cent of the males and 69 per cent of the females were completely drug free at the time of interview. Although the dosages were usually low and the duration of treatment short, patients on drugs seemed somewhat less likely to be classified into one of the types. For some reason this was particularly true among the women patients where only about a fifth of those on drugs were later classified. Another problem that had been anticipated was complete or partial muteness at the time of interview. This kind of patient made up 5 per cent of the sample. Since many of the syndromes rely heavily upon verbal behavior, it was expected that profiles of mute patients if classified at all would fall in certain types. This expectation was confirmed. Of the 16 mute male patients that were classified, six were of the Retarded–Motor Disturbed type, making up 20 per cent of that group. Another four of these males were in the Disoriented group. Of the 13 mute female patients classified, 10 were in the Retarded–Disorganized type, making up 20 per cent of that rather large group.

PSYCHIATRIC DIAGNOSIS

Table 6.4 presents the distribution of initial diagnoses of the types. Some of these diagnoses were especially helpful in defining

TABLE 6.4

Distribution of Initial Diagnoses of the Types in Percent

Type	N	Manic	Paranoid	Schizo-Affective	Acute Undiff.	Depressed	Simple	Catatonic	Chronic Undiff.
Males									
Excited	18	22	28	17	11	6	6		11
Excited-Hostile	39	13	67	8	5	2	2		2
Hostile Paranoid	28*		64	4	4	14	7		4
Hallucinated Paranoid	9		78					22	10
Grandiose Paranoid	21	5	71		5	5	6	5	6
Intropunitive	51	2	4	14	12	55	3	2	17
Retarded-Motor Disturbed	30		10	7	37	13	36	13	18
Disoriented	11**		9		9			18	11
Anxious Disorganized	19		42		37	5		5	9
All Males	374	4	41	6	16	14	4	4	
Females									
Excited	19	32	49	21	21	11		5	11
Excited-Hostile	37	24	8	14	8	5			8
Excited Disorganized	12**	33		8	25	8	6	8	15
Hostile Paranoid	34		79						
Hallucinated Paranoid	12		92		12				
Grandiose Paranoid	17		88		13				
Intropunitive	66***		11	14		48	5	2	5
Anxious Disorganized	13		31		31	8		23	8
Retarded Disorganized	54**		4	2	20	28	4	30	11
All Females	448	5	33	7	17	19	2	6	6

*Includes one passive **aggressive**

**Includes one hebephrenic.

***Includes one **inadequate personality with hysterical features**, one psychoneurotic conversion reaction, and one psychoneurotic anxiety reaction the types. In the males, 64 per cent of the Hostile Paranoid, 78 per cent of the Hallucinated Paranoid, and 71 per cent of the Grandiose Paranoid types were diagnosed as paranoid compared to the base rate of 41 per cent in the entire male sample. However, 67 per cent of the Excited–Hostile were also diagnosed as paranoid even though Paranoid Projection is not one of the principal defining syndromes of this type. These results strongly suggest that the psychiatric diagnosis of Schizophrenic reaction, paranoid type includes several identifiable subgroups. In the female sample, the same trend is present: 79 per cent of the Hostile Paranoid, 92 per cent of the Hallucinated Paranoid, 88 per cent of the Grandiose Paranoid, and 49 per cent of the Excited–Hostile types were given a diagnosis of Schizophrenic reaction, paranoid type. Manic patients of both sexes appeared most frequently in the various Excited types. Depressed patients were most prominent in the Intropunitive type. As a final example, 30 per cent of the female Retarded–Disorganized group was diagnosed as Schizophrenic reaction, catatonic type.

TYPE OF COMMITMENT AND WARD PLACEMENT

Sixty-three per cent of the males and 60 per cent of the females were involuntarily committed to the hospital. Intropunitive patients of both sexes tended to be voluntary admissions. The Anxious–Disorganized types of both sexes and the Excited–Disorganized women were voluntary admissions. All of the remaining female types contained more involuntarily committed patients than would be expected, as was also true of the male Hallucinated Paranoid and Disoriented types. These percentages are shown in Table 6.5 along with those for ward membership, and duration of current psychiatric episode.

The Intropunitive patients of both sexes are not as likely to be on completely closed wards as the sample as a whole. In the male sample there seems to be a tendency for them to be on partially open wards. Although at least half of the Hostile Paranoids are on closed wards, there are more of them on open wards (males) or partially open wards than is expected. However the Hallucinated–Paranoids of both sexes are on locked wards. Male Grandiose Paranoids also tend to be on closed wards.

TABLE 6.5

Description of the Types in Percent

Type	N	Commitment		Ward Membership			Duration of Current Episode	
		Vol.	Invol.	Closed	Open	Partial Open	< 10 mos.	> 9 mos.
Males								
Excited	18	33	67	72	22	6	94	6
Excited-Hostile	39	26	64	74	8	18	87	13
Hostile Paranoid	28*	36	64	50	25	25	79	18
Hallucinated Paranoid	9	22	78	78	22		89	11
Grandiose Paranoid	21	33	67	81	14	5	86	14
Intropunitive	51	47	53	33	16	51	78	22
Retarded-Motor Disturbed	30	30	70	77	3	20	80	20
Disoriented	11		100	64	9	27	55	45
Anxious Disorganized	19*	63	37	68	26		84	16
All Males	374	37	63	68	14	17	82	18
Females								
Excited	19	26	74	68	11	21	84	16
Excited-Hostile	37	19	81	73	8	19	84	16
Excited Disorganized	12	50	50	67	33		83	17
Hostile Paranoid	34	24	76	59	18	24	71	29
Hallucinated Paranoid	12	8	92	92		8	75	25
Grandiose Paranoid	17*	24	76	76	12	6	82	18
Intropunitive	66	68	32	55	27	18	83	17
Anxious Disorganized	13	69	31	62	31	8	92	8
Retarded Disorganized	54	30	70	80	9	11	87	13
All Females	448	40	60	72	17	11	85	15

* One unknown ward membership.

LENGTH OF ILLNESS

Sampling was restricted to patients with no more than one previous admission except for those patients with recurrent manic or depressive episodes. With this restriction in mind, the most interesting finding was that a third of the female Excited group had two or more previous admissions. There is not sufficient range in number of previous admissions to talk meaningfully about the relation of this variable to type membership. By definition, this is a relatively acute group of patients. This is also reflected in the last columns of Table 6.5 dealing with the duration of the current psychotic episode. For 82 per cent of the males and 85 per cent of the females, this was less than 10 months. Only the Disoriented males and the Hostile Paranoid females had appreciably greater percentages of chronically ill patients than the base rates.

TREATMENT AND OUTCOME

A follow-up questionnaire was obtained on all but 9 of the 822 patients 6 months after admission. These questionnaires provided information on the kind of primary and adjunct treatment the patients received, the number of days they were in the hospital during this period and their status after 6 months. Table 6.6 contains the data on primary treatment. Electric shock was used as the primary treatment for 8 per cent of the males, most frequently with the Hostile Paranoids. In the females, shock was given to the Intropunitive and Retarded Disorganized groups. Drugs of some sort were the primary treatment for over half the patients. Almost always these were one of the major tranquilizing drugs. When antidepressant drugs were used as the primary treatment, it was nearly always given the Intropunitive groups. Individual or group psychotherapy was the primary treatment for about 10 per cent of the sample. Intropunitive males seemed particularly likely to receive this treatment. Another large miscellaneous category of treatment consisted of milieu therapy, corrective therapy, industrial therapy, and so on. No trends are apparent.

Table 6.7 presents similar data for adjunct treatment. Higher proportions of patients received psychotherapy as a secondary treatment but the predominance of drug treatment is still evident. It was generally true that patients received several treatments,

8

TABLE 6.6

Primary Treatment Received by the Types In Percent

Type	N	Electric Shock	Drugs	Psycho-Therapy	Other
Males					
Excited	18		34	6	61
Excited-Hostile	38	8	58	3	32
Hostile Paranoid	28	25	35	4	28
Hallucinated Paranoid	9		44	11	44
Grandiose Paranoid	21		81	5	14
Intropunitive	49	6	43	28	21
Retarded-Motor Disturbed	30	13	47	3	37
Disoriented	11	18	45		36
Anxious Disorganized	19		32	21	47
All Males	368	8	50	10	33
Females					
Excited	19	5	52	15	26
Excited-Hostile	36	3	64	3	30
Excited Disorganized	12	17	16	17	50
Hostile Paranoid	34	6	77	9	9
Hallucinated Paranoid	12	8	58		33
Grandiose Paranoid	17	12	71	12	6
Intropunitive	66	24	44	14	18
Anxious Disorganized	13	8	39	16	38
Retarded Disorganized	54	24	43	4	30
All Females	445	12	53	8	26

sometimes several drugs, psychotherapy, as well as the usual hospital treatments. This accounts for the fact that the percentages in the table do not add to 100 per cent across the rows. The categories are not mutually exclusive and can not be added within the table and, with the exception of electric shock, can not be added to the primary treatment figures to get a combined percentage. To get a better picture of how prevalent drugs and psychotherapy were in the types either as a primary or secondary treatment, separate tallies had to be made. Drugs were given to 86 per cent of the males and 89 per cent of the females. There did not seem to be much variation between the types in treatments received, however. The Intropunitive and Hostile Paranoid males were somewhat less likely to receive drugs. Individual or group psychotherapy was received by 45 per cent of both sexes either as a primary or adjunct treatment. The Intropunitive and Anxious–Disorganized males and the Excited–Hostile females were particularly likely to get psychotherapy; Grandiose Paranoid and Disoriented males, and Grandiose Paranoid, Hallucinating Paranoid, and Hostile Paranoid women were less likely to be given psychotherapy. Electric shock treatment has already been discussed and the combined figures can be obtained from the two tables.

Table 6.8 shows the status of the patients 6 months after admission. The groups most likely to have received an approved discharge of some sort were the male Hallucinated–Paranoids and both Intropunitive groups. The male and female Grandiose Paranoids and the Disoriented males were likely to have had some other disposition. Sixty-three per cent of the latter group were still hospitalized as were a third of the male Retarded–Motor Disturbed group. The two Grandiose Paranoid groups tended to be discharged against medical advice, absent without leave, or transferred to some other installation.

Table 6.9 presents the information on number of days in the hospital during the 6 months follow-up period. This variable tended to be bimodal or U-shaped in distribution with a sizeable group spending the entire 6 months in the hospital and another large group that was only hospitalized 30 to 60 days. Although there was some variation in the average length of stay, the variability in every group was too large to reach any conclusions by inspecting the means. The Grandiose Paranoid males tended to spend less than 2 months in the hospital but the Disoriented

TABLE 6.7

Adjunct Treatment Received by the Types In Percent

Type	N	Electric Shock	Drugs		Psychotherapy		Other
			Tranquilizing	Anti-Depressant	Individual	Group	
Males							
Excited	18		56		33	11	39
Excited-Hostile	38	5	39	3	32	10	24
Hostile Paranoid	28		36	21	32	18	36
Hallucinated Paranoid	9	5	33		56	11	33
Grandiose Paranoid	21		14		10	5	14
Intropunitive	49		35	10	45	8	63
Retarded-Motor Disturbed	30		40	13	33	23	47
Disoriented	11	9	45	9	27		54
Anxious Disorganized	19	21	74		63	16	26
All Males	368	6	39	8	38	12	33
Females							
Excited	19	5	32	5	37	37	37
Excited-Hostile	36	3	42	11	50	19	33
Excited Disorganized	12		75		58	25	25
Hostile Paranoid	34	3	26	15	24	18	32
Hallucinated Paranoid	12		25	50	33		25
Grandiose Paranoid	17		18		6		18
Intropunitive	66	6	41	18	36	17	21
Anxious Disorganized	13	6	54	15	38	23	31
Retarded Disorganized	54	8	39	20	33	15	28
All Females	445	5	36	13	33	18	26

TABLE 6.8

Outcome Status of the Types Six Months After Admission In Percent

Type	N	Still Hospitalized	Approved Release	AMA or AWOL	Transferred
Males					
Excited	18*	17	67	6	6
Excited-Hostile	38	24	58	8	10
Hostile Paranoid	28	29	54	4	14
Hallucinated Paranoid	9		78		22
Grandiose Paranoid	21	5	48	24	24
Intropunitive	49	18	78	2	2
Retarded-Motor Disturbed	30	33	57	3	7
Disoriented	11	63	36		
Anxious Disorganized	19	15	63		21
All Males	368	20	63	5	10
Females					
Excited	19	25	63	10	6
Excited-Hostile	35	29	63	3	8
Excited Disorganized	12	8	75	8	6
Hostile Paranoid	34	27	68		8
Hallucinated Paranoid	12	8	75	8	6
Grandiose Paranoid	17	24	59	12	2
Intropunitive	66	13	82	5	8
Anxious Disorganized	13	8	77	8	
Retarded Disorganized	54*	20	76		
All Females	445	19	75	1	2

* 1 Deceased

TABLE 6.9

Length of Stay of the Types in Percent

Type	N	Days in Hospital		
		< 61	61-119	7119
Males				
Excited	18	44	28	28
Excited-Hostile	38	58	11	32
Hostile Paranoid	28	57	11	32
Hallucinated Paranoid	9	44	33	22
Grandiose Paranoid	21	62	19	19
Intropunitive	49	57	10	33
Retarded-Motor Disturbed	30	17	33	50
Disoriented	11	9	18	73
Anxious Disorganized	19	42	21	37
All Males	367	48	19	33
Females				
Excited	19	58	21	21
Excited-Hostile	36	36	31	33
Excited Disorganized	12	58		42
Hostile Paranoid	34	38	15	47
Hallucinated Paranoid	12	33	42	25
Grandiose Paranoid	17	47	24	29
Intropunitive	66	64	23	14
Anxious Disorganized	13	46	23	31
Retarded Disorganized	54	43	22	35
All Females	444	49	21	30

were more likely to stay in for over 4 months. The Retarded–Motor Disturbed men were not likely to get out of the hospital quickly but, after the first 2 months, they were released at greater than the expected rates. The Hallucinated Paranoid male spent an intermediate time in the hospital. Among female patients, the Intropunitive group tended to get out early rather than late, the opposite being the case with the Hostile Paranoid group. The Hallucinated–Paranoid tended to spend 2 to 4 months in the hospital. The Excited–Disorganized type was released quickly or tended to stay the full 6 months.

SUMMARY OF TYPE CHARACTERISTICS IN MALES

The Excited (1–10) patients are likely to be somewhat older, Protestant, high school or vocationally trained rather than college educated, have lower class jobs, have been married and are likely to be currently married. When admitted they were likely to be diagnosed as manics.

The Excited–Hostile (1–2–3–10) patients are older, of the Protestant faith and were more likely to be white. They are also likely to be diagnosed as manic or paranoid.

The Hostile Paranoid (2–3) type contains somewhat more non-white patients than expected. They come from non-rural areas and are from the middle socio-economic level. They typically receive a paranoid diagnosis, are more likely to be found on at least partially open wards, and are likely to receive electric shock as a primary treatment.

The Hallucinated Paranoid (3–5–8) contains a greater proportion of Negroes than most other types. They are less well educated, have lower class jobs but some come from upper class homes. They also tend to have been married at one time. They receive a paranoid or catatonic diagnosis, are likely to be involuntarily committed and are usually on locked wards. Despite this background they are likely to get an approved discharge within 6 months.

The Grandiose Paranoid (1–3–4–5) type also has a greater proportion of Negroes than the other types. These patients are a mixture of poorly educated and college trained, come from lower class homes, are likely to be married, diagnosed as paranoid, and kept on a closed ward. Many are likely to be discharged against medical advice, be absent without leave, or be transferred rather than get an approved discharge or remain in the hospital. Their hospital stay is accordingly shorter than most.

The Intropunitive (6) patients are 92 per cent white. Members are likely to be currently married and less likely than most to come from rural areas. Their fathers tend to have upper class jobs. Intropunitive patients are very likely to receive a diagnosis of Depressive reaction, to receive anti-depressant drugs and psychotherapy, and to get an approved discharge. They are usually placed on open wards.

The Retarded–Motor Disturbed (7–9) patients are younger, never married, come from rural areas, and tend to have lower class jobs. This type contains the most mute patients, is most likely to be diagnosed Schizophrenic reaction, acute undifferentiated or catatonic, and still be hospitalized after 6 months. When type members did leave the hospital they left in the last 4 months.

The Disoriented (7–8–9–10) group is made up primarily of the less educated, lower class, never married, rural patients. Mute during the interview type members are usually diagnosed as simple schizophrenic, catatonic, or chronic undifferentiated. They had been ill a long time before they were committed involuntarily to the hospital and tended to stay hospitalized for at least 6 months.

The Anxious Disorganized (3–4–6–7–8–9–10) type is likely to contain more younger, non-white, never married, voluntarily admitted and lower class, rural patients. The type is most likely to be diagnosed acute undifferentiated.

These descriptions are summarized in Table 6.10 for men and 6.11 for women.

SUMMARY OF TYPE CHARACTERISTICS IN WOMEN

The Excited (1–9–10) type is least likely to be Protestant or to have married than other patients. If married she is less likely to have remained so. She is less likely to be lower class, all come from urban areas and are very likely to be diagnosed Manic or Schizo-Affective. Her admission is likely to be involuntary usually with two or more previous admissions. She is also likely to leave the hospital in a nonapproved manner.

The Excited–Hostile (1–2–3–10) patient is older than most, and less likely to be nonwhite or Protestant. More college trained and fewer of the less educated are represented in this group. If she works she has a medium or unskilled job but her husband is likely to have an upper level job. She is more likely to be divorced, separated, or widowed than other patients and less likely to come from a rural area. She is quite likely to be diagnosed as Manic or Paranoid and to be committed involuntarily.

The Excited Disorganized (1–2–3–4–5–9–10) type contains more Negroes than expected but fewer Protestants. The type includes more of the less educated, fewer never-married and more still-married. Members of the type have middle and lower socio-economic level jobs but come from upper class homes. Members show a greater than usual tendency to be voluntary admissions, and are most often diagnosed as Manic. They are either released quickly or spend the entire 6 months in the hospital.

The Hostile Paranoid (2–3) woman is likely to be Protestant, be given a paranoid diagnosis, be committed, and be assigned to a partially open ward. Her current psychotic episode has been longer than most other patients. If married, her husband has a low level

TABLE 6.10.

SUMMARY OF CHARACTERISTICS OF THE MALE TYPES

	EXCITED	EXCITED-HOSTILE	HOSTILE-PARANOID	HALLUCINATED PARANOID	GRANDIOSE PARANOID	INTRO-PUNITIVE	RETARDED-MOTOR	DISORI-ENTED	ANXIOUS-DISORGANIZED
AGE	OLDER		OLDER				YOUNGER		YOUNGER
ETHNIC ORIGIN	WHITE	WHITE		1/3 NEGRO	1/3 NEGRO	WHITE			
RELIGION	PROT.	PROT.			PROT.				
EDUCATION	H. S.			8TH GR.	COLL. OR 8TH GR.			FEW COLL.	
MARITAL STATUS	MOST REMAR.			MOST MAR.			NEVER MAR.	NEVER MAR.	
RESIDENCE			CITY	RURAL		CITY	RURAL	RURAL	CITY
PATIENT OCCUP.		M. CLASS		L.&M. CLASS	L. & M. CLASS	U.CLASS	L.CLASS	L.CLASS	
FATHER OCCUP.				L. CLASS		M.& UP. CLASS		L.CLASS	
DIAGNOSIS	MANIC & PAR.	PAR.	PAR.	PAR.	PAR.	DEP.	ACUTE UNDIFF.	SIMPLE	PAR. & ACUTE UNDIFF.
COMMITMENT				INVOL.		VOL.		INVOL.	VOL.
WARD TYPE			OPEN OR PARTIAL	CLOSED	CLOSED	OPEN			
DUR. OF EPISODE	<10 MO.							>9 MO.	
PRIMARY TREAT.			ECT		DRUGS	PSYCHO THERAPY			PSYCHO THERAPY
ADJUNCT TREAT.	DRUGS		ANTIDEP. DRUGS						DRUGS
OUTCOME STATUS				APPROV.REL.	AWOL/AWA	APPROV. REL.	STILL HOSP.	STILL HOSP.	
LENGTH OF STAY				>119 DAYS	<61 DAYS		LONGEST	LONGEST	

job. She tends to remain in the hospital for most of the 6 months period.

The Hallucinated Paranoid (2–3–5) woman is most likely to be Catholic, less well educated, divorced or separated. If married her husband has a low level job. She is typically diagnosed as paranoid, committed, and allocated to a locked ward. She tends to spend 2 to 4 months in the hospital.

The Grandiose Paranoid (3–4–5) type contains many Negroes whose members are less well educated, diagnosed as paranoid, committed, and likely to leave the hospital in a nonapproved manner.

The Intropunitive (6) group contains almost no nonwhites. They are likely to come from upper class homes and to be currently married. They are very likely to receive a diagnosis of depressive reaction, to be committed, and to be placed on open or partially open ward. Intropunitive women receive electric shock or anti-depressant drugs. They tend to be discharged early rather than late with an approved discharge.

The Anxious Disorganized (3–5–6–7–9) type is younger, contains a fair number of nonwhites, and has never married. Members tend to have upper class jobs, to be voluntary admissions, and to be diagnosed as acute undifferentiated or catatonic.

The Retarded Disorganized (7–8–9) woman is more likely to be from a rural area. She is likely to be mute at the time of interview, diagnosed as catatonic, committed, and treated with electric shock.

EFFECT OF TREATMENT ON PROFILES

Re-ratings on IMPS were obtained on most patients just prior to their release from the hospital. Patients remaining in a hospital were re-rated approximately 6 months following the initial rating. The purpose of the re-ratings was to determine the differential effects of combined hospital and tranquilizer treatment on type profiles.

The mean syndrome scores of all re-rated members of a type were determined. These mean profiles are depicted on the standard score scale of the initial ratings. In other words, the scale units and the means are derived from the total sample at the time of admission to the hospital. The mean syndrome scores for each of

TABLE 6.11

SUMMARY OF CHARACTERISTICS OF THE FEMALE TYPES

	EXCITED	EXCITED-HOSTILE	EXCITED-DISORGANIZED	HOSTILE-PARANOID	HALLUCINATED PARANOID	GRANDIOSE-PARANOID	INTRO PUNITIVE	ANXIOUS-DISORGANIZED	RETARDED-DISORGANIZED
AGE		OLDER	OLDER					YOUNGER	
ETHNIC ORIGIN		WHITE	1/3 NEGRO			40% NEGRO	WHITE		
RELIGION			PROT.	PROT.	1/3 CATHOLIC				
EDUCATION		89% H.S. OR COLL.	MORE 8TH GR.		NONE COLL.	H.S. GRAD.			
MARITAL STATUS	1/3 UNMAR.		92% MARRIED				90% MAR.	1/3 UNMAR.	
RESIDENCE	CITY								1/4 RURAL
PATIENT OCCUP.					92% L. CLASS			L. & U. CLASS	74% L. CLASS
FATHER OCCUP.	UP. CLASS		UP. CLASS						M. CLASS
DIAGNOSIS	MANIC	PAR/MANIC	MANIC & ACUTE UND.	PAR.	PAR.	PAR.	DEP.	PAR/ACUTE UNDIFF.	DEP/CATA.
COMMITMENT	INVOL.	INVOL.		INVOL.	INVOL.	INVOL.	VOL.	VOL.	
WARD TYPE			OPEN		CLOSED		OPEN	OPEN	
DUR. OF EPISODE				>9 MO.	>9 MO.			<10 MO.	
PRIMARY TREAT.		DRUGS	OTHER			DRUGS	EST		EST
ADJUNCT TREAT.		PSYCHOTHERAPY	DRUGS, PSYCHOTHERAPY	ANTIDEP. DRUGS			APPROV. REL.		
OUTCOME STATUS			75% HOSP.			12% AWOL			
LENGTH OF STAY			>119 DAYS	>119 DAYS			<61 DAYS		

TABLE 6.12

Mean Syndrome Scores of the Types at Time of Follow-Up

Type	Syndrome									
	EXC	HOS	PAR	GRN	PCP	INP	RTD	DIS	MFR	CNP
Males										
Excited	.22	-.84	-.95	-.45	-.62	-.66	-.65	-.27	-.36	-.18
Excited-Hostile	.04	.10	-.47	-.34	-.65	-.64	-.85	-.46	-.69	-.52
Hostile Paranoid	-.45	.12	-.48	-.43	-.66	-.50	-.65	-.46	-.59	-.64
Hallucinated Paranoid	-.46	-.94	-.31	-.57	-.46	-.64	-.88	-.46	-.78	-.72
Grandiose Paranoid	-.24	-.83	-.77	-.14	-.37	-.53	-1.08	-.46	-.46	-.37
Intropunitive	-.46	-.58	-.92	-.50	-.64	-.02	-.94	-.46	-.56	-.74
Retarded-Motor Disturbed	-.64	-.48	-.32	-.53	-.40	.60	.22	-.46	-.10	-.55
Disoriented	-.63	-.50	-.78	-.60	-.57	-.76	.22	-.09	-.27	-.46
Anxious Disorganized	-.49	-.84	-1.06	-.46	-.58	-.53	.49	-.29	-.21	-.48
Females										
Excited	-.19	-.34	-.99	-.43	-.63	-.54	-.73	-.43	-.46	-.64
Excited-Hostile	-.05	5.11	-.40	-.38	-.67	-.58	-.60	-.43	-.63	-.50
Excited Disorganized	-.13	-.10	.24	.53	-.34	-.37	.01	-.43	-.25	-.15
Hostile Paranoid	-.59	-.37	-.74	-.37	-.62	-.53	-.80	-.43	-.56	-.76
Hallucinated Paranoid	-.70	-.84	-.75	-.55	-.48	-.60	-.75	-.43	-.91	-.63
Grandiose Paranoid	-.71	-.62	-.56	-.39	-.67	-.73	-.86	-.43	-.86	-.57
Intropunitive	-.54	-.62	-.99	-.52	-.64	.01	-.84	-.43	-.61	-.66
Anxious Disorganized	-.56	-.42	-.65	-.37	-.56	-.17	-.07	-.43	-.31	-.65
Retarded Disorganized	-.66	-.88	-.92	-.54	-.65	-.58	.25	-.01	-.25	-.48

types are given separately for men and women in Table 6.12. Figures 6.1–6.9 present the same information for men in the form of graphs. In addition the upper profiles present the mean syndrome scores manifested by the group as a whole at the time of the initial interview.

When the initial and the re-rating profiles are compared, it becomes evident that all patient types manifest substantial changes or "improvements" in level. The second impression given by the figures, especially for the men, is that while the level of the profile has decreased, the profile shape or general configuration has remained the same. The male Excited type still manifests greater than average excitement. Similarly the male Excited–Hostile class manifests a profile resembling the original although all scores have decreased. The male Hostile Paranoid's hostility scores remain highest for the profile. Anxious Intropunitiveness remains highest for the male Intropunitives. There are a few exceptions to this generalization concerning retention of the characteristic profile among the men. Among the Disoriented type members, Disorientation scores decrease more relative to Retardation and Apathy scores. As a consequence Retardation constitutes the peak score. The same observation may be made about the Retarded–Motor Disturbed group; Retardation scores are more resistant to treatment. It is also of interest to note that in the Anxious–Disorganized patients, Intropunitiveness and Retardation are most resistant to treatment. Scores on Paranoid Projection, Perceptual Distortion, and Motor Disturbance decrease. These results suggest that Intropunitiveness may be central to this pattern.

The effects of treatment are equally great on the women in the sample. However, the characteristic type profiles do not persist as strongly despite changes in level. The Excited, Excited–Hostile, and Excited–Disorganized patients manifest profiles relatively similar to those exhibited at admission. The same is true of the Intropunitives, Retarded–Disorganized, and Anxious–Disorganized types. On the other hand, the Hostile Paranoids, Hallucinated–Paranoids, and Grandiose–Paranoids manifest relatively flat profiles not easily recognized.

The findings thus suggest that the characteristic profile of each type tends to persist under treatment, especially in the case of the men. In general, the mean level of each profile including the

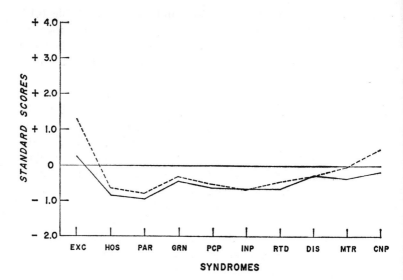

FIG. 6.1. Profile for Excited male type.

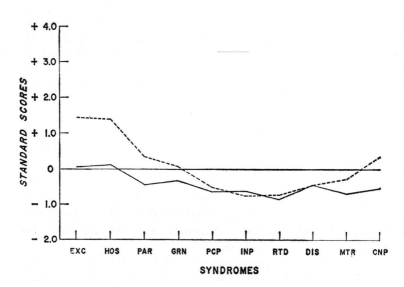

FIG. 6.2. Profile for Excited–Hostile male type.

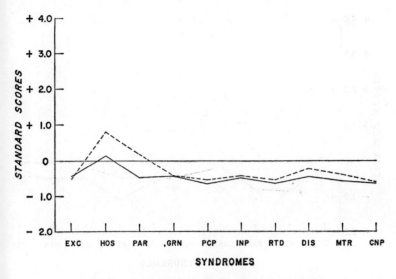

FIG. 6.3. Profile for Hostile Paranoid male type.

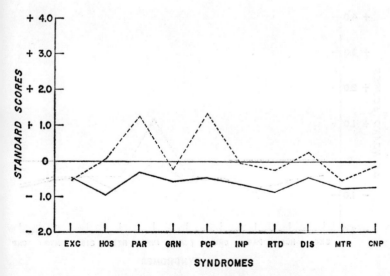

FIG. 6.4. Profile for Hallucinated Paranoid male type.

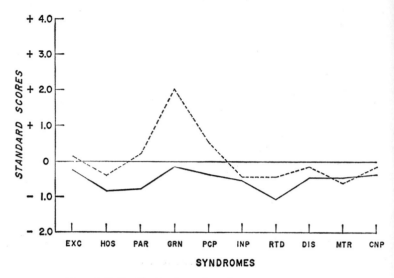

Fig. 6.5. Profile for Grandiose Paranoid male type.

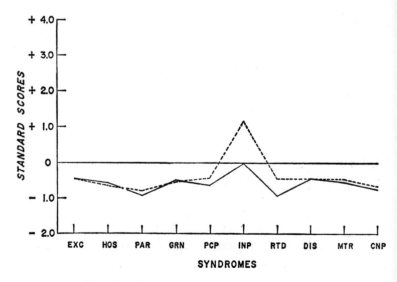

Fig. 6.6. Profile for Intropunitive male type.

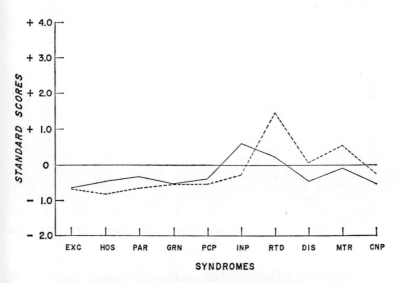

FIG. 6.7. Profile for Retarded–Motor Disturbed male type.

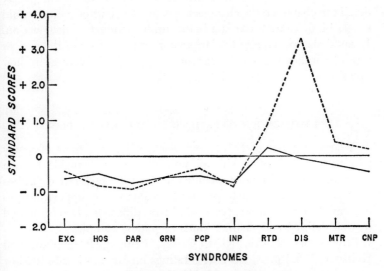

FIG. 6.8. Profile for Disoriented male type.

9

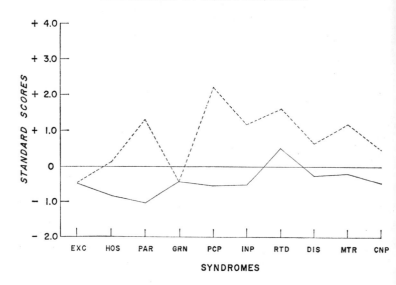

Fig. 6.9. Profile for Anxious–Disorganized male type.

characteristic peaks decrease with hospital and tranquilizer treatment. It would be of interest to obtain successive ratings on a large sample of newly admitted cases and to follow in greater detail the characteristic changes in profile. Such information would surely be of value towards a better understanding of drug action. It could also contribute to clarification of the nature of the patient types by indicating which syndromes appear to be central in their definition.

CLASSIFICATION OF PATIENTS FROM OTHER SAMPLES

A large number of IMPS and ward behavior ratings of newly admitted and chronic schizophrenic men were available from a series of drug evaluations included in the VA Cooperative Studies in Psychiatry. These data provided an interesting opportunity to determine if the various types would be differentially represented in well defined and distinct kinds of patient samples.

Project Six (Lasky, Klett, Caffey, Bennett, Rosenblum and Hollister, 1962) provided IMPS ratings on 505 newly admitted or readmitted patients from 32 VA Hospitals. About half of the patients were diagnosed as schizophrenic reaction, paranoid type and another third of them as acute or chronic undifferentiated type. The modal patient was 36 years old and had been hospitalized three or four times previously for a total duration of 18 to 24 months. All patients were under 55 years of age. The objective was to obtain a sample of schizophrenic patients with acute psychotic symptoms. However, because these patients were all veterans, they were older and ill a longer time than the patient sample previously discussed. Another 308 IMPS ratings were available from Project Twelve (Moseley, 1965) which was a partial replication of Project Six conducted in 20 VA Hospitals. The eligible patient sample was defined in the same manner as the earlier study and a very comparable sample was obtained. These two samples were pooled to form a group of 813 newly admitted, acutely psychotic schizophrenics.

The other three samples were clearly chronic. Project Nine (Caffey, Diamond, Frank, Grasberger, Herman, Klett, and Rothstein, 1964) was a study of drug discontinuation. The average patient was 40 years of age and had been hospitalized nearly 10 years. About a third of them were diagnosed as schizophrenic reaction, paranoid Type. The IMPS ratings used were from 153 patients interviewed after 4 months on placebo or at the time of their clinical relapse following withdrawal of tranquilizing medication. Patients from Project Ten (Honigfeld, Rosenblum, Blumenthal, Lambert and Roberts, 1965) were 54 to 74 years of age, the median age being 66 years. As in the previous study, all patients had been continuously hospitalized for at least 2 years but the average length of continuous stay of patients in this study was over 24 years. The sample contained a larger number of patients diagnosed as hebephrenic type than is usually obtained in VA studies. The 336 IMPS ratings were obtained 1 month after placebo capsules had been substituted for the patients' maintenance medication. Project Fourteen (Platz, 1965) was another evaluation of drug effectiveness in chronic schizophrenic patients. The average age in this sample was 41 years with an average of 9.5 years of hospitalization. The most common diagnoses were chronic undifferentiated (37 per cent), paranoid (27 per cent), and hebephrenic (19 per cent). The 308 IMPS ratings were obtained after 1 month on placebo capsules.

The IMPS ratings of the 1610 patients from these five studies were standardized using the means and standard deviations of the 374 males described in Chapter IV and were then evaluated for inclusion in the nine male types using the multiple cutting score program. Of these 1610, 656 or 41 per cent were classified, 36 per cent of the newly admitted, and 46 per cent of the chronic patients. Of those classified, 29 per cent were Disoriented, 27 per cent were Retarded–Motor Disturbed, and the remaining patients were represented in smaller numbers in the other seven types. The distribution of newly admitted and chronic into the types were somewhat different, however. Among the newly admitted, 21 per cent were classified into one of the two Excited types as opposed to 10 per cent of the chronics, 29 per cent of the newly admitted were one of the Paranoid types compared to 9 per cent of the chronics, 17 per cent newly admitted were Intropunitive but only 3 per cent of the chronics, 5 per cent of the newly admitted and 1 per cent of the chronic were Anxious–Disorganized. The chronic patients were most likely to be Retarded–Motor Disturbed—47 per cent compared to 6 per cent for the newly admitted—or Disoriented—30 per cent compared to 23 per cent for the newly admitted. It is of interest that 100 of the 171 chronic patients classified as Disoriented were from Project Ten, the study of older patients. These data are presented in another way in Table 6.13 where the percentage of newly admitted or chronic patients making up each type has been calculated.

TYPE MEMBERSHIP AFTER TREATMENT

Most of the newly admitted patients from Projects Six and Twelve had been rerated after 8 weeks of drug treatment. It was expected that their IMPS profiles would be depressed and flattened, leading to a smaller percentage of classifications. However, it seemed worthwhile to determine the extent to which the classification was stable over time for those who could be classified. Therefore, their IMPS profiles were also standardized and evaluated by the multiple cutting score program. Of the 719 available cases 32 per cent were classified but this included many patients who had not been classified initially. Essentially the same percentage of patients were represented in each type as had been observed prior to treatment, however, which suggests that drug treatment is not uniquely effective with any one of these types. Of the patients

TABLE 6.13

TYPE MEMBERSHIP OF OTHER SAMPLES

TYPES	NEWLY ADMITTED		CHRONIC		TOTAL
(MALES)	N	%	N	%	N
EXCITED	32	52	29	48	61
EXCITED–HOSTILE	28	76	9	24	37
HOSTILE PARANOID	40	68	19	32	59
HALLUCINATED PARANOID	16	70	7	30	23
GRANDIOSE PARANOID	27	79	7	21	34
INTROPUNITIVE	48	80	12	20	60
RETARDED–MOTOR DISTURBED	66	38	109	62	175
DISORIENTED	18	10	171	90	189
ANXIOUS DISORGANIZED	15	83	3	17	18
TOTAL	290	44%	366	56%	656

who were classified on both occasions, there was 64 per cent agreement. Moreover, many of the changes in type membership seem to have been to related types by an alteration of a portion of the profile. For example, an Excited–Hostile patient can become an Excited one by a decrease in the hostile paranoid elements of his profile or can become Hostile Paranoid if these elements are retained but he becomes somewhat less agitated. Many of the differences in type membership on the two occasions were of this nature.

WARD BEHAVIOR OF INTERVIEW TYPES

All of the newly admitted and chronic patients just described had also been rated at the same times by ward personnel. Project Six, Nine and Twelve patients had been rated using the Psychotic Reaction Profile (PRP) (Lorr, Klett and McNair, 1964). Project Ten and Fourteen patients had been rated using the Nurses Observation Scale for Inpatient Evaluation (NOSIE) (Honigfeld and Klett, 1965). Scores on these two scales were standardized using the means and standard deviations of all available patients. The factors or syndromes measured by PRP are as follows: Dominance, Hostile Belligerence, Resistiveness, Paranoid Projection, Anxious Depression, Seclusiveness, Retardation, Apathy, Motor Disturbances, Perceptual Distortion and Conceptual Disorganization.

The factor scores measured by NOSIE were reflected or reversed so that a high score represented pathology or deviation in an undesirable direction. Thus the seven scores can be described as (1) lack of Social Competence, (2) lack of Social Interest, (3) lack of Personal Neatness, (4) lack of Cooperation, (5) Irritability, (6) Manifest Psychosis, and (7) Paranoid Depression.

In general, the ward profiles are relatively flat and close to the mean. There are few sharp peaks or valleys. However, there is some consistency between the PRP profile and the defining variables of the IMPS. For the two Excited groups, Excitement, Hostility, and Perceptual Distortion are above the mean. However, the Paranoid scale does not achieve prominence in any of the three Paranoid types. The Intropunitive type is defined by Intropunitiveness and secondarily by Retardation. The Retarded–Motor Disturbed patients are highest on Retardation, Seclusiveness and Disorientation. The Disoriented type patients show peaks on Disorientation, Paranoid Projection and Conceptual Disorganization. The Anxious–Disorganized type scores highest on Intropunitiveness but shows a number of other variables above the mean. Thus agreement is fair for five of the types. The most marked failure is the lack of correspondence between the behavior of the Paranoid types in the interview and the wards. Perhaps this is because these groups are defined primarily by their ideation and only secondarily by their external behavior.

Inspection of the ward behavior scores reflected by NOSIE indicates that the Excited type is Socially Competent, Cooperative, Socially Interested and Personally Neat but somewhat Irritable. The Excited–Hostile type has a somewhat similar profile except Irritability is more prominent. The Hostile Paranoid type has an almost completely flat profile, below the mean on all variables. The Retarded–Motor Disturbed type shows a lack of Social Interest. The Disoriented type is lacking in Social Competence, Cooperation, Social Interest and Personal Neatness. The Anxious–Disorganized group has the most deviant profile of all the types on the NOSIE. However, the group is so small that inferences are hazardous. As in the case of PRP the correspondence in profiles is fair but nearly always plausible and consistent with the interview pattern in IMPS. It will be of interest to pursue this problem in future research on a more representative sample of psychotics.

SUMMARY

The available evidence for the validity of the types is scanty. Much additional information needs to be collected to determine how the types differ from each other in social and genetic background. The utility of the types for the selection of treatment and for the prediction of outcome has yet to be made. At most the findings presented offer suggestive support for differences in background, clinical condition and outcome. Related evidence in support of the types and their utility may be found in Chapter 8.

CHAPTER 7

CHRONIC PSYCHOTIC TYPES

Maurice Lorr

Earlier chapters presented a description of a set of types to be found among the more acutely disturbed psychotic patients. The sample as a whole was comprised of patients who either had not been previously hospitalized or had been hospitalized only once before. In the present chapter the several samples analyzed consisted of relatively more chronic psychotics. Evidence will be presented for the existence of a variety of psychotic types, many of which are similar to those found among the more acutely disturbed.

THE NORM SAMPLE

In the analysis reported here the problem was to determine the number and kinds of types to be found within a block of patients that provided the norm sample for IMPS (Lorr, Klett, McNair and Lasky, 1962). A cluster analysis of much of the data has been reported (Lorr, Klett and McNair, 1963), but a reanalysis was deemed worthwhile for several reasons. The typing process employed in the earlier analysis was less rigorous and systematic than the procedures applied in the present analysis. In the initial study the analyses were conducted without the aid of computers and thus involved smaller samples. Second, the separation of clusters was less rigorous, that is to say, a much higher level of between-cluster correlation was permitted. Third, search of the matrix for clusters was less systematic and complete.

The total sample consisted of 556 relatively chronic psychotic patients, all male. One sample of 207 was specially selected to assure representation of all likely sources of symptom variation. The second block of 359 cases were schizophrenics newly readmitted to a group of Veterans Administration Hospitals. In all, 44 state, federal, and private institutions contributed to the sample. The typical patient was 39 years old but the age range was from 20 to 75. The modal length of current hospitalization was a year or less but some patients had been hospitalized for as long as 15 years. Table 7.1 presents the diagnoses represented in the "core" sample of 207. It is important to note that patients were not on tranquilizers for several weeks preceding the interview, or at most were receiving light sedation. This arrangement was possible because the majority of cases constituted part of a nationwide sample studied to determine the effectiveness of several tranquilizers. Psychiatrists as well as psychologists played the role of interviewer and observer.

TABLE 7.1

DISTRIBUTION OF DIAGNOSES IN NORM "CORE" SAMPLE

DIAGNOSIS	No.	%.
SCHIZOPHRENIC, PARANOID	71	34.6
SCHIZOPHRENIC, UNDIFFERENTIATED	43	20.9
SCHIZOPHRENIC, CATATONIC	10	4.9
SCHIZOPHRENIC, SCHIZO-AFFECTIVE	7	3.4
SCHIZOPHRENIC, SIMPLE	3	1.5
SCHIZOPHRENIC, HEBEPHRENIC	19	9.3
MANIC DEPRESSIVE, MANIC	10	4.9
MANIC DEPRESSIVE, DEPRESSED	4	2.0
PSYCHOTIC DEPRESSIVE	15	7.3
INVOLUTIONAL PSYCHOTIC REACTION	7	3.4
OTHER	19	7.8
TOTAL	205	

Each patient was rated independently on IMPS by an interviewer and an observer following a 30 to 60 minute interview. The interviewer and observer ratings were combined into a total score for each syndrome. All syndrome scores were then standardized on the basis of the means and standard deviations of the total sample.

METHOD OF ANALYSIS

Three subsamples of 150 cases each were drawn randomly from the total sample. Random rather than sequential sampling was considered necessary for several reasons. First, the readmitted schizophrenics and the special normative sample cases were drawn in different ways. Another reason for randomization was that the hospitals contributing cases were represented in blocks and their subsamples were not necessarily drawn from similar populations. Limitations of the computer program prevented analysis of samples larger than 150.

The clustering program was applied separately to the correlations (Q) and the congruency coefficients (C) among the 150 cases represented in each of the three subsamples. The clusters were first matched within each subsample across the two indices of similarity. Next the clusters were matched across the three subsamples. Finally a stratified sample was selected as a further check on the cross-sample and cross-index matching. Each clearly defined type found in at least two subsamples was represented in the stratified sample in proportion to its relative frequency. Analysis of the stratified sample provided not only a check on the accuracy of the matching but provided a test of cluster invariance. Any type or class evolved should be replicable under changes in the sample of persons examined providing it is represented in sufficient numbers.

Matching within a subsample across similarity indices involved several steps. Two clusters defined by a high proportion of identical cases were judged identical. In addition, the ten standard scores of cluster members were averaged. Then congruency coefficients between the mean syndrome profiles of the two sets of clusters being compared were computed. Clusters were considered identical if the congruency coefficient between their profiles was at least 0.75.

Type matching across subsamples was also achieved by comparing the congruency coefficients between the mean syndrome profiles of the various clusters. Two clusters were judged identical if the congruency coefficient between their profiles was 0.75 or greater and all other indices of similarity were negative or close to zero. Such matching was checked by resort to the clusters identified in the stratified sample. When subsample clusters had been correctly matched their representatives in the stratified sample were nearly all found in the same cluster evolved. Thus the matching by congruency coefficient could readily be confirmed or rejected.

RESULTS OF MATCHING

The characteristic profile of a type can be described in terms of those mean syndrome scores that lie at some point above the sample mean on the standard score scale. For convenience and brevity each syndrome can be identified by a number. Let Excitement be denoted 1; Hostile Belligerence 2; Paranoid Projection 3; Grandiosity 4; Perceptual Distortion 5; Intropunitiveness 6; Retardation 7; Disorientation 8; Motor Disturbances 9; and Conceptual Disorganization 10. Then a 1–2–4–10 profile will mean that Excitement (1), Hostile Belligerence (2), Grandiosity (4), and Conceptual Disorganization (5) are elevated 0.15 above the sample mean of zero. This notation will be used hereafter to identify each of the types.

Some of the results of matching can be seen in Table 7.2. From five to seven clusters were identified in each of the three subsamples. Only five emerged in the stratified sample analysis. In most instances the same types emerged regardless of the index used to measure similarity. However, not every type emerged out of each subsample, perhaps because of the relative fewness of the type in the sample. Clusters listed as miscellaneous tended to be small (four members), inconsistent in the pattern manifested, unconfirmed in other subsamples, or collections of "flat", asymptomatic profiles. While there are no sharp differences, the two similarity indices do appear to influence the types emerging. In the stratified sample, for example, the 7–8–9–10 pattern appeared only in the Q analysis while 3–5–6–7–9–10 emerged only in the C analysis. The Retarded group (7) was best defined in the C analysis.

THE SEVEN TYPES

Members of each of the clusters found to be equivalent were pooled. The characteristic profile of each type was determined by computing the ten average standard scores of its members. Table 7.3 presents the mean syndrome scores of all types in the

TABLE 7.2

MATCHING Q AND C CLUSTERS THAT DEFINE

THE 7 PATIENT TYPES IN NORM SAMPLE

TYPE	SUBSAMPLE						
	1		**2**		**3**		STRATIFIED
	Q	C	Q	C	Q	C$_i$	Q	C
7-8-9-10	1	4	4	4	4	3	2	
6	2	5	2	2	3	1	5	3
2-3-5-6	3		3	3	5	4	4	5
1-2-4-10	4	3	1	1		7	1	1
1-2-3-4-5-10	5	6	6	1	2	2	3	1
3-5-6-7-9-10	6		5	6			-	4
7		1			1	6	(2)	2
MISCELL.	7	2		5,7	6,7	5		

Norm sample. Figures 7.1 to 7.7 show the mean profiles of the seven types and indicate, as well, the extent of variation around the mean scores. The shaded areas enclose the central 68 per cent of scores around the mean.

Not all syndromes are relevant in defining a type. The crucial syndromes are those on which (a) all members score above the total sample mean; (b) all members score below the mean. A syndrome on which members score equally often below as above the mean is undiscriminating.

The Excited–Hostile Type

The 1–2–4–10 profile is defined mainly by Excitement and Hostility. Grandiosity and Conceptual Disorganization play lesser roles. Paranoid Projection and Motor Disturbances may also be present but are not essential. Included within this Excited–Hostile type are a small group who are primarily excited; their hostility

TABLE 7.3

MEAN SYNDROME SCORES OF 7 PSYCHOTIC TYPES IN NORM SAMPLE

TYPE	SYNDROME									
	EXC	HOS	PAR	GRN	PCP	INP	RTD	DIS	MTR	CNP
EXCITED-HOSTILE	1.88	1.08	.02	.19	-.60	-.46	-.68	-.39	-.03	.37
GRANDIOSE PARANOID	.77	.35	.70	2.51	.79	-.41	-.46	-.33	-.02	.66
HOSTILE PARANOID	-.32	1.28	.94	-.24	.00	.06	-.33	-.29	-.45	-.55
INTROPUNITIVE	-.51	-.53	-.74	-.55	-.34	1.54	-.03	-.34	-.49	-.66
RETARDED	-.74	-.69	-.84	-.58	-.46	-.50	1.15	-.38	-.38	-.45
ANXIOUS-DISORGANIZED	-.57	-.04	1.03	.06	2.02	1.70	1.03	-.38	.31	.72
RETARDED-DISORGANIZED	-.41	-.52	-.60	-.45	-.15	-.55	.59	1.89	1.25	.79

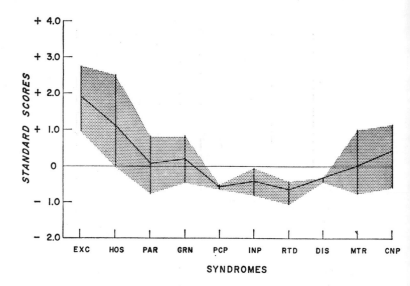

Fig. 7.1. Profile of Excited–Hostile type.

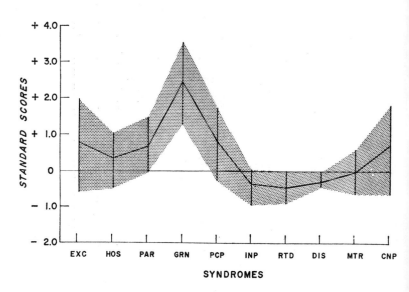

Fig. 7.2. Profile of Grandiose Paranoid type.

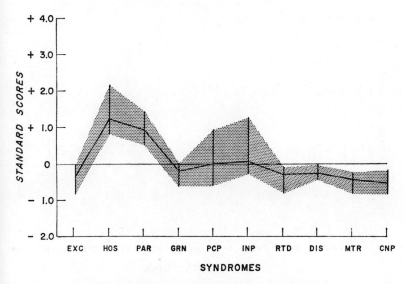

FIG. 7.3. Profile of Hostile Paranoid type.

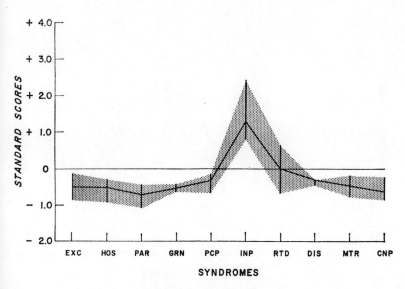

FIG. 7.4. Profile of Intropunitive type.

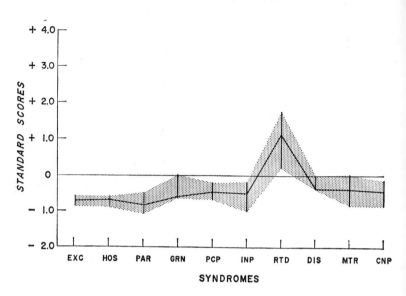

FIG. 7.5. Profile of Retarded type.

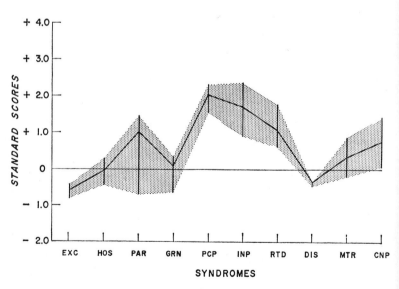

FIG. 7.6. Profile of Anxious–Disorganized type.

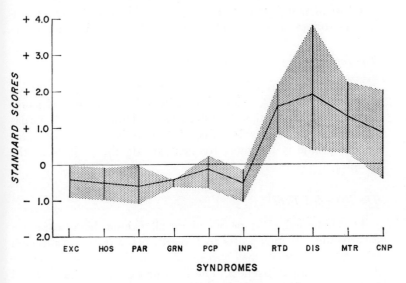

FIG. 7.7. Profile of Retarded–Disorganized type.

scores are below the average of the total sample. The excited group without hostility is more common in acute samples where it separates out as a distinctive type.

The Grandiose Paranoid Type

The Grandiose Paranoid (1–2–3–4–5–10) type is primarily grandiose as all members have highly elevated scores on this syndrome. Scores on Excitement, Hostility, Paranoid Projection, Conceptual Disorganization, and Perceptual Distortion are usually but not always elevated. Typically other syndrome scores such as Anxious Intropunitiveness, Retardation and Disorientation are below the general mean.

The Hostile Paranoid Type

The Hostile Paranoid (2–3) type represents another paranoid group. In this type, Hostility and Paranoid Projection are uniformly elevated above the sample mean. Some members also have elevated scores on Perceptual Distortion and Anxious Intropunitiveness.

Excitement as well as Grandiosity are notably absent. The remaining syndromes are nearly always below the general mean.

The Intropunitive Type

Intropunitive (6) type members all have elevated scores on Intropunitiveness. Occasionally members also have elevated scores on Perceptual Distortions and Retardation. However, the Retardation scores are always less than Intropunitiveness scores. This patient profile is the most frequent among the patients in the sample.

The Retarded Type

The Retarded (7) type members all exhibit high scores on Retardation. All other scores are typically below the mean although an occasional patient may also manifest some hostility or a slight degree of intropunitiveness. The Retarded group is clear-cut and fairly numerous among chronic patients. While a few similar profiles are found within an acute sample, they are less common and hence become confused with the next type to be described.

The Retarded–Disorganized Type

Retardation is always elevated, while Disorientation and Motor Disturbances are usually prominent in this patient type. Conceptual Disorganization, on the other hand, is somewhat less common; in a third of the cases this score is below the Norm mean.

The Anxious–Disorganized Type

Class members all have scores elevated above the mean on Perceptual Distortion, Intropunitiveness and Retardation. In addition, many also have high scores on Paranoid Projection, Motor Disturbances and Conceptual Disorganization.

DIFFERENTIATION OF THE TYPES

What is the evidence for separation or differentiation of the more chronic patient types? Since one goal of the study was the identification of mutually exclusive patient classes, the problem of differentiation is an important one. Tables 7.4 and 7.5 present the average correlations and the average congruency coefficients among the clusters identified in the stratified sample. If the non-diagonal entries are inspected it is seen that no positive correlation is greater than 0.07, and no positive congruency coefficient is greater than 0.21. Thus the evidence indicates that the clusters are well distinguished from each other. The average coefficients among the clusters found in the three subsamples are equally small and thus are not presented. Table 7.6 presents the congruency coefficients among the seven mean syndrome profiles of the pooled subsamples. These results are not as valid as those given in the preceding tables because correlations among averages do not always represent the average correlations among cluster members. Nevertheless, the coefficients do indicate a satisfactory separation of the clusters.

The diagonals of Tables 7.4 and 7.5 give the average relationships among cluster members. High values of the similarity indices indicate high profile consistency among members. Inasmuch as the indices are not less than 0.65, the clusters can be regarded as substantially homogeneous with respect to membership.

What can be said about the number of cases classified within the various patient classes? A desirable property of any typing procedure of typing scheme is the inclusion of a high proportion of all cases. Table 7.7 lists the numbers of cases defining each

TABLE 7.4

AVERAGE CORRELATIONS AMONG CLUSTERS

OF STRATIFIED SAMPLE OF NORM DATA

CLUSTER	1	2	3	4	5	6
1	.65					
2	-.30	.74				
3	.05	-.30	.78			
4	-.39	00	-.07	.67		
5	-.30	.03	-.23	.02	.73	
6	.07	-.47	00	.05	-.05	.74

TABLE 7.5

AVERAGE CONGRUENCIES AMONG CLUSTERS

OF STRATIFIED SAMPLE OF NORM DATA

CLUSTER	1	2	3	4	5	6	7
1	.80						
2	-.45	.71					
3	-.21	-.06	.71				
4	-.02	-.05	-.39	.67			
5	.08	.01	.10	-.09	.68		
6	.21	-.51	.12	-.21	-.17	.78	
7	.06	-.05	-.32	.03	-.57	.12	.68

TABLE 7.6

CONGRUENCY COEFFICIENTS AMONG THE MEAN

PROFILES OF THE 7 PSYCHOTIC TYPES

TYPE		A	B	C	D	E	F
1-2-4-10	A						
1-2-3-4-5-10	B	.37					
2-3	C	.19	.02				
6	D	-.42	-.57	-.07			
7	E	-.50	-.59	-.31	.37		
3-5-6-7-9-10	F	-.43	.15	-.07	.13	-.20	
7-8-9-10	G	-.35	-.30	-.54	-.21	.32	.02

cluster in the three subsamples and in the stratified sample. The correlation-based analyses included 51 per cent of all cases while the congruency-based analyses classified 48 per cent. In the stratified sample 71 and 58 per cent of the 150 cases were classified in the Q and C analyses.

TABLE 7.7

NUMBER OF CASES DEFINING EACH CLUSTER

WITHIN THE NORM SUBSAMPLES

	SUBSAMPLE							
	1		2		3		STRATIFIED	
INDEX	Q	C	Q	C	Q	C	Q	C
CLUSTER 1	24	30	19	17	14	18	30	12
2	22	11	19	17	10	17	16	16
3	12	9	11	11	14	14	21	18
4	9	9	14	9	9	6	21	17
5	7	8	8	7	7	6	13	9
6	6	7	8	5	6	5	6	8
7	4			6	5	4		7
TOTAL	84	74	79	72	65	70	107	87
%	55	49	53	48	43	47	71	58

TABLE 7.8

NUMBER IN NORM SAMPLE ASSIGNED TO EACH TYPE BY

CLUSTER ANALYSIS AND CORRELATION COEFFICIENT

TYPE	CLUSTER ASSIGNED	CORRELATION ASSIGNED	PER CENT ASSIGNED
EXCITED-HOSTILE	36	23	18
GRANDIOSE PARANOID	28	15	13
HOSTILE PARANOID	27	18	14
INTROPUNITIVE	40	24	20
RETARDED	25	18	13
ANXIOUS-DISORG.	13	10	7
RETARDED-DISORG.	31	17	15
TOTAL	200	125	100

Following the stratified sample analyses, matched clusters were pooled. The size of the patient classes is shown on Table 7.8. The Intropunitives (6) and the Excited–Hostile (1–2–4–10) represent the largest types. The smallest class is the Anxious–Disorganized (3–5–7–9–10). Next each profile in the sample of 450 was correlated with each of the mean syndrome profiles of the seven types. Patients were then assigned to that class with which they correlated highest providing the coefficient was at least 0.55. The value of 0.55 was chosen because a correlation based on ten measures is significant at $p < 0.05$ at this point. While the pooled subsample types included only 44 per cent of cases, use of the correlation coefficient resulted in a total of 325 out of 450 or 72 per cent classified. Note that the percentages are relative to the total classified and not to the total sample. Thus a relatively large proportion of all cases can be classified into one of the seven types. In subsequent studies an effort will be made to check these findings on an independent comparable sample.

COMPARISON WITH PRIOR FINDINGS

The patient types identified in the present analysis can be compared with the original six types (Lorr, Klett and McNair, 1963), and with the types described in Chapter 4. The original analysis types were labeled Excited–Hostile, Hostile Paranoid, Intropunitive, Retarded, Disorganized, and Excited–Grandioes. The first five original types correspond very closely to the re-analysis types labeled Excited–Hostile, Hostile Paranoid, Intropunitive, Retarded and Retarded–Disorganized. However, an Excited–Grandiose type did not separate out in the reanalysis in any of the subsamples. Instead Excited–Grandiose members appear to have been separated into the Grandiose Paranoid and the Excited–Hostile (1–2–4–10) types. The seventh or Anxious–Disorganized appears only in the reanalysis.

It will be recalled that nine psychotic types were found among the men and women of the acute sample. Of these nine types, six were identical for men and for women. A seventh type (3–5–6–7–8–9–10) was similar in shape but more elevated on Disorientation and Motor Disturbances in men. The major difference between the sexes was in the separation of a Retarded–Motor Disturbed type and a Disoriented type in men from a Retarded–Disorganized

TABLE 7.9

CONGRUENCY COEFFICIENTS BETWEEN

CHRONIC (NORM) AND ACUTE PSYCHOTIC TYPES

CHRONIC TYPE (NORM)	C	ACUTE TYPE
EXCITED–HOSTILE	.95	EXCITED–HOSTILE
GRANDIOSE–PARANOID	.85	GRANDIOSE–PARANOID
HOSTILE–PARANOID	.75	HOSTILE–PARANOID
INTROPUNITIVE	.96	INTROPUNITIVE
ANXIOUS–DISORGANIZED	.89	ANXIOUS–DISORGANIZED
RETARDED–DISORGANIZED	.86	DISORIENTED

type in women. As Table 7.9 shows, agreement between six of the male acute and six of the more chronic types is quite close. The Excited–Hostile (1–2–4–10) chronic type exhibits less paranoid ideation and more grandiosity than the Excited–Hostile (1–2–3–10) of the acute sample. The chronic Hostile Paranoid (2–3) is more anxious and hallucinated than the corresponding acute type. The chronic Grandiose Paranoid (1–3–4–5) is less hostile and excited among the acute patients. The Intropunitive (6) types in the two samples appear to differ in insignificant ways. The chronic patients of the Retarded–Disorganized type (7–8–9–10) are less disoriented but more retarded than the acute patients in the Disoriented class. Finally, the chronic Anxious–Disorganized type manifests fewer elevated scores on Disorientation than the acute type.

In conclusion it can be said that the reanalyzed chronic patient type profiles can be regarded as identical (a) with five types in the original analysis, and (b) with six types identified in the acute psychotic sample.

THE CHRONIC LONG-TERM SAMPLE

The norm sample included a fair proportion of chronically ill cases who had been hospitalized three and four times. Yet the norm sample was not selected with emphasis on chronicity and long-term hospitalization. In view of the high proportion of such patients in psychiatric hospitals, further investigation seemed to be of considerable interest. Accordingly a sample of 450 cases was obtained. The IMPS ratings had been made in connection with the two nationwide Veterans Administration studies of the tranquilizers.

One-third of the sample came from a drug reduction and drug discontinuation study. All of these 150 cases were male schizophrenics under 56 years of age who had been hospitalized for a total of 2 or more years. Lobotomized cases and cases with central nervous system disease were excluded. Patients had been on a stable tranquilizer treatment program for 3 or more months preceding the study. IMPS ratings were completed on most patients 16 weeks after discontinuation of drug treatment. On the remainder ratings were completed when the physician noted that the patient had definitely become worse and needed to be re-established on treatment.

A second sample of 300 cases was taken from a study of the selective action of 3 drugs on chronic schizophrenics grouped as "hyperdynamic" and "hypodynamic". All cases were male schizophrenics under 56 years of age who had been hospitalized for a period of 3 or more years. Interviews and ratings were conducted by teams of raters at the end of the 4-week period of discontinuation of previous medication. The so-called hyperdynamic patient was characterized by "disjointed motivation, projection, and frequent hyperkinetic manifestations". In addition he was described as "irritable and cantankerous and communicating with others regardless of the content or meanings of his verbalizations". The hypodynamic patient, on the other hand, is characterized "by autism, lethargy, lack of spontaneity, and anergic reactions. Mental activity is decreased; the patient is autistic and may be withdrawn, showing no apparent interest in his surroundings and no obvious desire to approach or communicate with others".

METHOD OF ANALYSIS

The procedures applied to the IMPS scores for the chronic long-term sample were much the same as previously described. The clustering program was separately applied to the correlations and the congruencies among the 150 cases of the 3 subsamples of 150 cases. The clusters emerging were then matched across the similarity indices and across subsamples. However, a stratified sample was not assembled or analyzed as was done in the norm sample analysis.

TABLE 7.10

NUMBER OF CASES DEFINING EACH CLUSTER IN THE THREE SUBSAMPLES

OF CHRONIC LONG-TERM PATIENTS

| | SUBSAMPLE | | | | | |
| | 1 | | 2 | | 3 | |
CLUSTER	Q	C	Q	C	Q	C
1	34	33	30	37	35	25
2	21	17	12	34	16	34
3	7	5	8	6	8	8
4	7	6	5	6	5	7
5			4	4		4
6			5			

Table 7.10 presents the initial results of the analysis. The proportions classified in the clusters are not too different from other analyses. However, the number of clusters were fewer than for the norm sample. In Table 7.11 may be found the seven types matched across subsamples. A "flat" or asymptomatic profile was quite prominent. Evidently quite a few patients did not relapse following discontinuation of drugs.

THE CHRONIC PATIENT TYPES

After matching equivalent clusters were combined. The characteristic syndrome profile was then determined for each type. This process consisted of computing the average standard score of type members on each of the ten syndromes. Table 7.12 presents the type profiles and their tentative names.

TABLE 7.11

MATCHING Q AND C CLUSTERS THAT DEFINE THE

CHRONIC LONG-TERM SAMPLE TYPES

	SET					
	1		2		3	
TYPE	Q	C	Q	C	Q	C
1-7-9-10	3	3		3	4	
2-9			5	5		
3-5			6		3	4
6			4	4		
7			3			
7-8-9	2	2	1	2	1	1
7-9			2		2	5
FLAT .	1	1		1	2	
MISCELL.	4	4				3,6

The Excited–Disorganized Type

Members of this patient group (1–7–9–10) all have strongly elevated scores on Motor Disturbances and Conceptual Disorganization. Nearly all have average or above-average scores on Excitement. At the same time about two-thirds of the group also score above average on Retardation and Apathy. It seems likely that it is the ratings on Apathy that are the effective elements in this score. The general pattern suggests a "catatonic-like" excitement.

The Hostile–Motor Disturbed Type

This patient type (2–9) is small and defined mainly by elevated scores on Hostile Belligerence. Scores on Motor Disturbances are frequently but not always above the mean of the sample. Further data will be needed to evaluate the stability of this type.

TABLE 7.12

MEAN SYNDROME SCORES OF PSYCHOTIC TYPES

CHRONIC LONG-TERM SAMPLE

TYPE	SYNDROME									
	EXC	HOS	PAR	GRN	PCP	IMP	RTD	DIS	MTR	CNP
EXCITED-DISORGANIZED	1.27	-.38	-.36	-.10	-.34	-.71	.28	.03	2.03	2.12
HOSTILE-MOTOR DISTURBED	-.26	.66	-.49	-.46	-.49	-.36	-.27	-.46	.33	-.65
HALLUCINATED PARANOID	-.36	-.44	.71	-.25	1.93	.13	-.46	-.33	.53	-.59
INTROPUNITIVE	-.37	-.87	-.91	-.35	-.27	.95	-.47	-.46	-.44	-.73
RETARDED	-.75	-.98	-1.15	-.52	-.62	-.68	.21	-.46	-.94	-.70
RETARDED-MOTOR DISTURBED	-.53	-.93	-1.01	-.58	-.61	-.64	1.08	-.37	.86	-.17
DISORIENTED	-.48	-.94	-.99	-.55	-.59	-.88	1.12	4.38	1.07	-.11

The Hallucinated Paranoid Type

The profile of the Hallucinated Paranoid (3–5) is much like the type of the same name found among acute patients. All members exhibit highly elevated scores on Perceptual Distortion. Nearly all have moderately elevated Paranoid Projection scores. Although the mean level on Motor Disturbances is moderately high, it can be accounted for by a few extreme scores. Thus the latter syndrome is not differentiating for this type. Intropunitive scores also are moderately elevated for half of the group.

The Intropunitives

As might be anticipated, few Intropunitives (6) are found in the sample. However, the profile is quite characteristic of this patient type; only Anxious Intropunitiveness is above the general mean for all members. Although the type emerged only in one sub-sample, its verification in several other studies left no doubt about its existence.

THE RETARDED TYPE

The Retarded (7) patients exhibit only a mild psychomotor Retardation and Apathy. All other syndromes are uniformly low. The profile is very similar to that found in the norm sample. It is likely that this is the group described as autistic, seclusive and "hypodynamic".

The Retarded–Motor Disturbed Type

This patient group (7–9) is the same as the patient class found among the acute psychotic sample of men. Nearly all have above-average scores on Retardation and Motor Disturbances. The remaining elements of the profile are all depressed below the mean.

The Disoriented Type

Nearly all members of the Disoriented patient type (7–8–9) manifest extreme Disorientation scores. Also, except for a few members, all are characterized by distinctly elevated scores on Retardation and Motor Disturbances. Members of the type constitute a fairly high proportion of all cases in the sample. Among acute psychotics, on the other hand, the Disoriented patient is relatively rare.

TABLE 7.13

CONGRUENCY COEFFICIENTS BETWEEN MEAN PROFILES

OF CHRONIC LONG TERM TYPES

		A	B	C	D	E	F
EXCITED-DISORGANIZED	A						
HOSTILE-MOTOR DISTURBED	B	-.15					
HALLUCINATED PARANOID	C	-.20	-.17				
INTROPUNITIVE	D	-.44	.20	.03			
RETARDED	E	-.35	.35	-.23	.62		
RETARDED-MOTOR DISTURBED	F	.31	.32	-.19	.24	.60	
DISORIENTED	G	.20	-.14	-.22	-.15	.08	.34

DIFFERENTIATION OF THE TYPES

The average correlations among the clusters, within subsamples, were uniformly low; none exceeded 0.30. Thus the evidence supports the differentiation of the types within subsamples. The similarity of the mean syndrome profiles of the chronic types was also evaluated. Table 7.13 presents the congruency coefficients among these profiles. Examination of the table shows that a few of the coefficients are moderate in size. However, none are sufficiently high to justify elimination of the types involved.

COMPARISON WITH OTHER SAMPLES

The more chronic long-term psychotics, as judged by the types evolved here, appear not to be strikingly different from the chronic or even the acute. However, the samples analyzed were by no means representative of long-term chronics found in psychiatric hospitals. The selection procedure for the second sample, in particular, was directed towards hyper- and hypodynamic cases.

Four of the types are evidently the same as those identified in the Acute sample. These are the Hallucinated Paranoid (3–5), the Retarded–Motor Disturbed (7–9), the Disoriented (7–8–9) and the Intropunitive (6). Table 7.14 gives the congruency coefficients between these types. The coefficients are all fairly high except for the coefficient between the two Hallucinated Paranoid groups, which is borderline. The Retarded patient type (7) was checked against a similar group identified in the norm sample. The chronic Excited–Disorganized (1–9–10) was compared with the acute male Excited (1–10) pattern but the match was poor.

SUMMARY

In this chapter the results of two typing studies were reported. In the first analysis, the standardization sample for the Inpatient Multidimensional Psychiatric Scale (IMPS) provided the basic data. Identification procedures disclosed seven male patient types. Five of the types were the same as those found in the acute patient sample. A Retarded and a Retarded–Disorganized group constituted the two new patient classes.

The sample in the second analysis consisted of chronic long-term Schizophrenics whose drug treatment had been discontinued. Again seven patient types were identified of which two had not been previously found. These were an Excited–Disorganized group and a Hostile–Motor Disturbed group. All of the remaining types could be found among acute or norm sample types.

CHAPTER 8

TYPES BASED ON
REPEATED MEASUREMENT

CHARLES E. RICE AND NILS B. MATTSSON

As is evident from the other chapters in this book, most of the approaches to typing psychiatric patients have been static in the sense that, typically, a patient is assessed at one point in time and patients are classified according to these "one-shot" profiles of measures. But clinical observation suggests that the total pattern of symptomatology often changes over time so that a static typing approach may indicate that we have types A and B when in reality, if we could take a more longitudinal approach, we might conclude that A and B are but separate phases of type C. The possibilities of investigating such shifts in symptom patterns have been mentioned by Lorr, Klett, and McNair (1963) among others, but opportunity and appropriate methods for investigating these shifts have generally been lacking. This chapter describes some admittedly tentative approaches for typing patients with respect to how they change over time.

There are two general types of approach which could be used to study the change over time in patterns of psychopathology. The first of these would involve the identification of a number of patient types, perhaps by the use of methods like those developed by Lorr and his associates (1963). The patients in these types could then be observed over a period of time, repeated measures on a number of variables obtained, and changes in symptom profiles noted. Several schemes for dealing with the data are suggested. One scheme would consist of typing the patients at each of a number of assessment periods and then noting the extent to which patients exhibiting Profile A at Time 1 will, at time $t(t > 1)$, exhibit Profiles A, B, C, etc. The data could be utilized in another manner, however. The various profile elements (these are variously

151

labeled as "symptoms" or "syndromes"), or rather their measures, may be plotted as a function of time and their paths or trajectories noted. In this way the rise and fall over time of the various aspects of psychopathology would be exhibited.

A second scheme for studying change in psychopathology over time, and the one pursued by the authors, is the attempt to classify patients into types with respect to the manner in which they change. Two patients would fall into the same type if they exhibited similar patterns of change over time. If we assume that a sample of patients has a profile of scores at each of several time periods, three methods of utilizing these data to detect types of change suggest themselves. These methods correspond to three different ways of viewing patterned change over time.

The approach to studying change over time in psychopathology which we have used is, as has been mentioned, a typological one. Before presenting empirical data we shall now turn to a more complete explication of these methods.

THREE BASIC MODELS

The inclusion of time as a formal parameter in data-reduction problems in psychology of which typology studies are an example, was triggered by the work of Cattell (1946) and more recently has been considered in an expanded but tentative manner by Tucker (1963) and Horst (1963). The introduction of time-series analysis into psychology has been fostered by the work of Mefferd, Moran, and Kimble (1958) and by Holtzman (1962). Our efforts have involved the use of more familiar statistical techniques even though some similarity with the above mentioned models can be noted.

The three basic concepts underlying our work are (1) a set of attributes which characterize human behavior or functioning, (2) a set of time curves corresponding to these symptoms, and (3) the concept of an attribute profile. These three notions will be examined prior to a description of the disease process models.

With regard to the first notion, a set of behavioral attributes, there is much that can be noted, but we will arrange a necessarily brief discussion around two considerations. The first of those pertains to what might be called the level of observation. Behavior may be observed at several levels ranging from molecular physiological events to more molar behavior in a social setting. In the study of behavior pathology observations are mostly of a more molar sort, although there have been notable exceptions. Our thinking has involved only molar aspects of behavior and without prejudging the desirability of mixing molar and molecular variables we will assume a set of attributes all of which are at a level above the strictly physiological. In the realm of psychopathology the type of attributes we have in mind are often called symptoms, but our work has dealt with more abstract attributes, called syndromes by Lorr, Klett and McNair (1963), which are inferred from the observation of more discrete behavior often on the basis of a technique such as factor analysis.

The second consideration regarding the attribute set pertains to its exhaustiveness. In any study of psychopathology it is difficult to decide just what aspects of behavior are to be observed and measured. All one can hope to do is to try to cover the field as adequately as possible so as to include all that is relevant, hopefully without being redundant. We assume a fairly exhaustive and non-redundant set of attributes such as those developed by factor-analytic studies like those of Lorr and Wittenborn.

A second concept underlying our models is the idea of a time curve for each attribute. We conceive of each attribute of a person's behavior being measured on a series of occasions with variation over time being expressed as a curve. It is not assumed that each attribute follows a unique course over time. These time curves, also called time-series, may well be cyclic or periodic, although this is not assumed. The number and spacing of time-sequential observations are important considerations, a detailed discussion of which could lead to an extended digression. However, a few remarks are in order at this point.

First, it is obvious that the behavior of a person should be observed over a period of time which is long enough to permit the identification of important long-term trends in the curves. Secondly, observations should be frequent enough to catch important short-term trends. Further, the total number of measurement occasions should be as great as is practicable so that appropriate statistical techniques can be employed. Finally, we may mention that equally-spaced measurement occasions are certainly most desirable, but more important for our work has been the

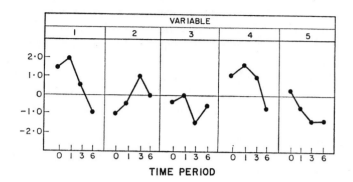

FIG. 8.1.

requirement that their spacing is the same for all patients being studied.

Our final basic notion is a familiar one, namely that of a profile of attributes for a person as measured on a given occasion. Such a profile is useful in that it shows the patterns of relationships between a person's behavioral attributes at a given point in time.

With these basic concepts in mind we may proceed to describe the three ways of conceptualizing change-types. (In the medical or psychiatric realm these could perhaps be called disease-processes.)

Model 1. A given change-type may be identified by a characteristic set of attribute time-curves. One such possible set is represented in Fig. 8.1 for a set of five attributes measured on four occasions. Measurement on each attribute is assumed to be on a common metric.

Model II. A given change-type may be identified by a characteristic time-sequential ordering of attribute profiles. Figure 8.2 illustrates this for the same attribute measures.

Model III. A given change-type may be identified by a characteristic set of attribute time-curves *in conjunction with* a characteristic sequential ordering of profiles. A graphic representation is not provided for this, but it should be clear that a three-dimensional surface would be required to portray such a change-type.

As has been mentioned in earlier chapters, one of the important steps in any typology approach is the selection of a similarity

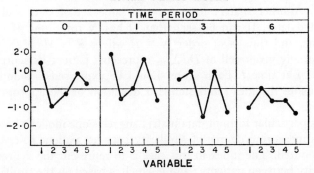

FIG. 8.2.

index to be used in correlating persons prior to clustering or classifying them into types. We shall discuss three ways of organizing and utilizing the same set of basic data to compute similarity indices. These three methods correspond to the three models for change-types.

The Within-Score Method

In order to fix ideas we shall describe, in a more precise fashion, the type of data which is to be employed in the change models to be discussed. Let us assume we have a sample of N patients $(1, 2, \ldots i \ldots N)$ each measured on M variables $(1, 2, \ldots j \ldots M)$ at each of T periods $(1, 2, \ldots t \ldots T)$ of time. We may then conceive of D, a basic data matrix, which may be represented as follows:

$$1 \ldots \ldots \ldots j \ldots \ldots M$$
$$1 \ldots t \ldots T \quad 1 \ldots t \ldots T \quad 1 \ldots t \ldots T$$

1
2
.
.
i
.
.
N

The rows of this matrix correspond to patients. The columnar arrangement should be noted carefully. Columns corresponding to variables are subdivided into columns corresponding to time periods. D may thus be called the periods-within-variables data matrix. Another matrix form for the same set of data will be presented later. It can be seen that D has N rows and $M \times T$ columns, and thus is of order $N \times R$ where $R = M \times T$. The value in any given cell of D, X_{ijt}, represents patient i's score on variable j at time t. Each score should be expressed in standard form, using the mean and standard deviation of the appropriate column.

This particular form of data matrix suggests one model whereby indices measuring degree of similarity between patient pairs may be computed. The index in this case is to represent the degree of similarity between patients i and k which is based on the similarity of their attribute time curves. More precisely, what we propose is to compute a correlation between i and k based on the within-variable sums of squares and sums of cross products.

If we think in terms of the conventional product-moment correlation the index may be expressed as

$$r_{i,\,k} = \frac{\sum\limits_{j=1}^{M} \sum\limits_{t=1}^{T} (X_{ijt} - \bar{X}_{ij.})(X_{kjt} - \bar{X}_{kj.})}{\sqrt{\sum\limits_{j=1}^{M} \sum\limits_{t=1}^{T} (X_{ijt} - \bar{X}_{ij.})^2} \; \sqrt{\sum\limits_{j=1}^{M} \sum\limits_{t=1}^{T} (X_{kjt} - \bar{X}_{kj.})^2}}$$

$$(1)$$

where, for example, $\bar{X}_{ij.}$ represents the mean of patient i's scores on variable j over the t time periods.

In effect, what is actually being done here is first to correlate two patients on a single variable in terms of the patients' deviations from their own means on this variable. Two patients will correlate highly if their time curves on this variable are of the same shape. But we are also summing over several variables and are thus obtaining an average correlation so that two patients will correlate highly only if their time curves for each variable are similarly shaped. The reader familiar with Cattell's (1946) covariation designs will note that this within-variable correlation approach can be viewed as an extension of a type S design.

The above method, with its attendant computations, involves several assumptions which are important to note.

1. The covariance matrices for each variable are equal. This assumption is not only necessary as a rationale for the operation of summing over variables, but is highly desirable in that homogeneity

of covariances between patients i and k over all variables enhances the possibility of detecting stable typologies.

2. The scores corresponding to variables at any one time period are uncorrelated. Assumed independence of the variables provides another rationale for the summation operation. This suggests the use of scores derived from an orthogonal factor solution.

3. The measures of each variable are uncorrelated over time. The existence of sizeable serial correlations, unfortunately to be anticipated in using data obtained from repeated measurements on the same patients, creates two problems. First, our estimate of the true correlation between two patients will likely be an underestimate unless the time curves are in exactly the same phase and cycle. Consequently, we would be erring on the conservative side and because of lowered similarity indices we could fail to detect important patient types. The second difficulty as noted by Holtzman (1962), is that the degrees of freedom are reduced for testing the significance of the correlation between patients. However, even though this might possibly result in the mistaken inference that two patients are exhibiting the same type of change pattern, this fact can be detected at a later stage of the typing process.

In summary, what we are attempting to do with the within-scores approach is to compare patients with respect to their respective sets of attribute time-curves. A group of patients will be highly intercorrelated, and thus of the same change type, if they exhibit highly similar sets of time-curves.

The Within-Period Method

The basic data matrix may be arranged column-wise in a different form. Columns would now correspond to periods or occasions and sub-columns to variables. This is the variables-within-period form of the data matrix. Each patient now is represented, following along a given row, by a time-sequential ordering of score profiles. Two patients may now be correlated by employing the within-period sums of squares and sums of cross-products. This may be expressed as

$$r_{i,\,k} = \frac{\sum\limits_{t=1}^{T} \sum\limits_{j=1}^{M} (X_{ijt} - \bar{X}_{i.t})(X_{kjt} - \bar{X}_{k.t})}{\sqrt{\sum\limits_{t=1}^{T} \sum\limits_{j=1}^{M} (X_{ijt} - \bar{X}_{i.t})^2} \sqrt{\sum\limits_{t=1}^{T} \sum\limits_{j=1}^{M} (X_{kjt} - \bar{X}_{k.t})^2}} \tag{2}$$

where $\bar{X}_{i.t}$ represents the mean of patient i's scores on variable j at time t.

With this approach, two patients' profiles are being correlated at each time period and an "average" correlation over time periods is being computed. Two patients will be highly correlated if, period for period, they have similarly shaped profiles. This can be viewed as an extension of Cattell's type Q design involving a summation over occasions or periods.

The same three basic assumptions underlying the within-score method hold for the present approach. Existence of autocorrelation is perhaps a less serious problem for the within-period model, but the assumption of independent measures at any given period is, on the other hand, more important. If patient profiles consist of scores which are highly correlated this could result in an underestimate of the correlation between two patients. This would have the effect of making it more difficult to find homogeneous patient types.

A "Total" Correlation Method

A third type of agreement index would, ideally, have a high value only if two patients displayed similarly shaped time-curves as well as similar time-sequences of profiles. Several different techniques have been tried by the authors, none too satisfactory.

One approach was based on deviations from the grand means of patients' $R(R = M \times T)$ measures, and thus utilized the total sums of squares and cross-products. One problem which arose is what might be termed "cross-over". Two patients might display similarly shaped sets of time-curves or profiles but unless they maintain their positions with respect to the levels of their curves they will not be highly correlated using this method.

Another approach utilized scores deviated from both sets of ipsative means, i.e. deviated from the appropriate period and score means. It was thus based on a residual sum of squares and cross-products. The types based on this agreement index were far too "loose". Additional techniques are currently under investigation.

In summary, we may briefly compare the three approaches to identifying types of change-process (or disease process, in the realm of psychopathology). The within-score method is based on the notion that a given change-type can be identified by a characteristic set of time-curves corresponding to a set of behavioral measures (symptoms, syndromes). Relationships between the measures are ignored. Persons are correlated using the within-score sums of squares and sums of cross-products.

The within-period method is based on the concept of a given change process being identified by a characteristic time sequence of behavioral profiles ("phases", symptom profiles). Here, relationships between the measures are emphasized while the specific time-curves of the measures are, relatively speaking, ignored. People are correlated using the within-period sums of squares and sums of cross-products.

A total correlation method assumes that a given change process can best be identified by a characteristic set of time-curves along with a time-sequence of phases. Here, the time-courses of the variables and their interrelationships are given equal emphasis. Work is currently being undertaken to develop an appropriate total correlation index.

RESULTS*

Repeated measurement data of the type required for the application of the "dynamic" typology methods is, for the most part, hard to come by. Such data became available as a result of the first collaborative study conducted by the Psychopharmacology Service Center of the National Institute of Mental Health (1964: see also Goldberg, Cole and Clyde, 1963; and Goldberg, Klerman, and Cole, 1965).

This study was designed to compare the effectiveness of three phenothiazine drugs in the treatment of newly-admitted acute schizophrenic patients. The repeated measures, of concern to us, were psychiatric ratings obtained just prior to treatment and at three periods during the treatment phase of the study. The

* The data employed in this work were collected during a study supported by NIMH grants numbered; MH 04661, MH 04663, MH 04667, MH 04673, MH 04674, MH 04675, MH 04679, and MH 04803; and by NIMH contract no. SA–43–ph–3064. Acknowledgement is gratefully extended to Jonathan O. Cole, M.D. and Solomon C. Goldberg, Ph.D. of Psychopharmacology Service Center, NIMH, for permission to use the data.

change-types we attempted to isolate are thus types of response to phenothiazine drugs. More precisely, they should be regarded as types arising from the interaction of drug treatments with various types of psychotic disease processes. The unequivocal identification of the psychotic processes would, ideally, require that no psychotropic drugs be administered during the study. However, as will be shown, types emerge which bear a strong resemblance to those identified in previous typology studies.

The Sample and Data

The sample we used consisted of 222 newly-admitted schizophrenic patients from nine hospitals, all of these patients were administered one of three phenothiazine drugs (chlorpromazine, fluphenazine, or thioridazine); the three drug groups were pooled for the work reported in this chapter. The sample of 222 did not include patients who were dropped from the collaborative study because of undesirable side effects or insufficient improvement, a procedure necessary so as to avoid missing entries in the basic data matrix. This introduces one obvious bias in that a great many of the patients are thus *drug-improvers*. A group of placebo patients which remained in the study during the entire treatment phase was deemed too small to be included in the present work.

The variables employed as a basis for typing were the ten IMPS factor scores or syndromes described in earlier chapters, and will be referred to by their "code" designations as previously given. Patients were rated on the IMPS immediately prior to treatment and at one, three, and six weeks on drug by each of two raters. The scores were based on the ratings of the more senior or experienced rater in each case.

In addition to the IMPS a number of other measures were obtained. Although the types were obtained on the basis of the IMPS factor scores, the other measures provide concurrent evidence which adds clinical depth to the obtained types.

The Burdock Ward Behavior Rating Scale (Burdock *et al.*, 1959) was one of these concurrent instruments. Nurses rated the ward behavior of the patients at pre-treatment and again at one, three and six weeks on drug. A factor analysis, conducted as a part of the collaborative study, yielded seven factors. The seven scales, along with their abbreviations, are as follows (some of the factor names are changed slightly from their original titles):

1. Withdrawal (WITH)
2. Irritability (IRR)
3. Personal Neglect (NEGL)
4. Sadness (SAD)
5. Feelings of Unreality (UNR)
6. Resistiveness (RES)
7. Confusion (CONF)

A high score on each scale indicates disturbed behavior. All scores were converted to standard form prior to computing mean profiles for each type.

In addition to ratings based on clinical interviews and observation of ward behavior, patients' self-ratings of affect were obtained on the Clyde Mood Scale (Clyde, 1963). Ratings were obtained at pre-treatment and at three and six weeks of therapy. Patients receive measures on six factor scores:

1. Friendly (FR)
2. Aggressive (AGG)
3. Clearthinking (CLTH)
4. Sleepy (SL)
5. Unhappy (UNH)
6. Dizzy (DIZ)

High scores reflect an elevated degree of each mood. Again, all scores were converted to standard form prior to undertaking statistical analysis.

The amount of drug, measured in number of capsules per week, was recorded for each patient at each week of treatment. Each capsule contained either 100 mg of chlorpromazine, 100 mg of thioridazine, or 1 mg of fluphenazine. Physicians were permitted a flexible dosage schedule but were not to exceed 112 capsules per week. Intramuscular medication could also be employed, but we did not employ these data in our analyses.

Each patient, upon admission to the study, was diagnosed by a psychiatrist. Inasmuch as the collaborative study was supposed to be restricted to schizophrenics, the physician was not provided with non-schizophrenic diagnostic labels to check on the admission form. As a result, despite the provision of an "other" category, the diagnoses were not too diverse. Nevertheless, the predominant diagnoses for each type will be presented.

Abundant follow-up information was obtained for some patients but because much of the data is incomplete we used just three measures:

1. A global rating of improvement obtained at the end of treatment. This is a seven-point scale with low scores reflecting greater improvement.

2. A global rating of severity of illness obtained six months from the date the patient was admitted to the study, even if the patient was in the community. This was also a seven-point scale with high scores reflecting severe pathology.

3. A rating of social functioning, also obtained at six months. This was a five-point scale; a low score reflects a more adequate level of social functioning.

Statistical Procedures

The basic data matrix contained forty columns because, as noted above, each patient received a score on ten syndromes at each of four points in time. For the computation of the within-score correlation the data was arranged in the periods-within-score form so that the index of agreement between two patients may be viewed as an average taken over ten variables, each with four repeated measures. The scores-within-period or profile form was used for the within-period correlation; the index here is an average of four correlations, each based on ten observations.

It is to be noted that shapes of curves and profiles were of prime interest in the computation of agreement indices. Information concerning level and dispersion is lost by using a correlation coefficient. Other indices, such as the congruency coefficient, which utilizes information about level, have been employed in a within-score and within-period manner by the authors. Results based on these indices will not be presented here.

Each of the forty scores for a patient was converted to standard form using the means and standard deviations of the distributions of all 222 patients. All computations described below were performed on digital computers.

Two sub-samples, one of 89 patients and another of 90, were drawn randomly from the larger sample. The patients in each sub-sample were intercorrelated using each of the three correlation methods. In each case patient clusters were extracted using a variation of Holzinger's (1941) method of cluster analysis. Clusters were retained for further analysis only if they contained four or more patients.

Centroids (vectors of mean scores) were then computed for each cluster. The within-score centroids from each sub-sample were cross-correlated, using the within-score method. Only clusters which correlated at least 0.50 with a cluster from the other sub-sample were considered to be replicated. Any others were discarded at this stage. A similar procedure was followed for the within-period and total correlation clusters, using the appropriate index of correlation in each case.

The surviving clusters from the sub-sample of 89 were augmented by attempting to classify each of the remaining patients from the sample of 222 into one of the groups. This was done by correlating each of these patients' centroids with each group centroid using the appropriate correlational method. Patients were classified only if they correlated at least 0.40 with a given group centroid and then only if this maximal correlation squared exceeded their squared correlations with any other group by at least 0.11. All patients not meeting these criteria remained unclassified.

At this point the sample of 222 was partitioned into several clusters or types, this being done on the basis of each of the three correlational approaches. The augmented groups were then subjected to a factor-space D^2 analysis (Overall and Gorham, 1960). This was done to determine if the clusters were significantly separated from each other in the space spanned by orthogonal dimensions derived from a principal components analysis of the pooled within-groups correlation matrix. The types based on each correlational method will now be described in detail.

The Within-Score Types (W–S)

A total of nine groups was extracted using the method just described. IMPS centroids, based on standard scores for these groups are presented in Tables 8.1–8.3. The type VII time-curves are displayed in graphic form in Fig. 8.3. (Time-curves for the other types will not be presented because of space limitations.) The Burdock centroids are displayed in Tables 8.5–8.7, Mood scale centroids in Table 8.8, and drug dosage centroids in Table 8.9.

The nine group centroids were found to be quite independent of one another as is revealed by the array of D^2 coefficients displayed in Table 8.4. The D^2 values were based on a space of those six orthogonal dimensions which accounted for the largest share of the common variance; no attempt was made to interpret those dimensions.

The Burdock centroids were also found to be statistically separate. Multiple discriminant analysis yielded an F-value of 1.92, significant beyond the 0.001 level ($df = 224/548$). No comparable statistical analysis was attempted with the Mood Scale centroids because N, in some groups, varied markedly from period to period.

A repeated-measures analysis of variance of the dosage centroids revealed a significant period $\times$ type interaction ($F = 1.61$, significant beyond the 0.01 level); this suggests that the dosage curves for the nine types differ with respect to slope.

The within-score types are described below. The IMPS pattern for a given type will be described first, followed by a discussion of the Burdock and Mood Scale patterns for the group. The drug dosage pattern will then be described followed by a mention of the major admission diagnoses for the patients in the group.

Type I

IMPS (Table 8.1). Drug response is manifested primarily by marked improvement in RTD, DIS, and MTR; the patients' symptomatology was most florid at pre-treatment on these syndromes.

Ward behaviour (Table 8.5). These patients, at pre-treatment, were rated high on Withdrawal, Confusion, and Personal Neglect. Improvement on these factors, especially the latter, was most marked.

Mood (Table 8.8). Only three patients were able to complete the Clyde Mood Scale at pre-treatment so that the Period 0 means may be regarded as unstable. These patients rated themselves highly on Aggressive, Sleepy, and Dizzy at this point in the study. These scores were considerably lower by Period 3, but patients rated themselves as feeling more dizzy after six weeks of drug treatment.

TABLE 8.1

Centroids for Within-Score Types I-III

Standard Score Units

IMPS Syndrome	TYPE I N = 13				TYPE II N = 7				TYPE III N = 26			
	Time Period				Time Period				Time Period			
	0	1	3	6	0	1	3	6	0	1	3	6
EXC	-0.23	0.11	-0.10	-0.16	0.00	-0.36	-0.52	-0.16	-0.35	-0.23	0.09	0.02
HOS	-0.42	0.46	0.45	0.31	-0.38	-0.51	-0.55	-0.25	-0.12	-0.25	0.11	0.64
PAR	-0.94	0.02	0.22	0.17	-0.60	-0.57	0.25	0.26	0.13	-0.01	0.13	0.78
GRN	-0.48	0.22	0.22	0.39	-0.43	-0.43	-0.47	-0.15	-0.19	-0.22	-0.07	0.00
PCP	-0.49	0.20	0.17	-0.07	-0.04	0.06	0.80	-0.27	-0.03	-0.23	-0.03	0.21
INP	-0.59	-0.03	-0.57	-0.36	-0.23	-0.03	0.62	0.03	0.01	-0.17	0.50	1.02
RTD	1.09	0.52	-0.34	-0.14	1.36	1.51	1.13	0.08	-0.20	0.05	0.41	1.00
DIS	2.86	-0.21	-0.08	-0.08	1.09	4.44	0.50	-0.08	-0.45	-0.21	-0.14	-0.08
MTR	0.89	0.20	0.15	-0.15	1.36	1.18	0.53	-0.13	-0.51	-0.18	0.08	0.76
CNP	-0.26	0.53	0.06	-0.18	0.64	0.57	0.55	-0.06	-0.13	-0.19	0.10	0.86

TABLE 8.2

Centroids for Within-Score Types IV–VI

Standard Score Units

IMPS Syndrome	TYPE IV N = 21 Time Period				TYPE V N = 12 Time Period				TYPE VI N = 11 Time Period			
	0	1	3	6	0	1	3	6	0	1	3	6
EXC	-0.06	-0.30	-0.50	-0.46	-0.72	-0.48	-0.61	-0.47	1.39	1.37	0.98	-0.26
HOS	0.82	-0.07	-0.36	-0.54	-0.89	-0.67	-0.63	-0.43	0.40	0.63	-0.15	0.05
PAR	0.63	0.07	-0.65	-0.41	-0.53	-0.62	-0.56	-0.57	0.30	0.30	0.13	-0.23
GRN	-0.59	-0.29	-0.40	-0.39	-0.12	-0.60	-0.38	-0.40	1.35	1.53	1.47	-0.14
PCP	0.06	-0.40	-0.39	-0.30	0.59	-0.33	-0.30	-0.25	-0.01	-0.41	0.28	-0.02
INP	0.47	-0.31	-0.57	-0.73	0.47	-0.04	-0.70	-0.58	-0.47	-0.14	-0.31	0.02
RTD	-0.03	-0.18	-0.54	-0.45	1.18	-0.37	-0.47	-0.58	-0.79	-0.45	-0.34	-0.09
DIS	0.03	-0.15	-0.19	-0.08	-0.10	-0.21	-0.19	-0.08	-0.51	-0.21	-0.19	-0.08
MTR	-0.07	-0.03	-0.57	-0.53	0.51	-0.33	-0.61	-0.17	-0.46	-0.34	-0.07	-0.31
CNP	-0.22	-0.22	-0.34	-0.36	-0.25	-0.61	-0.56	-0.50	0.33	0.49	0.34	-0.31

TABLE 8.3

Centroids for Within-Score Types VII-IX

Standard Score Units

IMPS Syndrome	TYPE VII N = 9				TYPE VIII N = 11				TYPE IX N = 8			
	Time Period				Time Period				Time Period			
	0	1	3	6	0	1	3	6	0	1	3	6
EXC	0.84	-0.35	-0.16	-0.25	-0.20	-0.01	-0.21	-0.24	-0.10	0.88	0.97	1.63
HOS	1.06	0.40	0.34	-0.41	0.08	0.06	0.55	-0.65	0.19	0.37	-0.42	0.19
PAR	0.47	0.15	0.73	-0.40	0.74	0.77	0.67	-0.51	-0.41	-0.21	-0.72	-0.21
GRN	0.14	-0.39	0.20	-0.05	0.65	0.45	-0.11	-0.36	-0.10	0.30	0.63	0.71
PCP	-0.32	-0.31	-0.36	-0.23	1.30	2.64	0.03	-0.16	-0.57	-0.37	-0.49	-0.30
INP	-0.29	-0.16	-0.07	1.49	0.48	0.58	0.40	-0.35	0.18	0.10	-0.61	-0.13
RTD	-0.13	0.27	0.48	-0.29	-0.46	-0.11	-0.11	-0.31	-0.73	-0.62	-0.49	-0.36
DIS	-0.13	-0.07	0.09	-0.08	-0.20	-0.10	-0.19	-0.08	-0.51	-0.21	-0.19	-0.08
MTR	0.64	0.09	0.24	-0.18	-0.29	0.40	-0.02	-0.15	-0.86	-0.19	-0.01	0.61
CNP	1.16	0.18	-0.01	-0.29	-0.05	0.20	0.00	-0.34	-0.31	0.27	0.07	-0.09

TABLE 8.4

Mahalanobis' D^2 Between Pairs

of Within-Score Types

		I	II	III	IV	V	VI	VII	VIII
II	D^2	*6.47							
	F	3.54							
	DF	6/13							
III	D^2	***17.05	***27.30						
	F	21.30	21.04						
	DF	6/32	6/26						
IV	D^2	***9.40	***22.77	***3.71					
	F	10.61	16.09	6.38					
	DF	6/27	6/21	6/40					
V	D^2	***9.01	***24.36	***5.66	1.53				
	F	7.34	12.67	6.67	1.63				
	DF	6/18	6/12	6/31	6/26				
VI	D^2	***27.82	***36.64	***6.76	***8.33	***11.26			
	F	21.35	17.96	7.46	8.35	8.21			
	DF	6/17	6/11	6/30	6/25	6/16			
VII	D^2	***15.78	**26.05	0.83	*3.09	*5.51	*6.56		
	F	10.49	10.99	0.79	2.67	3.48	3.91		
	DF	6/15	6/9	6/28	6/23	6/14	6/13		
VIII	D^2	***29.03	***33.99	***12.19	***15.03	***18.39	***12.96	***17.27	
	F	22.28	16.66	13.46	15.07	13.40	8.91	10.29	
	DF	6/17	6/11	6/30	6/25	6/16	6/15	6/13	
IX	D^2	***17.49	***27.71	*5.55	*3.30	*5.99	1.86	4.13	**15.18
	F	10.63	10.61	4.77	2.60	3.46	1.01	1.94	8.27
	DF	6/14	6/8	6/27	6/22	6/13	6/12	6/10	6/12

*** = $p < .001$,   ** = $p < .01$,   * = $p < .05$

Dosage (Table 8.9). Dosage was increased rapidly for this group up to the second week. At this point the curve reached a plateau with patients receiving an average of over 50 capsules of phenothiazine per week.

Diagnosis. Most of these patients were diagnosed as catatonic schizophrenics.

Type II

IMPS (Table 8.1). It can be noted from an examination of Table 8.1 that this group resembles Type I in that both show striking improvement with respect to RTD, DIS, and MTR. However, the two types differ in that they appear to be "out of phase", i.e. they show similar time-curves, but the type I patients improve much more rapidly than those in type II.

Ward behavior (Table 8.5). These patients, like those in type I, received high pre-treatment ratings on Withdrawal, Personal Neglect, and Confusion. Little improvement was manifested until the patients had been on drug for six weeks. Another interesting feature is the rather abrupt increase in Sadness, noted by the nurses after the patients had been on drug for one week; an equally abrupt decrease on this factor occurs after six weeks of treatment.

Mood (Table 8.8). As was the case with the first group, few type II patients were able to complete the Mood Scale prior to treatment. The data suggest that these patients felt more sleepy and dizzy after three weeks on drug than at the start of treatment, but that these manifestations subsided considerably by the end of treatment. In addition, the patients rated themselves as feeling more friendly and aggressive at the termination of drug therapy.

Dosage (Table 8.9). The dosage for this group was gradually stepped up to a maximum average of 61 capsules per week by the fourth week and then dropped slightly.

Diagnosis. Most of these patients were diagnosed as schizophrenia, catatonic type.

Type III

IMPS (Table 8.1). This group shows a relative decrement (remembering that scores are in standard form) on almost all syndromes. Examination of the raw score means, which we do not display, reveals that these patients exhibited virtually no florid symptomatology at pre-treatment and that they showed no improvement to speak of and, on some syndromes, an absolute decrement. It is clear, of course, that the IMPS scales left little room for improvement in the case of this group.

Ward behavior (Table 8.5). A gradual rise on all factor scores can be noted, especially on Irritability and Feelings of Unreality.

Mood (Table 8.8). The major features of the Mood Scale curves were increased feelings of unhappiness and decreasing feelings of friendliness.

12

TABLE 8.5

Centroids for Within-Score Types I-III
on Burdock Ward Behavior Rating Scale Factors

Standard Score Units

WBRS Factor	TYPE I Time Period				TYPE II Time Period				TYPE III Time Period			
	0	1	3	6	0	1	3	6	0	1	3	6
WTH	0.75	0.56	0.30	0.07	0.57	0.58	0.66	-0.35	-0.32	-0.29	0.02	0.09
IRR	0.31	-0.31	-0.25	-0.10	-0.03	-0.44	-0.69	-0.41	-0.07	0.15	0.35	0.89
NEGL	1.33	0.27	-0.05	0.26	1.03	0.99	1.37	-0.06	-0.66	-0.31	-0.02	0.58
SAD	-0.05	-0.19	-0.32	-0.38	-0.03	0.41	0.71	-0.43	0.27	0.08	0.38	0.64
UNR	-0.26	0.40	0.17	0.07	0.18	-0.64	-0.12	0.39	-0.04	-0.07	-0.11	0.66
RES	0.16	-0.07	0.14	0.36	-0.43	-0.73	-0.74	-0.05	-0.25	0.06	0.23	0.54
CONF	0.69	0.59	-0.21	0.04	0.57	0.44	0.92	0.58	-0.26	-0.21	0.07	0.50

TABLE 8.6

Centroids for Within-Score Types IV - VI

on Burdock Ward Behavior Rating Scale Factors

Standard Score Units

WBRS Factor	TYPE IV Time Period				TYPE V Time Period				TYPE VI Time Period			
	0	1	3	6	0	1	3	6	0	1	3	6
WTH	0.38	0.33	-0.15	-0.12	0.62	-0.25	-0.64	-0.46	-0.14	-0.79	-0.48	0.23
IRR	-0.08	-0.17	-0.38	-0.25	-0.12	-0.48	-0.38	-0.30	0.29	0.19	0.02	-0.24
NEGL	0.19	0.19	-0.39	-0.27	0.07	-0.48	-0.40	-0.39	-0.08	-0.36	-0.40	-0.16
SAD	0.39	0.47	-0.28	-0.49	0.36	0.26	-0.55	-0.24	-0.68	-0.44	-0.84	-0.24
UNR	-0.16	-0.18	-0.43	-0.37	-0.46	-0.64	-0.37	-0.19	0.60	0.48	0.85	-0.19
RES	0.05	0.31	-0.02	-0.60	0.19	-0.13	-0.27	-0.50	0.39	-0.02	0.04	0.27
CONF	-0.03	-0.12	-0.43	-0.29	0.62	-0.23	-0.50	-0.32	-0.21	-0.38	-0.27	-0.79

TABLE 8.7

Centroids for Within-Score Types VII - IX
on Burdock Ward Behavior Rating Scale Factors

Standard Score Units

WBRS Factor	TYPE VII Time Period				TYPE VIII Time Period				TYPE IX Time Period			
	0	1	3	6	0	1	3	6	0	1	3	6
WTH	-0.75	-0.44	-0.24	-0.04	-0.11	0.60	0.19	0.14	-0.52	-0.58	0.22	-0.27
IRR	-0.09	-0.22	0.21	0.11	0.38	-0.22	-0.43	-0.24	-0.49	-0.01	0.35	0.33
NEGL	0.00	-0.03	-0.08	-0.10	-0.08	0.21	-0.40	0.15	-0.83	-0.40	-0.55	-0.39
SAD	-0.67	-0.97	-0.10	0.26	-0.30	-0.15	-0.15	-0.18	-0.95	-0.79	-0.03	0.30
UNR	-0.22	0.29	-0.50	-0.37	0.60	0.48	0.31	-0.19	-0.03	0.11	1.39	1.05
RES	-0.25	0.20	0.14	0.13	0.19	0.31	-0.17	-0.17	-0.20	-0.45	-0.06	-0.17
CONF	0.15	0.01	0.01	0.60	0.17	-0.01	0.03	-0.40	-0.66	-0.53	0.03	-0.40

Dosage (Table 8.9). The patients in this group, perhaps because they showed little florid symptomatology, were dosed very lightly during the first week. Dosage was then stepped up but never reached the mean dosage level of drug administered to most of the other within-score types.

Diagnosis. Paranoid and acute undifferentiated schizophrenia were the major diagnoses for this type.

Type IV

IMPS (Table 8.2). This is a group which entered the study high on HOS, PAR, and INP, and which had improved markedly by the end of one week on drug.

Ward behavior (Table 8.6). All factor scores show a drop which, unlike the IMPS, is not manifest until the third week of the study.

Mood (Table 8.8). The most marked features of the Mood Scale time-curves are increased Friendly and Clearthinking scores and a marked decrease in unhappiness.

Dosage (Table 8.9). This group received a fairly low dosage during the first week of treatment and then was stepped up somewhat during the second week. The group was then maintained at this relatively low dosage level for the remainder of the study.

Diagnosis. Nearly all of the patients in type IV received an admission diagnosis of paranoid schizophrenia.

Type V

IMPS (Table 8.2). This group, like type IV, appears to be another "quick response" type. Sharp improvement, most of it occurring during the first week of the study, can be noted for RTD, PCP, and MTR.

Ward behavior (Table 8.6). The Burdock centroids reveal a marked first week improvement in Withdrawal, Personal Neglect, and Confusion along with a later decrease in Sadness.

Mood (Table 8.8). These patients rated themselves as feeling extremely friendly throughout the study. A sharp increase on Clearthinking is noted during the third week, along with decrease on Sleepy and Unhappy. Also of interest is a sharp rise in feelings of dizziness at Period 6.

Dosage (Table 8.9). These patients were maintained at a low level of dosage throughout the six week treatment period.

Diagnosis. Diagnostically, this group was quite diverse, with the labels of catatonic, paranoid, and acute undifferentiated schizophrenia predominating.

Type VI

IMPS (Table 8.2). These patients entered the study very much elevated on EXC and GRN. Improvement was rather minimal until the group had been on drug for six weeks.

Ward behavior (Table 8.6). The group entered the study elevated on Feelings of Unreality and Resistiveness, the former remaining high until the sixth week, and the latter showing an early drop but a later increase. Withdrawal and Sadness were quite low, but the patients became somewhat more withdrawn by the end of the study.

Mood (Table 8.8). The patients reported feeling very aggressive and clearthinking; these scores dropped sharply at Period 6. A sharp drop in sleepiness occurred by the third week.

Dosage (Table 8.9). Dosage was continually increased throughout the treatment period until, by the sixth week, these patients were receiving more than any other within-score group.

Diagnosis. Six of the nine patients in this group were diagnosed as paranoid schizophrenia.

Type VII

IMPS (Table 8.3 and Fig. 8.3). A complex patterning of change was displayed by the patients in type VII. Rapid improvement can be noted on EXC, HOS, and CNP. However, equally noteworthy is the sharp increase in INP symptomatology between the third and sixth week on drug. Examination of the raw score means revealed that this was a rise in absolute as well as in relative terms.

Ward behavior (Table 8.7). The patients entered the study with low scores on Withdrawal and Sadness. The most notable changes were increases on Sadness and Confusion at the end of the study.

Mood (Table 8.8). The most noteworthy features of the Mood Scale time-curves were a sharp sixth week drop on Clearthinking and a third week rise on Unhappy.

TABLE 8.8

Centroids for Nine Within-Score Types

on Clyde Mood Scale Factors

Standard Score Units

CMS Factor	TYPE I			TYPE II			TYPE III		
	Time Period			Time Period			Time Period		
	0	3	6	0	3	6	0	3	6
FR	0.06	0.02	-0.04	-0.14	0.25	0.62	-0.05	-0.30	-0.38
AGGR	0.59	0.03	-0.07	-0.25	-0.48	0.43	-0.08	-0.02	0.03
CLTH	0.28	-0.03	0.04	-0.27	-0.70	-0.12	-0.14	-0.41	-0.16
SL	0.38	-0.30	-0.13	0.27	0.82	-0.60	0.02	0.08	0.27
UNH	0.10	-0.07	-0.04	-0.49	-0.21	-0.66	-0.05	0.17	0.52
DIZ	0.32	0.01	0.35	-0.04	0.84	0.38	-0.20	0.12	-0.29

	TYPE IV			TYPE V			TYPE VI		
FR	-0.11	0.01	0.32	0.65	0.48	0.51	-0.49	0.06	-0.39
AGGR	-0.69	-0.43	-0.42	-0.16	-0.09	-0.22	0.84	0.51	-0.25
CLTH	0.20	0.51	0.37	-0.65	0.12	0.24	0.70	0.51	-0.09
SL	0.16	-0.16	-0.03	-0.12	-0.64	-0.36	0.46	-0.59	-0.24
UNH	0.51	-0.01	-0.04	-0.02	-0.66	-0.24	-0.80	-0.19	-0.45
DIZ	0.30	-0.05	-0.02	-0.16	-0.09	0.48	-0.02	-0.62	-0.28

	TYPE VII			TYPE VIII			TYPE IX		
FR	0.08	0.09	-0.24	0.31	-0.08	0.04	-0.15	0.02	0.36
AGGR	-0.26	0.01	-0.28	0.85	0.14	-0.04	0.37	0.30	0.22
CLTH	0.43	0.59	-0.13	0.18	-0.03	0.18	-0.12	-0.17	0.02
SL	-0.13	0.17	0.04	0.45	0.47	0.14	-0.08	-0.80	-0.41
UNH	-0.28	0.28	0.23	0.09	0.12	-0.20	-0.18	-0.48	-0.38
DIZ	-0.10	-0.12	-0.18	0.12	-0.28	-0.50	-0.01	-0.43	0.05

Dosage (Table 8.9). These patients received heavier dosages of phenothiazine than any other within-score type during the first week of the study. The mean dosage level was then increased sharply, but declined somewhat during the fifth week of the study.

Diagnosis. Type VII was another group diagnosed predominantly as paranoid schizophrenia.

Type VIII

IMPS (Table 8.3). Type VIII patients exhibited florid symptomatology on PCP, PAR, and GRN prior to treatment. These syndromes showed a sharp decrease late in the study.

Ward behavior (Table 8.7). Nurses rated these patients as being high on Feelings of Unreality; a sharp drop on this factor can be noted at Period 6. Also of interest are the sharp spike on Withdrawal during the first week and the decrease in irritability during the same interval.

WITHIN- SCORE MODEL

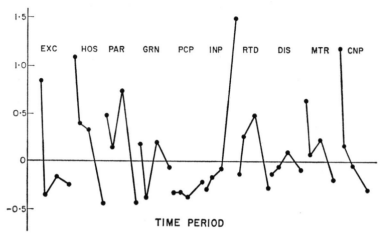

FIG. 8.3.

Mood (Table 8.8). Sharp decreases in feelings of friendliness and aggressiveness occurred at the third week. A decrease in sleepiness can be noted by the sixth week for this type.

Dosage (Table 8.9). These patients received a steadily increasing amount of drug up to the final week of the study, at which point a decrease in mean dosage occurred.

Diagnosis. This was yet another group of paranoid schizophrenics.

Type IX

IMPS (Table 8.3). The most clear-cut features of the IMPS time-curves for this small group were the steady increases on EXC, GRN, and MTR.

Ward behavior (Table 8.7). Steep increases on Irritability, Sadness, and Feelings of Unreality are quite evident for these patients.

Mood (Table 8.8). The time-curves for the Mood Scale did not show such spectacular changes as the IMPS and Burdock curves. The patients reported feeling rather aggressive throughout the study. A sharp decrease in sleepiness occurred at the third week.

Dosage (Table 8.9). Although a steady dosage increase can be noted during the first three weeks of treatment, followed by a

TABLE 8.9

Within-Score Types

Dosage Centroids over Six Weeks on Treatment

and Means of Follow-up Ratings

W-S Type	Mean Number of Capsules For Week Number						Improvement at 6 weeks	Severity at 6 months	Social Functioning at 6 months
	1	2	3	4	5	6			
I	37.3	55.4	53.8	52.6	57.2	58.4	1.8	2.0	2.7
II	28.8	52.4	56.8	62.0	59.4	54.2	1.9	1.4	1.7
III	25.2	35.8	43.8	46.2	49.7	48.2	3.0	3.4	3.8
IV	28.8	44.6	48.5	47.9	49.3	46.6	1.4	2.2	2.8
V	33.6	43.7	41.4	34.2	29.8	28.4	1.4	2.5	2.4
VI	35.7	46.1	52.1	53.1	65.7	65.1	2.1	2.5	3.0
VII	48.4	72.4	68.1	67.3	59.0	54.8	2.1	2.7	2.4
VIII	30.7	45.0	54.1	64.6	69.7	57.6	1.5	2.6	3.6
IX	26.8	35.9	45.3	42.6	37.0	38.9	2.4	2.8	2.6

slight reduction, the dosage level for this group was rather low compared to the other within-score types.

Diagnosis. Four of the eight patients were diagnosed as paranoid schizophrenics; the remainder were classified as acute undifferentiated schizophrenia.

The mean follow-up ratings for the within-score types are displayed in Table 8.9. Analysis of variance ($F = 8.58$, significant beyond the 0.001 level) revealed that the nine types differed significantly at the end of the study with respect to physicians' ratings of global improvement. Types IV, V, and VIII showed the greatest amount of improvement while type III clearly improved the least.

The six-month severity of illness ratings did not differentiate the groups ($F = 1.49$), but the types did differ significantly with respect to six-month ratings of social functioning. ($F = 2.47$, significant beyond the 0.05 level.) Type II patients were rated as functioning at the highest level, while type VIII was rated the lowest in this regard.

Any attempt to generalize about the reactions of acute schizophrenics to phenothiazine treatment, based on these types, must be tempered by the fact that the data available to us were not ideal for the within-score method. For one thing, there were not enough measurement periods. More are needed to permit the more rigorous identification of types which show the same basic change processes but are merely out of phase. Typing patients on the basis of a within-score agreement index will probably always yield more groups because, ideally, the different phasings of the same basic processes will fall out as separate types. Another difficulty, already alluded to, is the fact that the measurement periods were not evenly spaced. This fact, coupled with the small number of periods makes it hazardous to draw any definitive conclusions about the shapes of the time-curves for any type.

Another problem resides in the fact that because the method is quite sensitive to picking up fluctuations over time, it also is more susceptible to whatever errors of measurement reside in the repeated observations of the same patients. There was very likely a great deal of "noise" in the data so that the types extracted are probably based on the most spectacular trends in the time-curves.

There is one final objection to the within-score approach which we can mention. The method may be criticized on clinical grounds because, in effect, the patient is being considered as a bundle of symptoms each of which is followed independently over time. This atomistic emphasis, however, may be justified in studies where one is primarily interested in following the time courses of several symptoms as a basis for identifying response to treatment.

The within-score approach does, however, reflect the course of treatment. The data reveal that, for example, types IV and V were "drug-responder" types in a general sense, while type IV is a group which exhibited generalized decrement. The other groups showed either improvement or decrement with respect to certain key symptoms or else "mixed" reactions of improvement on some syndromes coupled with decrement on others.

On the whole, we are quite encouraged by the fact that, in many cases, the nurses' Burdock ratings and the patients' self-ratings of mood show patterns of change which appear clinically similar to those observed on the IMPS. The IMPS time-curves, on which the within-score typology is based, do not thus appear to have been fortuitous.

The Within-Period Types (W-P)

Clustering based on the use of the within-period agreement index yielded seven types. The results germane to this typology are displayed in Tables 8.10–8.16. The profiles for type I are graphically shown in Fig. 8.4. Factor-space D^2 analysis (Table 8.12) revealed that the IMPS profiles for the within-period types are markedly separated; only types IV and VII failing to be significantly separated.

Burdock centroids are shown in Tables 8.13 and 8.14, Mood Scale means in Table 8.15, and dosage means in Table 8.16. Mutiple discriminant analysis revealed that the seven Burdock centroids differed significantly. ($F = 1.61$, significant beyond the 0.001 level; $df = 168/443$.) Analysis of variance of the drug dosage data yielded a significant interaction effect. ($F = 1.58$, significant beyond the 0.05 level); again, as in the case of the within-score types, the dosage slopes differ. The Mood Scale data, for reasons already mentioned, were not subjected to statistical analysis.

We shall describe these types using a format identical to that followed in the discussion of the within-score types.

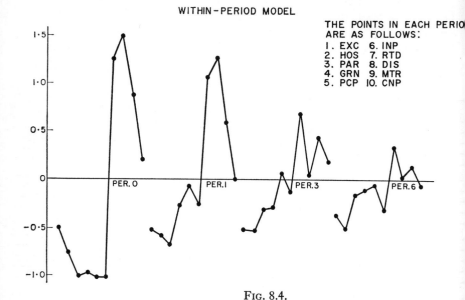

Fig. 8.4.

Type I

IMPS (Table 8.10 and Fig. 8.4). The IMPS mean profile at pre-treatment clearly resembles the Disorganized Type identified by Lorr *et al.* (1963); the peaks on RTD, DIS, and MTR typify such a group. The shape of the profile holds up at each successive time period except that DIS vanishes by the third week. Successive profiles become "damped" because of a regression toward the mean on all syndromes. A close check of the data revealed that this type primarily contains patients from within-score types I and II.

Ward behavior (Table 8.13). The pretreatment mean profile shows peaks on Withdrawal, Personal Neglect, and Confusion along with a low score on Resistiveness. The profile holds up well with the passage of time, although becoming damped.

Mood (Table 8.15). No real peaks appear in the Mood Scale pretreatment profile. Aggressive and Clearthinking are, however, very low. The reduced N for this group prior to treatment makes these Period 0 means somewhat suspect. The Period 3 and Period 6 profiles show peaks on Sleepy and Dizzy.

Dosage (Table 8.16). Dosage was increased sharply during the second week and remained at this fairly high level during the remainder of the study.

TABLE 8.10

Centroids for Within-Period Types I-IV

Standard Score Units

Time Period	PATIENT TYPE I N = 24									
	EXC	HOS	PAR	GRN	PCP	INP	RTD	DIS	MTR	CNP
0	-0.51	-0.79	-1.03	-0.49	-0.51	-0.51	1.25	1.47	0.88	0.20
1	-0.53	-0.59	-0.69	-0.26	-0.06	-0.25	1.05	1.25	0.59	0.00
3	-0.52	-0.54	-0.32	-0.30	0.04	-0.15	0.67	0.04	0.41	0.16
6	-0.39	-0.51	-0.19	-0.12	-0.06	-0.33	0.32	0.01	0.11	-0.06
	PATIENT TYPE II N = 20									
0	-0.37	0.81	1.00	-0.28	0.34	-0.17	-0.56	-0.35	-0.47	-0.51
1	-0.25	0.82	1.30	-0.15	0.01	-0.02	-0.18	-0.21	-0.05	-0.27
3	-0.31	0.84	1.11	-0.14	0.77	-0.04	-0.21	-0.19	-0.33	-0.30
6	-0.01	0.88	1.05	0.00	0.43	0.10	-0.05	-0.08	-0.19	-0.04
	PATIENT TYPE III N = 27									
0	1.36	0.34	0.23	1.41	-0.19	-0.55	-0.80	-0.43	-0.28	0.24
1	1.33	0.45	0.34	1.61	-0.32	-0.26	-0.50	-0.21	-0.23	0.32
3	1.33	-0.18	-0.07	1.35	-0.08	-0.40	-0.34	-0.19	-0.05	0.23
6	0.73	0.17	-0.15	0.96	-0.10	-0.23	-0.21	-0.08	-0.05	-0.11
	PATIENT TYPE IV N = 14									
0	-0.65	-0.47	0.78	-0.12	1.64	-0.19	0.13	0.06	-0.04	-0.76
1	-0.43	-0.66	-0.12	-0.25	0.70	-0.45	-0.22	-0.12	-0.26	-0.48
3	-0.48	-0.72	-0.38	-0.11	0.20	-0.75	-0.72	-0.19	-0.34	-0.61
6	-0.40	-0.61	-0.45	-0.06	-0.08	-0.56	-0.51	-0.08	-0.35	-0.51

TABLE 8.11

Centroids for Within-Period Types V-VII

Standard Score Units

Period	PATIENT TYPE V N = 11									
	EXC	HOS	PAR	GRN	PCP	INP	RTD	DIS	MTR	CNP
0	0.65	1.35	-0.16	-0.35	-0.63	0.30	-0.17	-0.25	0.01	-0.08
1	1.10	1.37	-0.22	-0.32	-0.45	-0.28	-0.45	-0.21	0.01	0.25
3	0.44	0.95	-0.03	-0.26	-0.42	-0.44	-0.47	-0.19	-0.13	0.06
6	0.81	0.16	-0.44	-0.08	-0.30	-0.52	-0.50	-0.08	-0.20	0.47
	PATIENT TYPE VI N = 17									
0	-0.38	-0.08	0.29	-0.54	-0.35	1.04	0.33	-0.34	-0.14	0.05
1	-0.50	-0.21	0.01	-0.56	-0.11	0.97	0.86	-0.21	0.05	-0.12
3	-0.63	0.15	0.48	-0.47	-0.25	1.07	1.56	-0.19	0.61	0.11
6	-0.47	-0.06	-0.19	-0.40	-0.14	1.44	1.42	-0.08	0.49	-0.06
	PATIENT TYPE VII N = 9									
0	-0.40	-0.60	-0.53	-0.23	-0.05	1.22	-0.50	-0.33	-0.28	-0.69
1	-0.41	-0.71	-0.66	-0.13	-0.10	1.22	-0.46	-0.21	0.05	-0.55
3	0.06	-0.71	-0.68	-0.31	-0.49	0.35	-0.50	-0.19	-0.12	-0.64
6	0.25	-0.47	-0.52	-0.26	-0.30	-0.17	-0.62	-0.08	0.17	-0.48

TABLE 8.12

Mahalanobis' D^2 Between Pairs

of Within-Period Types

		I	II	III	IV	V	VI
II	D^2	*** 10.12					
	F	16.20					
	DF	6/37					
III	D^2	*** 18.58	*** 11.34				
	F	35.33	19.29				
	DF	6/44	6/40				
IV	D^2	*** 5.79	*** 7.93	*** 11.62			
	F	7.34	9.18	15.57			
	DF	6/31	6/27	6/34			
V	D^2	*** 12.01	** 6.08	*** 5.83	*** 9.04		
	F	12.81	5.95	6.54	7.26		
	DF	6/28	6/24	6/31	6/18		
VI	D^2	*** 6.02	*** 10.61	*** 28.40	*** 15.01	*** 14.17	
	F	8.70	13.93	43.50	15.90	12.74	
	DF	6/34	6/30	6/37	6/24	6/21	
VII	D^2	** 4.73	*** 8.04	*** 12.60	2.19	* 5.85	*** 9.58
	F	4.33	6.77	12.09	1.52	3.49	7.44
	DF	6/26	6/22	6/29	6/16	6/13	6/19

*** = p < .001,   ** = p < .01,   * = p < .05

Diagnosis. Half of the patients in this group were diagnosed as catatonic schizophrenics, while acute undifferentiated was the second most popular diagnosis for these patients.

Type II

IMPS (Table 8.10). Type II, with its Period 0 peaks on HOS and PAR, also closely resembles a type described by Lorr *et al.* (1963). The profile remains rather intact at each successive period except for the sudden emergence of PCP at the third week. The profiles do not become damped as treatment progresses indicating that improvement on these syndromes was minimal.

Ward behavior (Table 8.13). The pretreatment profile shows peaks on Irritability and Resistiveness. The profile remains intact, without damping, with two exceptions; Resistiveness drops out briefly during Period 1, and Withdrawal becomes emergent during the third week.

Mood (Table 8.15). The Period 0 mean profile features a peak on Clearthinking and a very low score on Friendly. The profile changes at Period 3 with a very sharp peak on Dizzy.

Dosage (Table 8.16). Dosage was stepped up at a brisk rate until, by Period 6, these patients were receiving more medication than any other within-period type. This might well account for their increased feelings of dizziness!

Diagnosis. Nearly all of these patients received an admission diagnosis of paranoid schizophrenia.

Type III

IMPS (Table 8.10). The pretreatment profile for type III, with its peaks on EXC and GRN, corresponds to Lorr's Excited–Grandiose Type. This pattern is maintained quite well with some damping during the final week suggesting late improvement. It is interesting to note that almost all of the patients from W-S VI fall into this group. The reader will recall that the former exhibited elevated EXC and GRN time-curves which did not drop until the final week.

Ward behavior (Table 8.13). The mean pretreatment profile for this type shows peaks on Feelings of Unreality and Resistiveness. This profile undergoes little change except for damping late in the study.

Mood (Table 8.15). Friendly, Aggressive, and Clearthinking scores are peaks for the initial profile of this group. This configuration holds up fairly well as time passes; Clearthinking becomes a more pronounced feature late in the study.

Dosage (Table 8.16). The dosage pattern is very similar to that for type I.

Diagnosis. Although paranoid schizophrenia was the most predominant diagnosis for this group (14 cases), acute undifferentiated and schizoaffective were other popular labels (seven and five cases, respectively).

Type IV

IMPS (Table 8.10). This type, at pretreatment, may best be described as paranoid hallucinatory; PAR and PCP were the most

TABLE 8.13

Centroids for Within-Period Types I - IV

on Burdock Ward Behavior Rating Scale Factors

Standard Score Units

Time Period	PATIENT TYPE I						
	WTH	IRR	NEGL	SAD	UNR	RES	CONF
0	0.64	-0.29	0.97	0.46	0.13	-0.52	0.68
1	0.60	-0.51	0.56	0.50	-0.34	-0.63	0.65
3	0.32	-0.47	0.48	0.35	0.14	-0.45	0.56
6	0.07	-0.35	0.24	-0.08	-0.03	-0.10	0.32
	PATIENT TYPE II						
0	0.10	0.43	-0.05	-0.13	-0.24	0.39	-0.40
1	0.19	0.42	0.29	-0.15	-0.02	-0.07	-0.23
3	0.58	0.46	0.09	0.08	-0.10	0.45	-0.08
6	0.25	0.36	-0.16	-0.06	0.07	0.49	0.15
	PATIENT TYPE III						
0	-0.54	0.14	-0.33	-0.76	0.56	0.40	-0.48
1	-0.57	0.44	-0.24	-0.59	0.55	0.35	-0.29
3	-0.24	0.12	-0.07	-0.59	0.73	0.24	0.07
6	0.05	-0.11	-0.18	-0.34	0.11	0.32	-0.27
	PATIENT TYPE IV						
0	0.48	-0.11	-0.15	0.13	0.18	0.08	-0.01
1	0.48	-0.39	-0.07	-0.04	0.09	0.02	-0.02
3	-0.26	-0.67	-0.42	-0.56	-0.16	-0.38	-0.27
6	-0.11	-0.47	0.00	-0.27	-0.37	-0.37	-0.35

prominent features of the Period 0 mean profile. The profile becomes quickly damped indicating rapid improvement under phenothiazine treatment. Successive profiles assume somewhat different shapes as PAR quickly loses its prominence in the syndrome pattern.

Ward behavior (Table 8.13). The Period 0 profile has only one distinguishing feature—a sharp peak on Withdrawal. By the third week all standard scores, including Withdrawal, are negative, a pattern similar to that observed for the IMPS profiles.

Mood (Table 8.15). High scores are virtually absent from the Time 0 mean profile. Aggressive, on the other hand, is very low. A profile change at third week is evident with a peak on Friendly and a very low Unhappy score. By the end of the study, yet another configuration emerges; Aggressive is high and Clearthinking very low.

TABLE 8.14

Centroids for Within-Period Types V - VII

on Burdock Ward Behavior Rating Scale Factors

Standard Score Units

Time Period	PATIENT TYPE V						
	WTH	IRR	NEGL	SAD	UNR	RES	CONF
0	-0.03	0.02	0.17	0.11	-0.53	0.10	-0.26
1	-0.09	0.07	-0.24	0.24	-0.36	0.80	-0.17
3	0.07	-0.02	-0.21	-0.10	-0.20	0.72	-0.44
6	-0.51	-0.05	-0.05	-0.36	0.03	-0.10	0.09
	PATIENT TYPE VI						
0	-0.24	-0.27	-0.38	0.36	-0.38	-0.18	-0.11
1	-0.03	-0.31	-0.41	0.19	-0.13	-0.25	0.04
3	0.37	-0.08	0.20	0.79	-0.18	-0.47	0.44
6	0.36	0.02	0.11	0.97	-0.16	-0.51	0.28
	PATIENT TYPE VII						
0	0.03	-0.23	-0.22	0.28	0.18	-0.29	0.14
1	-0.42	-0.37	-0.12	0.41	-0.46	-0.42	0.02
3	-0.49	-0.37	-0.44	-0.03	-0.31	-0.30	-0.16
6	-0.35	-0.23	0.50	0.27	-0.37	-0.52	-0.42

Dosage (Table 8.16). The patients were maintained on a very low level of phenothiazine throughout the study.

Diagnosis. This was predominantly a paranoid schizophrenic group.

Type V

IMPS (Table 8.11). Type V exhibits a pretreatment IMPS mean profile which has been referred to in previous studies as Excited–Hostile (Lorr *et al.*, 1963). The profile shows little damping over time. However, the syndrome pattern changes in that, although EXC remains prominent, HOS drops out of the picture by the final week and CNP becomes quite notable at this time.

Ward behavior (Table 8.14). No real peak is evident prior to treatment for this group's profile. At the same time, Feelings of Unreality is rated low. After one week on drug the profile changes somewhat in that Resistiveness becomes prominent. From this point on in the study a damping of the profile can be noted.

13

Mood (Table 8.15). Pretreatment peaks on Clearthinking and Sleepy can be noted. Profile changes then occur. Sleepiness drops out and feelings of friendliness emerge by the sixth week.

Dosage (Table 8.16). Dosage is increased somewhat during the second week, but then remains at a relatively low level for the remainder of treatment.

Diagnosis. This was almost exclusively a paranoid schizophrenic group.

Type VI

IMPS (Table 8.11). The pretreatment profile for type VI bears some resemblance to Lorr's Intropunitive type. INP is the most prominent feature of this profile, but PAR and RTD are also somewhat elevated. No damping can be noted as treatment continues. In fact, INP becomes even more pronounced. The configuration of the profile changes rather markedly in that RTD becomes increasingly more elevated and MTR emerges during the last half of the treatment period.

Ward behavior (Table 8.14). A pretreatment peak on Sadness, with all other factor scores low, initially characterizes the Burdock profiles for this type. At Period 3 Withdrawal and Confusion emerge and this changed configuration continues to the end of treatment.

Mood (Table 8.15). Patients' self-ratings on Aggressive and Unhappy are the only ones resembling peaks on the Period 0 profile. Friendly and Clearthinking, on the other hand, are very low. Sleepiness is prominent at the third week along with increased unhappiness. This configuration, with Friendly and Clearthinking remaining very low, continues at Period 6.

Dosage (Table 8.16). Dosage increases continue up to the fifth week until an intermediate level of about seven capsules per day is reached.

Diagnosis. This group was quite mixed diagnostically; catatonic, paranoid, and acute undifferentiated schizophrenics were all represented.

Type VII

IMPS (Table 8.11). This is more clearly an Intropunitive type with a sharp Period 0 peak on INP. The profile becomes markedly

TABLE 8.15

Centroids for Seven Within-Period Types on Clyde Mood Scale Factors

Standard Score Units

Time Period	FR	AGGR	CLTH	SL	UNH	DIZ
			TYPE I			
0	0.06	-0.77	-0.44	0.00	-0.31	0.00
3	-0.02	-0.27	-0.54	0.32	-0.18	0.29
6	-0.05	-0.12	-0.24	0.05	-0.23	0.36
			TYPE III			
0	0.69	0.70	0.36	-0.49	-0.18	-0.33
3	0.44	0.60	0.68	-0.31	-0.19	-0.41
6	0.27	0.25	0.61	-0.27	-0.17	-0.12
			TYPE V			
0	0.01	-0.23	0.35	0.35	0.04	-0.04
3	-0.11	0.10	0.63	-0.09	-0.13	-0.36
6	0.40	0.01	0.44	-0.10	-0.20	-0.26
			TYPE VII			
0	-0.12	-0.36	-0.42	-0.13	0.44	-0.04
3	-0.03	-0.35	-0.41	-0.28	-0.09	-0.31
6	0.11	-0.28	-0.30	-0.12	-0.20	-0.40

Time Period	FR	AGGR	CLTH	SL	UNH	DIZ
			TYPE II			
0	-0.54	-0.18	0.41	0.24	0.24	0.01
3	-0.10	-0.26	-0.11	-0.06	0.01	0.54
6	0.00	-0.05	-0.04	-0.10	0.02	0.47
			TYPE IV			
0	0.12	-0.52	0.03	0.17	-0.05	0.15
3	0.36	-0.28	-0.03	-0.01	-0.60	0.07
6	0.05	0.25	-0.68	0.06	-0.15	-0.01
			TYPE VI			
0	-0.50	0.16	-0.50	-0.08	0.17	-0.24
3	-0.69	0.05	-0.70	0.34	0.55	-0.06
6	-0.96	-0.04	-0.53	0.23	0.42	-0.46

damped by the third week of treatment, suggesting considerable improvement.

Ward behavior (Table 8.14). Sadness is the most prominent feature early in the study. At Period 3 this drops out; all scores were negative at this point. Of no little interest is the sudden emergence of Personal Neglect at Period 6.

Mood (Table 8.15). A high Unhappy score and low Clearthinking score can be noted at Period 0. This configuration remains fairly intact but becomes damped on successive profiles.

Dosage (Table 8.16). The dosage curve for this group is almost precisely the same as for type VI.

Diagnosis. Most of the patients in this group were diagnosed as acute undifferentiated schizophrenics.

The mean follow-up ratings for the within-period types are displayed in Table 8.16. The seven groups differed significantly with respect to the sixth week global improvement ratings ($F = 2.55$, significant at the 0.05 level). Types IV and VII were rated as most improved, while type VI was rated as least improved.

The types also differed with respect to the six-month global ratings of severity of illness ($F = 2.52$, significant at the 0.05 level). The groups rank in the same order as they did for the six-week ratings. This rank order also held up for the six-month social functioning ratings, but the mean differences are not statistically significant ($F = 1.61$).

One of the most striking features of the within-period types is that in each case, despite profile changes which occur during the course of treatment, pretreatment profiles correspond rather closely with types found through the work of Lorr and his associates. This finding can be considered as confirmatory, of course, but several other considerations are of importance here.

Because our sample of 222 was, by and large, a group of improvers on drug treatment, the variance for each syndrome became smaller as treatment progressed. Thus, there was more variance to be shared during the early phases of the study. This, coupled with the fact that there were only four assessment occasions, produced types which were perhaps disproportionately determined by the syndrome pattern of pretreatment.

However, we were encouraged by the fact that the Burdock and Clyde Mood profile sequences were, with few exceptions, configurations which were expected and meaningful. These concurrent

TABLE 8.16

Within-Period Types

Dosage Centroids over Six Weeks on Treatment
and Means of Follow-up Ratings

W-P Type	Mean Number of Capsules For Week Number						Improvement at 6 weeks	Severity at 6 months	Social Functioning at 6 months
	1	2	3	4	5	6			
I	31.9	52.7	56.1	54.3	55.1	54.9	1.9	2.7	2.8
II	34.0	56.8	66.8	69.1	73.4	74.5	2.4	2.7	2.8
III	33.5	48.1	52.9	55.3	59.1	57.2	2.2	3.0	3.0
IV	26.7	37.2	34.2	35.2	34.9	31.9	1.6	2.2	2.7
V	26.8	42.8	44.4	37.0	41.2	36.0	1.8	2.6	2.6
VI	26.3	36.7	43.1	50.7	49.5	45.1	2.6	4.3	4.1
VII	26.4	43.0	49.8	51.4	47.4	48.3	1.8	2.4	2.7

measures provide evidence for the clinical potential of the within-period approach.

Another point is in order. The types based on within-period correlation may have more appeal to the clinician than the within-score types. This is because the patterning of syndromes is emphasized, i.e. the approach is more configurational in nature.

CONCLUDING REMARKS

The methods described in this chapter are admittedly tentative attempts to attack a very difficult problem—the inclusion of time as another dimension in the typing of persons. However, it is particularly important to come to grips with this problem because a dynamic concept of personality suggests that we consider some such notion as "patterned variability over time".

Accordingly, our aim was to develop methods for classifying persons into types with respect to the manner in which they change over time on a number of behavior measures. To this end, three techniques for computing the degree of similarity between persons have been considered, two of which are sufficiently developed so as to warrant detailed discussion in this chapter. The first of these is based on the notion that a type may be characterized by a set of time-curves and a second method arose from the idea that a type may be characterized by a time-ordered sequence of profiles.

It should be emphasized again that, despite the fact that the data were obtained from interviews with patients undergoing treatment with phenothiazine drugs, no inferences are being advanced about the action of these drugs. Rather, the aim has been to explore the efficacy of our methods. (The one observation we would make at this point, however, is that, in the therapy situation, terms such as "improvement" are misleadingly simple; there appear to be many varieties of improvement, as the change patterns indicate.) The results indicate that the use of both the within-score and within-period agreement indices yields patient groupings which are replicable (in the limited sense described) and "statistically separate".

In addition, the concurrent measures which were obtained suggest that the IMPS-based patterns of change are clinically valid and meaningful. For example, despite the fact that factor names may often be misleading, one would expect that, for a given type if a certain shaped time-curve for INP occurs, similar curves for nurses' ratings of sadness and patients' self-ratings of unhappiness should also be noted. This was quite often the case.

One would also expect to find that the use of both similarity indices would yield types which differ with respect to post-treatment ratings of improvement. This was the case for both the within-score and the within-period types. Six-month differences with respect to severity of illness and level of social functioning were found for the within-period and within-score types, respectively. Thus, some degree of predictive validity was demonstrated.

Some problems remain, of course, many of which have been mentioned. Failure to meet the assumptions underlying the computation of the agreement indices and the difficulty caused by patients being "out of phase" are among the most serious of these problems. Another difficulty resides in the classical problem of what constitutes reliable change in the use of repeated measures. However, despite the fact that measurement error resides in the data, if the identification of replicable and clinically meaningful patterns of change can be accomplished, the existence of this error may not constitute a serious problem.

The further development of the rather simple techniques described in this chapter would seem to offer promise for research in personality and psychopathology. Diagnostic classes could then be defined with respect to patterned change over time on a number of variables. Types of response to various classes of treatments could be determined as has been suggested by the data we have presented. In this regard, it should be noted that such types would have prognosis "built into" them.

We would, at this point, suspend judgment as to whether use of the within-score or within-period agreement indices yields the most useful types. Both are techniques which can be used with the same body of data. As already mentioned, they represent complementary views of patterned change over time, the within-score approach emphasizing the time-curve aspects of change and the within-period method emphasizing the configurational aspects. Much depends on the purposes of the investigator.

PART III

WARD AND COMMUNITY BEHAVIOR TYPES

CHAPTER 9

WARD BEHAVIOR TYPES

Maurice Lorr

In previous chapters evidence was offered for the existence of psychotic types based on behaviors observed in an interview. There is general recognition that the sample of behaviors restricted to an hour and involving only two or three individuals may not be sufficient. The hospital ward offers a broader and more representative sampling of the patients' characteristic interpersonal interactions with a variety of other individuals. There is opportunity to observe his relationships to other patients, nurses, ward aides, physicians, and other types of hospital personnel. For these reasons it is of interest to explore the behavior types occurring within ward settings.

AIMS AND SAMPLE

In this chapter a report will be given of an exploratory investigation of ward behavior types. The aim was to identify the classes of homogeneous profiles within a sample of hospitalized psychotics. The measuring instrument was the revised Psychotic Reaction Profile (PRP), a ward behavior inventory measuring 11 dimensions of patient ward behavior. It will be shown that seven patient types, most very similar to those found in a psychiatric interview, emerge in successive analyses.

The sample consisted of 348 patients rated by nurses and aides after three days of observation at five state and university hospitals. Of this group 204 were women and 144 were men. The typical patient was 29 years old but the ages ranged from 16 to 60. The sample included broad spectrum of functional psychotics. Newly admitted cases as well as more chronic cases from all possible types of wards were represented.

The Psychotic Reaction Profile (Lorr, O'Connor and Stafford, 1960) has been factored twice (Lorr and O'Connor, 1962; Lorr, Klett and McNair, 1964). In the second analysis the correlations among 85 behavior statements were factored to yield 11 factors five of which confirmed a previous analysis. The 11 ward factors or syndromes were labeled Hostile Belligerence, Paranoid Projection, Resistiveness, Dominance, Anxious Depression, Seclusiveness, Retardation, Apathy, Perceptual Distortions, Motor Disturbances, and Conceptual Disorganization. As the titles imply, the inventory was deliberately designed to measure the same behavior syndromes observed in the interview as well as additional patterns unique to the ward.

The original form was modified with a view (a) to increasing the reliability of the shorter syndrome measures, and (b) to measuring three additional syndromes of Excitement, Disorientation, and Supervisory Care Needed. The revised PRP consisted of 105 behavior statements each to be rated on a four-point scale of frequency of occurrence following a three-day period of observation. It was designed to measure all of the factors previously identified except Dominance which was dropped. In addition statements were included to measure constructs of Excitement, Disorientation, and Supervisory Care Needed. The factor analysis of the data confirmed all 13 factors hypothesized.

Eleven syndromes were selected to represent the domain of ward behavior. Although Apathy and Seclusiveness can be discriminated factorially, the two clusters of variables are too highly correlated to be scored separately. Resistiveness, similarly, is quite close to Hostile Belligerence. For this reason variables representing Apathy and Seclusiveness were combined, as were measures of Hostile Belligerence and Resistiveness. Table 9.1 presents a set of statements that illustrate the nature of the 11 syndromes measured by PRP. From four to eleven statements defined each of the syndromes. The correlations among the raw scores of the 11 syndromes are presented in Table 9.2. The independence of the classificatory criteria can be judged from the table.

METHOD OF ANALYSIS

The typing procedure sketched in Chapter 3 was followed in the present analysis. The first 300 cases were subdivided into two samples of 150 cases each. To establish a common unit of measure each of the 11 factor scores was transformed into standard score form. Correlations and congruency coefficients were then computed among all members of each subsample. Next the typing procedures

TABLE 9.1

STATEMENTS EXEMPLIFYING THE 11 SYNDROMES

OF PRP

SYNDROME	STATEMENT
EXCITEMENT	TALKS IN A LOUD OR INTENSE VOICE.
	ACTS GAY; "ON TOP OF THE WORLD".
HOSTILE BELLIGERENCE	LOSES TEMPER WHEN DEALING WITH OTHER PATIENTS.
	THREATENS TO ASSAULT OTHERS.
PARANOID PROJECTION	ACTS AS THOUGH THE HOSPITAL IS PERSECUTING HIM..
	THINKS HE IS BEING CONFINED IN A PRISON.
PERCEPTUAL DISTORTIONS	SEEMS TO HEAR THINGS THAT ARE NOT THERE.
	SAYS VOICES THREATEN PUNISHMENT OR TORTURE.
INTROPUNITIVENESS	LOOKS WORRIED AND NERVOUS.
	SEEMS SCARED OR PANICKY WITH FRIGHT.
RETARDATION	SPEAKS SOFTLY; DIFFICULT TO HEAR.
	LOOKS TIRED AND "ALL WORN OUT."
SECLUSIVENESS	IGNORES THE ACTIVITIES AROUND HIM.
	SHOWS INTEREST IN THE PROBLEMS OF OTHERS.
DISORIENTATION	KNOWS THE NAMES OF WARD AIDES.
	ACTS CONFUSED OR BEWILDERED.
SUPERVISORY CARE	REQUIRES HELP IN DRESSING.
	REQUIRES HELP TO TAKE A SHOWER.

(TABLE CONTINUED ON NEXT PAGE)

TABLE 9.1—*(continued)*

SYNDROME	STATEMENT
MOTOR DISTURBANCES	GIGGLES IN A SILLY WAY WITHOUT GOOD REASON. MAKES STRANGE MOVEMENTS THAT DO NOT MAKE SENSE.
CONCEPTUAL DISORGAN.	IT IS DIFFICULT TO UNDERSTAND WHAT HE IS SAYING. REPEATS WORDS AND PHRASES IN A MEANINGLESS WAY.

TABLE 9.2

CORRELATIONS AMONG THE 11

WARD BEHAVIOR FACTORS

	FACTOR									
	EXC	HOS	PAR	PCP	INP	RTD	SEC	DIS	SUP	MTR
EXC										
HOS	.57									
PAR	.37	.66								
PCP	.11	.33	.39							
INP	-.06	.13	.30	.31						
RTD	-.27	-.04	.01	.16	.47					
SEC	-.41	.02	.08	.30	.33	.51				
DIS	.01	.15	.23	.48	.28	.38	.49			
SUP	.06	.29	.26	.44	.28	.36	.38	.62		
MTR	.33	.37	.24	.50	.03	.11	.14	.40	.36	
CNP	.32	.27	.26	.42	.23	.22	.22	.61	.39	.54

described in Chapter 3 were applied to the similarity indices among members of each subsample.

The correlation (Q) and congruency (C) clusters with each subsample were compared and matched on the basis of (a) the proportion of members identical in the two clusters, and (b) the degree of similarity in their mean syndrome profiles as measured by the congruency coefficient.

The subsample clusters were first compared and matched on the basis of the degree of similarity between their mean syndrome profiles. Two clusters were considered the same if the value of C was at least 0.75 and if all other coefficients were negative or small and positive. As a final check a stratified sample was assembled. It consisted of a random sample of members of each of the clusters matched at least once. The stratified sample was then subjected to a typing analysis. A type was considered to be confirmed if a high proportion of all members of a stratified sample cluster consisted of those cases assigned to it. Although not matched in the initial analysis the group defining an Intropunitive type was included in the stratified sample. Intropunitive patients were known to occur frequently in interview data and thus it seemed plausible to expect such a type to emerge in ward data as well.

RESULTS OF MATCHING

The characteristic profile of a type can be described in terms of those syndromes whose scores lie at some point above the sample mean on the standard score scale. For convenience and brevity of description each syndrome will be identified by a number. Let Excitement be denoted 1, Hostility 2, Paranoid Projection 3, Perceptual Distortion 4, Intropunitiveness 5, Retardation 6, Seclusiveness 7, Disorientation 8, Supervisory Care Needed 9, Motor Disturbance 10, and Conceptual Disorganization 11. This notation will be used in the tables to identify each type. The 1–2 type, for example, consists of a group who have scores elevated on Excitement (1) and Hostility (2).

The results of matching the Q and C clusters that define the seven ward behavior types are presented in Table 9.3. Between five and eight clusters were identified in the three analyses. Forty to forty-seven per cent of all cases were included in the clusters that emerged. Since a high proportion of the sample had been

TABLE 9.3

MATCHING Q AND C CLUSTERS THAT DEFINE

THE 7 WARD BEHAVIOR TYPES

TYPE	SUBSAMPLE					
	1		2		STRATIFIED	
	Q	C	Q	C	Q	C
1-2	2	5	1	3	1	2
2-3	4	4	3		5	4
2					6	
5	5				4	7
6-7	1	1	2	1	2	1
4-6-7-8-9-10-11	3	2	4	4	3	3
1-2-3-4-5-8-9-10-11				2		6
MISCELL.	6	3	5,6	5		5,8
PER CENT INCLUDED	47	44	44	40	63	65

receiving drug treatment, many were relatively asymptomatic. Consequently their syndrome profiles would tend to be flat. Thus drug treatment probably accounts for the comparatively small proportion of all cases classified. It should be noted that the proportion classified in the stratified sample is 63 to 64 per cent. It therefore seems likely that a fairly high proportion of patients not on drugs could be assigned to one of the types.

THE WARD BEHAVIOR TYPES

The mean syndrome scores of the seven ward types are given in Table 9.4. The figures present the typical patient profiles.

The Excited–Hostile pattern (1–2) is marked primarily by excited behavior as all cases are elevated above the total sample mean.

TABLE 9.4

MEAN WARD BEHAVIOR SYNDROME SCORES FOR 7 PATIENT TYPES

TYPE	WARD SYNDROME										
	EXC	HOS	PAR	PCP	INP	RTD	SEC	DIS	SUP	MTR	CNP
EXCITED-HOSTILE	1.56	.13	-.34	-.59	-.71	-.84	-1.35	-.75	-.43	-.20	-.22
HOSTILE PARANOID	.32	1.47	2.48	-.18	.04	-.57	.07	-.27	-.40	-.26	-.17
HOSTILE	-.45	.79	-.46	-.38	-.45	-.21	.09	-.79	-.52	-.46	-.49
INTROPUNITIVE	-.43	-.53	-.43	-.38	1.68	-.29	-.26	-.70	-.48	-.46	-.53
RETARDED-SECLUSIVE	-.69	-.51	-.51	-.43	.08	1.11	.58	.09	-.19	-.54	-.36
RETARDED-DISORGANIZED	-.56	-.33	-.37	.59	-.10	.74	.94	1.68	1.06	1.23	-1.43
EXCITED-DISORGANIZED	1.94	2.68	2.25	2.07	.54	.13	-.25	.92	1.21	2.38	1.26

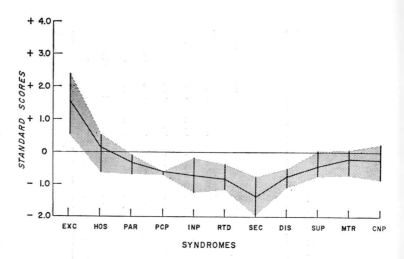

FIG. 9.1. Profile for Excited–Hostile ward type.

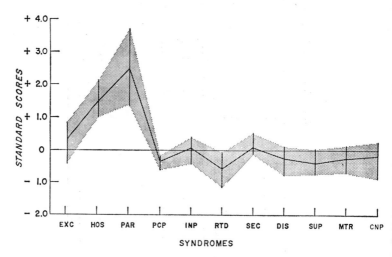

FIG. 9.2. Profile for Hostile Paranoid ward type.

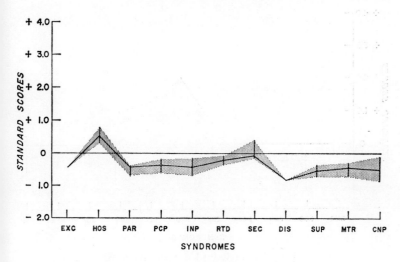

FIG. 9.3. Profile for Hostile ward type.

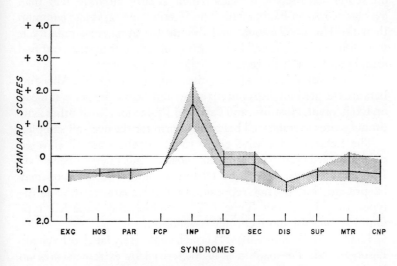

FIG. 9.4. Profile for Intropunitive ward type.

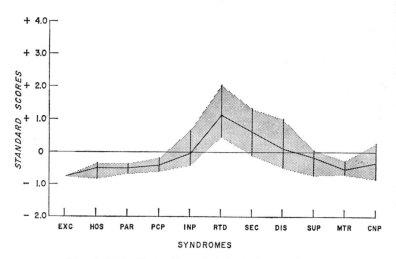

FIG. 9.5. Profile for Retarded–Seclusive ward type.

Hostility is usually but not always present. The type is also characterized by scores below the mean on Perceptual Distortion, Anxious Depression, Seclusiveness, and Retardation.

The Hostile–Paranoid type (2–3) members have scores elevated on scores descriptive of their label. Nearly all have less than average scores on Excitement. The Hostile type (2) is less common than the Hostile–Paranoid and despite the apparent similarity is well differentiated. The Hostile group emerged from the stratified sample and thus will require further verification.

The Intropunitive type (5) is quite distinctive in profile. All members are elevated on Intropunitiveness and below the general mean on Excitement, Hostility, and Paranoid Projection. Most other syndrome scores average well below the norm for the over-all sample.

The Retarded–Seclusive group (6–7) members are all elevated on the Retardation syndrome and most are not rated as Seclusive. Intropunitiveness, Perceptual Distortion, and Disorientation may be present, but do not represent uniform characteristics of the type. In this respect Type 6–7 resembles the Retarded type found among the more chronic psychotics.

The (1–2–3–4–5–8–9–10–11) type is tentatively labeled Excited–Disorganized. The pattern is characterized by extreme scores on Excitement, Hostile Belligerence, Paranoid Projection, and

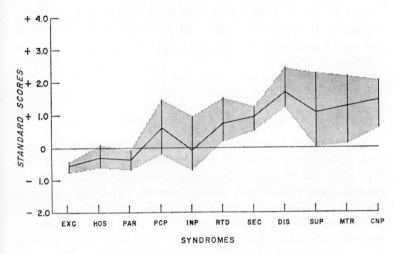

FIG. 9.6. Profile for Retarded–Disorganized ward type.

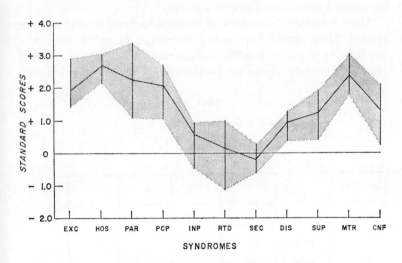

Fig. 9.7. Profile for Excited–Disorganized ward type.

Perceptual Distortion. The more schizophrenic syndromes—Need for Supervisory Care, Motor Disturbances, and Conceptual Disorganization—are also sharply elevated.

The (4–6–7–8–9–10–11) type will be called Retarded–Disorganized. It is characterized by all of the syndromes that mark the withdrawn and disorganized schizophrenic. Members are disoriented, hallucinated, disturbed in motor behavior, conceptually disorganized, and somewhat retarded and seclusive.

DIFFERENTIATION OF THE TYPES

Are the ward behavior types adequately distinguishable from each other? Are members of a type sufficiently similar in profile? Tables 9.5 and 9.6 present the average correlations and the average congruencies within and among clusters. The highest mean correlation between clusters of the stratified sample is 0.16 while the highest congruency coefficient is 0.36. Thus the types are well separated or differentiated. Negative correlations can be ignored as they imply profiles opposite in slope and direction. The values in the diagonals of the two tables are 0.64 or higher. Since these values represent mean correlations or congruencies, they imply substantial agreement among members.

After matching, members of clusters deemed identical were pooled. Their profiles have been presented in Table 9.4. But it was not feasible to recompute the average correlations between pooled clusters. Instead congruency coefficients were computed between

TABLE 9.5

AVERAGE CORRELATIONS AMONG CLUSTERS

OF STRATIFIED WARD SAMPLE

CLUSTER	1	2	3	4	5	6
1	.73					
2	−.51	.70				
3	−.24	.07	.70			
4	−.18	.12	−.42	.76		
5	.08	−.25	−.38	−.02	.67	
6	.04	.06	−.29	.03	.16	.74

TABLE 9.6

AVERAGE CONGRUENCY COEFFICIENTS AMONG CLUSTERS
OF STRATIFIED WARD SAMPLE

CLUSTER	1	2	3	4	5	6	7	8
1	.67							
2	-.03	.76						
3	-.26	-.49	.64					
4	-.23	.03	-.20	.65				
5	.08	-.17	.14	-.31	.66			
6	-.62	.06	.23	.23	-.07	.66		
7	.22	.16	-.38	-.06	-.21	-.29	.67	
8	.36	-.54	.25	-.11	-.08	-.26	-.01	.69

TABLE 9.7

CONGRUENCY COEFFICIENTS AMONG THE MEAN
PROFILES OF 7 WARD BEHAVIOR TYPES

TYPE		A	B	C	D	E	F
1-2	A						
2-3	B	.10					
2	C	.27	.14				
5	D	-.02	-.17	.18			
6-7	E	-.49	-.46	.18	.28		
4-6-7-8-9-10-11	F	-.64	-.37	-.62	-.46	.11	
1-2-3-4-5-8-9-10-11	G	-.05	.49	-.43	-.50	-.67	.33

the mean profile of each type and every other type. The results are
presented in Table 9.7. It is quite evident that the pooled types
are sufficiently differentiated.

COMPARISONS

Are the ward behavior types the same or different from those identified in interview data? It is not possible to give a precise answer to this question yet. It would first be necessary to demonstrate that most of the ward and interview syndromes are measures of the same behavioral or ideational tendencies; then to show that the types evolved out of interview and ward data correspond.

Since the ward types presented here are tentative, the comparisons offered are tentative and couched in qualitative terms. The ward Excited–Hostile type (1–2) appears very similar to the interview Excited–Hostile group (1–2–3–10). In addition to the excitement and hostility, many patients in the ward type manifest paranoid thinking just as the interview group does.

The ward Hostile Paranoid (2–3) resembles the interview Hostile Paranoid type in most respects except that more members in the ward group are also mildly excited. The Hostile (2) type appears to be included among the Hostile Paranoids in interview data. The Intropunitive (6) ward group is closely similar in profile to the corresponding interview group. No syndrome except Intropunitiveness is elevated above the mean of the sample.

The Retarded–Seclusive group (6–7) resembles the Retarded type found among more chronic patients. Seclusiveness, not observable in the interview, appears to be the added element. The Retarded–Disorganized group (4–6–7–8–9–10–11) is quite similar in profile to the interview type of similar name. Patients are slowed up, disoriented, disturbed in thinking and in motor behavior and in need of supervisory care for drinking, washing, etc. The ward Excited–Disorganized patient type closely resembles its correlative class identified in interview data. Both groups included excited and disordered patients. Only the grandiose element is missing in the ward description since no such syndrome was included.

In summary it can be said that a typing analysis of the revised Psychotic Reaction Profile resulted in the identification of seven ward behavior classes. Six of these patient classes correspond closely to interview types when judged qualitatively in terms of elevated mean syndrome profiles. The findings are thus supportive of the interview types. In Chapter 6 on validity of the acute psychotic types indirect evidence is presented that ward behavior is consistent with behavior manifested in the interview.

CHAPTER 10

BEHAVIOR PATTERNS OF SCHIZOPHRENICS IN THE COMMUNITY

Martin M. Katz, Henri A. Lowery and Jonathan O. Cole

In this chapter, we will attempt to review a series of studies which were designed to extend the descriptive-phenomenologic approach in psychopathology to the behavior of schizophrenics in the community.

The major impetus for these investigations derives from the confusion which exists concerning some basic concepts in psychopathology. The concept of schizophrenia does not, for example, appear to be any clearer today than it ever has been. Rümke (1960) lists some ten contradictions concerning its etiology, manifestations and course, and although he seems to feel that they are all resolvable, it will be clear to most investigators in the field that certain of them are not. The confusion over such concepts has contributed to a decline in the care with which schizophrenia is identified and described, and a lessening of the ability of clinicians and theoreticians to communicate to each other about what it means.

We will describe the development of an observational rating method, the attempt to relate measures of behavior obtained in the community to similar measures in the hospital, and will detail the development of a typology based on patterns of social behavior and symptomatology which are manifested in the community. Finally, the results of investigations of the validity of the typology, both with regard to the visibility of the types to other observers, and its predictive utility with regard to drug treatment, will be reported.

We have felt that the descriptive-phenomenologic approach has not been utilized as well or as comprehensively as it might be in psychopathology, and see the present work as a contribution to clarifying certain of the conceptual issues and to establishing a basic descriptive framework for other types of research in the field.

It has been clear for some time now that there has been a major gap in the attempt to describe comprehensively the occurrence and manifestation of psychopathology in the psychoses. The majority of the research which is aimed at describing and separating out patterns of symptomatology and behavior in the psychoses has dealt with their manifestations as they are observed in the hospital setting. The effort to objectify and quantify observations of pathology as these occur in the hospital has not been extended to other settings, despite the fact that pathology is initially discovered and identified in the community. This situation has existed because careful description and observation requires a controlled setting and the availability of trained observers.

The trained observers required to carry out this type of research are psychiatrists and psychologists, who are viewed as the experts in the art of detecting the more subtle manifestations of pathology, and the semi-professionals, the nurses and ward attendants, who, because they work in the living situation of patients, are in an advantaged position for the observation of their day-to-day behavior. The schedules of items of behavior which are provided for these observers for ratings have grown out of various theories of psychopathology and out of experience with what it is in the patient's behavior that can be observed and rated reliably. The outcome has been the development of sets of dimensions of pathology which are based on observations by the professionals of the patient's behavior in the interview situation (Lorr et al., 1962; Wittenborn, 1951), and other sets of dimensions (Lorr and O'Connor, 1962; Goldberg et al., 1963), which are based on the analysis of observations in the ward situation. There should be some overlap of dimensions between these two situations, the interview and ward, but it would be very strange, given the differences in settings and the types of observers, if there were complete agreement between the two. There are, in fact, indications in the research referred to that different areas of behavior are covered in the two settings, which simply point up the need for extending similar observational methods to other significant observers and to other critical situations.

The general aim of the large majority of such research is the objective description of psychopathology in all of its manifestations. Although the "descriptive, phenomenologic" approach views description and classification as values in themselves, there is the implicit assumption that if the important phenomena are set out, described in objective, unbiased terms, then it is more likely that the basic dimensions underlying these phenomena will be manifested, and the opportunities for understanding the roots of pathological behavior will, therefore, be enhanced.

The major gap referred to earlier has to do with the absence of objective information on the patient's behavior *prior* to entering the hospital. It is in the community that what is designated as psychopathology is initially manifested and identified. It is usually on the basis of such symptoms or behavior that the patient is subsequently hospitalized, and despite the availability of detailed knowledge of his behavior following hospitalization, little knowledge exists of the relationship between behaviors in these two very different settings. That these relationships may not be very strong is evidenced in research, which demonstrates that the level of pathology at discharge is not very predictive of future adjustment in the community (Ellsworth and Clayton, 1959). Further, if one were to approach the community situation and to obtain information on patient behavior prior to hospitalization, one could then ask whether the "behavioral dimensions" which would be derived in this process, would, in fact, closely resemble the dimensions which have been developed from behavioral observations within the hospital.

In the remainder of this chapter, we will take up this problem by reporting research on the following:

(1) A description of a method for obtaining objective, quantifiable information on the symptomatology and social behavior of patients prior to hospitalization.

(2) The relationships of the various behavioral measures, which are derived, to similar measures which are based on ratings of the patient in the interview and ward situations.

(3) The development of a typology from a sample of patient profiles, which identifies a set of discrete patterns of behavior in the community.

(4) The attempt to validate the typology through investigations of (a) its pattern of relationships with behavior as viewed by professionals (psychiatrists and psychologists) in the interview, and as viewed by nurses and attendants on the ward, and (b) its utility in the prediction of response to drug treatment.

THE RELATIVE'S RATING SCALE

In the attempt to apply the descriptive-phenomenologic approach to the study of the psychopathology of schizophrenia, the authors felt that it would be salutary to depart from the expert's framework and to attempt, through the eyes of the lay observer, to reconstruct the nature of the behavioral pathology of schizophrenics—to determine, for example, whether lay people would put the same kinds of behavior together that professionals do. Further, given the limitations of the expert observer, e.g., his theoretical preconceptions, restricted period of observation, and the limitations and influences of the milieu in which the observations go on, it was felt that the key observer selected should ideally meet the following requirements: He should (a) be in a position to observe the patient's behavior over a period of time in the patient's natural environment, (b) be naive about formal theories of psychopathology, (c) be somewhat detached emotionally as far as the patient is concerned, so that his judgments could be viewed as reasonably objective. It is unfeasible to locate any observer who meets all of these qualifications. In this research we selected the close relative of the patient, who satisfies the first two criteria and tried to construct the reporting scheme, a rating inventory. It was believed that the influence of his probable emotional involvement would thus be minimized.

The rating inventory, described in detail elsewhere (Katz and Lyerly, 1963), is comprised of two kinds of items: psychiatric symptoms which have been translated into lay language, and items which describe social behavior. The inventory is further characterized by the attempt to be as comprehensive as possible in its inclusion of items in the symptom and social behavior areas. It focuses as much as possible on concrete behaviors rather than on phenomena requiring judgments or inferences on the part of the observer. A format was used which would permit quantification and the development of a set of scores or a profile of the patient's behavior. It was intended that the inventory could be used both to describe a patient's behavior prior to entrance into treatment, and as part of a set of scales, to assess clinical and social adjustment at various intervals following treatment.

After a preliminary test found it to be generally valid in discriminating between extreme groups on the dimension of "adjustment", the inventory was administered to the relatives of approximately 100 newly admitted psychotic patients at Spring Grove State Hospital in Maryland. The relative was asked to describe the patient's behavior just prior to his entrance into the hospital.

These data were used to determine, through a factor analytic method, whether a set of measures could be developed to provide a profile of symptomatic and social behavior. On the basis of this analysis, which was reported previously (Katz and Lyerly, 1963), 77 of the original 128 items were assigned to one of twelve clusters which, from the cluster analysis and from a second order factor analysis, appeared to be measuring such factors as social obstreperousness, psychoticism (bizarreness and panic), withdrawal and depression, suspiciousness, and nervousness. The twelve clusters were then used to develop a formal scoring system for the inventory. These clusters are presented in Table 10.1.

COMMUNITY VERSUS HOSPITAL BEHAVIOR

The validation of the separate clusters measured is a complex undertaking in itself. For the current problem we sought to establish the nature of the relationships between these measures which have as their base the patient's behavior in the community, and measures reflecting his behavior during hospitalization. Is the patient's behavior as reported by the relative predictive of his behavior in the hospital?

In the National Institute of Mental Health Collaborative Study of Drugs and Schizophrenia (1964), it was possible to investigate in a large sample of acute schizophrenics the relationships between, on the one hand, such variables as "belligerence" reported by the relative, and, on the other, "hostility", as rated by the psychiatrist on the Inpatient Multidimensional Psychiatric Scale (IMPS) (Lorr et al., 1962), "irritability", as rated by the nurse on the Ward Behavior Scale (Burdock et al., 1960), and "aggressiveness", as rated by the psychiatrist on the Clyde Mood Scale (Clyde, 1963).

Table 10.1

KAS[a] Form R1: Relatives' Ratings of Patient Symptoms and Social Behavior

Subtest Clusters

(1) Belligerence[b]

28. Got angry and broke things
50. Cursed at people
45. Got into fights with people
113. Threatened to tell people off

(2) Verbal Expansiveness

100. Shouted or yelled for no reason
106. Talked too much
99. Spoke very loud
105. Kept changing from one subject to
     another for no reason
118. Bragged about how good he was

(3) Negativism

46. Was not cooperative
36. Acted as if he did not care about
     other people's feelings
47. Did the opposite of what he was asked
48. Stubborn
56. Critical of other people
51. Deliberately upset routine
59. Lied
37. Thought only of himself
60. Got into trouble with law

(4) Helplessness

93. Acted as if he could not make decisions
74. Acted helpless
92. Acted as if he could not concentrate on
     one thing
3.   Cried easily

(5) Suspiciousness

40. Thought people were talking about him
107. Said people were talking about him
43. Acted as if he were suspicious of people
108. Said that people were trying to make him
     do or think things he did not want to

(6) Anxiety

19. Afraid something terrible was going to happen
122. Said that something terrible was going to
     happen
18. Had strange fears
111. Talked about people or things he was afraid of
23. Got suddenly frightened for no reason
125. Talked about suicide

(Table continued on next page)

[a]Katz Adjustment Scales.

[b]Items within a cluster are listed in order of importance for interpretation of the cluster. Order is based
on part-whole correlations of individual items with the cluster.

Table 10.1 Continued

(7) Withdrawal and Retardation

76. Moved about very slowly
8. Just sat
80. Very slow to react
70. Quiet
17. Needed to do things very slowly to do them right
84. Would stay in one position for long period of time

(8) General Psychopathology

5. Acted as if he had no interest in things
12. Felt that people did not care about him
30. Acted as if he had no control over his emotions
31. Laughed or cried at strange times
32. Has mood changes without reason
33. Had temper tantrums
34. Got very excited for no reason
42. Bossy
44. Argued
52. Resentful
55. Got annoyed easily
67. Stayed away from people
71. Preferred to be alone
73. Behavior was childish
79. Very quick to react to something said or done
90. Acted as if he were confused about things; in a daze
91. Acted as if he could not get certain thoughts out of his mind
94. Talked without making sense
97. Refused to speak at all for periods of time
98. Spoke so low you could not hear him
110. Talked about how angry he was at certain people
119. Said the same things over and over again
121. Talked about big plans he had for the future
127. Gave advice without being asked

(9) Nervousness

20. Got nervous easily
21. Jittery
38. Showed his feelings
22. Worried or fretted

(10) Confusion

85. Lost track of day, month, or the year
86. Forgot his address or other places he knows well
88. Acted as if he did not know where he was

(11) Bizarreness

116. Talked about strange things that were going on inside his body
26. Did strange things without reason
25. Acted as if he saw people or things that weren't there
124. Believed in strange things
24. Had bad dreams

(12) Hyperactivity

7. Had periods where he could not stop moving or doing something
13. Did the same thing over and over again without reason
6. Was restless

In investigating the relationships among variables in the two settings, it is clear that the relationships between certain of the relatives' rating variables and the hospital variables, because of their obvious communality in meaning, can be hypothesized in advance (such as the examples presented above) and where the relationship is demonstrated, can be interpreted as evidence of predictive validity. Any significant relationship which occurs in an empirical correlational analysis of this type and this size, will have to be interpreted with regard to its meaningfulness and the actual magnitude of the correlation. To be considered, also, in the interpretation of the correlations is the fact that in the Collaborative Study there are nine hospitals from different areas of the country, representing various types of settings, and including some twenty psychiatric raters and twenty nurses. The correlations are, therefore, likely to be in the modest direction and to underestimate the extent of any given relationship.* With these qualifications in mind the results of a set of comparisons of patient behavior in the community with patient behavior and mood in the interview situation and on the ward, based on a sample of 242 patients in the Collaborative Study, are presented in Table 10.2.

Generally speaking the relationships are as expected modest, but it is clear that they are in the anticipated directions and indicate a certain amount of consistency across all situations. "Belligerence", as rated by the relatives, predicts "hostility"† as viewed by the psychiatrist in the interview, and "irritability", on the ward, as rated by the nurse. Further, "belligerence" is, also, likely to be associated with the psychiatrist perceiving "ideas of persecution" and the nurse recording that there is "denial of illness" and an absence of "depression" (appearance of sadness). The "verbal expansiveness" reported by the relative, is related positively as expected, to the psychiatrist's rating of "manic speech", and negatively to the nurse's ratings of depression and lack of social participation. In another realm, both of these variables are related

* The "Relatives' Rating Scale" also differs from the IMPS and Ward Behavior Scale in that in the former every patient is rated by a different rater—which introduces another limiting factor where correlations with other variables are concerned.

† The IMPS was scored in accord with a system developed from a factor analysis of the item data on the 404 patients in the NIMH–PSC study. The rationale and the scoring system are described in Goldberg et al., 1963.

Table 10.2

Predictive Validity of Relatives' Ratings: Correlations with Interview, Ward Behavior, and Mood Ratings during first week following Hospital Admission[a]

Relatives' Ratings of Patients' Pre-Admission Symptoms and Social Behavior (KAS:R1)	Initial Interview: Psychiatric Ratings of Symptoms (IMPS)		Ward Behavior: Nurses Ratings (WBS)		Mood: Doctors' Ratings (CMS)[b]	
1. Belligerence	Ideas of Persecution	.23[c]	Appearance of sadness	-.32	Unhappy	-.22
	Hostility	.20	Denial of illness	.30	Clear-thinking	-.14
	Slower speech & movements	-.19	Irritability	.24		
	Manic speech	.18	Confusion	-.14		
	Guilt	-.17	Global rating of mental illness	.14		
2. Verbal Expressiveness	Slower speech & movements	-.29	Appearance of sadness	-.39	Aggressive	.21
	Manic speech	.29	Confusion	-.25	Unhappy	-.19
	Memory deficit	-.17	Social non-participation	-.22		
	Hostility	.15	Denial of illness	.21		
	Guilt	-.14				
	Indifference	-.14				
	Ideas of Persecution	.14				
3. Negativism	Guilt	-.23	Denial of illness	.30	Unhappy	-.19
			Appearance of sadness	-.25		
			Irritability	.17		
4. Helplessness	Guilt	.18	Irritability	-.16	Unhappy	.19
	Hostility	-.14			Aggressive	-.15
					Friendly	.14

a Based on N of 222 acute schizophrenic patients from nine hospitals in the NIMH-PSC Collaborative Study of Drugs and Schizophrenia.
b Clyde Mood Scale.

(Table continued on next page)

Table 10.2 Continued

Relatives' Ratings of Patients' Pre-Admission Symptoms and Social Behavior (KAS:RI)	Initial Interview: Psychiatric Ratings of Symptoms (IMPS)		Ward Behavior: Nurses' Ratings (WBS)		Mood: Doctors' Ratings (CMS)[b]	
5. Suspiciousness	<u>Ideas of Persecution</u> Incoherent speech Auditory hallucinations	.22 -.16 .14	Denial of illness	.14		
6. Anxiety	Incoherent speech	-.16	Irritability	-.16		
7. Withdrawal & Retardation	<u>Manic speech</u> Hostility	-.23 -.18	Social Non- Participation Irritability	.23 -.19	Aggressive	-.20
9. Nervousness	Delusions of grandeur Auditory hallucinations Manic speech	-.18 -.14 .14			Unhappy Friendly	.20 .16
10. Bizarreness	<u>Auditory hallucinations</u> Delirium Memory deficit	.17 .17 .16	Global rating of mental illness Self-care Feelings of unreality	.16 .15 .14		
11. Hyperactivity	Guilt	-.17	Appearance of sadness	-.18	Unhappy	-.18

c For N of 222 r = .14: significant at .05 level; r = .18: significant at .01 level. All significant relationships between the Relatives' Ratings variables and variables from the IMPS, WBS, and CMS are recorded in the table. The correlates which were predicted are underlined (see text).

to the patient's general mood being rated as "not unhappy" (on the Clyde Mood Scale).

Without attempting to integrate and explore in detail the many other relationships here, some of which are not consistent with expectations, the interrelationships are reasonably clear and suggest a similarity in patterns of behavior across the two situations, the community and the hospital, which will be explored in more detail in the remainder of this report. Despite the consistency in patterning, the general level of correlation which exists throughout indicates that the amount of overlap is limited, and that given a certain amount of uncommon but valid variance in all of these scales, it is likely that they contribute different pieces of information about similar theoretical constructs.

What interests us here in the long run, however, is not so much the direct relationships between individual variables, but the likelihood that patterns of relationships among variables in one setting are very likely to be related to similar patterns in the other setting. The fact that the second order factor of social obstreperousness, which would include the measures of belligerence, verbal expansiveness and negativism, has consistent, meaningful relationships with the IMPS and Ward Behavior variables—as does another second order factor, withdrawal and helplessness (although of a very different kind)—supports the idea that the patterns manifested both in the community and hospital situations are likely to be similar. Despite these consistencies, it is clear that we are also dealing with a large amount of independent variance, and that it will take a good deal of thought and further analysis before the areas of overlap and independence are completely understood.

DEVELOPMENT OF THE TYPOLOGY

Having developed a set of reliable measures whose interrelationships are known (Katz and Lyerly, 1963) and on which a good deal of evidence for validity exists, we turned to the problem of determining whether an empirical analysis of the profiles of behavior manifested within a population of schizophrenic patients would lead to the development of a typology, i.e. a method for classifying patients on the basis of their patterns of behavior in the community. It is from an analysis of a sample of patient profiles from the Spring Grove State Hospital population that

Table 10.3

Factor Patterns Based on Analysis of Relatives' Ratings of 24 Schizophrenic Patients

Patient Type I - Agitated, Belligerent, Suspicious [a]

High Scores	Low Scores
Nervousness [b]	Bizarreness [b]
Belligerence	Withdrawal and Retardation
Hyperactivity	Anxiety
Negativism	Verbal Expansiveness
Suspiciousness	

Patient Type II - Withdrawn, Periodically Agitated

High Scores	Low Scores
Withdrawal and Retardation [b]	Remaining Clusters
Nervousness [b]	
Hyperactivity [b]	

Patient Type III - Acute Panic State

High Scores	Low Scores
Helplessness [b]	Negativism [b]
Nervousness [b]	Belligerence [b]
Anxiety [b]	Verbal Expansiveness
	Hyperactivity

Patient Type IV - Withdrawn, Helpless, Suspicious

High Scores	Low Scores
Suspiciousness [b]	Verbal Expansiveness [b]
Withdrawal and Retardation [b]	Anxiety
Helplessness [b]	Nervousness
	Bizarreness

Patient Type V - Agitated, Helpless

High Scores	Low Scores
Hyperactivity [b]	Suspiciousness
Helplessness	Anxiety
	Verbal Expansiveness
	Negativism

Patient Type VI - Agitated, Expansive, Bizarre, Suspicious

High Scores	Low Scores
Hyperactivity [b]	Belligerence [b]
Suspiciousness [b]	Helplessness
Verbal Expansiveness	Anxiety
Bizarreness	Withdrawal and Retardation
	Negativism

Note - Patients were randomly drawn from a sample of 200 at the Spring Grove State Hospital, Catonsville, Maryland. The data was provided by Dr. Mary Michaux, Research Department.

[a] Titles for types are based on interpretations of the patterns.

[b] One or more standard deviations above or below the profile mean for the patient type. Entries without the **b** are between .5 and 1 SD above or below the profile mean.

the typology was derived. Through a principal components analysis of the correlations among a sample of patient profiles randomly selected from a larger population, a set of prototypes was constructed. The sample of patients was relatively small (24)—but the clusters of patients were clear, and whether one approached this matrix with the more precise principal components analysis or a simpler form of cluster analysis, the result was the same, i.e. sets of clusters derived from the two procedures were very similar. The six patterns are presented in Table 10.3. Five have been extensively studied and we will refer only to these in the descriptions. There are three "paranoid" subtypes:

Type I.   An agitated, belligerent—fairly well integrated type.
Type IV. A withdrawn, helpless type.
Type VI. A more expansive, hostile but less integrated type.

There are two basically withdrawn types, one of which (II) is periodically agitated, and the other (IV), as mentioned, is helpless and paranoid. Type III appears to be more acute than the others in the sense that these patients are high on anxiety (panic), helplessness, nervousness, and bizarreness. The types would appear to make good clinical sense.

The more important question one is faced with here, however, is not how sensible the patient types look, or not even so much how the typology was derived (i.e. whether one develops the system on the basis of theory or finds the patterns empirically, or applies some elaborate statistical technique to the problem of which patients cluster together) but whether the typology is valid, whether the classes of patients really exist, and then, whether the classification system is useful, either theoretically or practically. It is these questions about validity which are more troublesome—from a conceptual standpoint—in this area than anything else, and for which there appear to be very limited guidelines.

THE CONCURRENT VALIDITY OF THE TYPOLOGY

If the typology is valid, if the types identified in this analysis of relative ratings really are discrete, then other observers ought to describe the different types as having different patterns of characteristics. In attempting to investigate the concurrent validity of the typology, we set the following questions:

(1) Will psychiatrists and psychologists, who subsequently see and rate these patients on the basis of a psychiatric interview, perceive the various types as manifesting different patterns of symptoms? If so, will the content and the pattern of the symptomatology described by the psychiatrists correspond to the description of the patient type identified by the relatives? In other words, do the psychiatrists and relatives appear to be describing the same types of patients?

(2) Will the nurses perceive the different patient types as manifesting different patterns of behavior on the ward? If so, will the nurses and relatives agree with regard to the pattern of behavior presented by a given patient type?

In the National Institute of Mental Health Collaborative Study of Drugs and Schizophrenia (1964), the availability of some 400 acute schizophrenic patients from nine hospitals made tests of these validity questions possible.

In accord with previously derived criteria, 62 per cent of the total sample of patients were assigned to one of the six types on the basis of the relative's rating inventory, which was completed at admission.* These patients were also interviewed during the first week of their hospital stay and an Inpatient Multidimensional Psychiatric Scale was completed by two raters, usually a psychiatrist and a psychologist. A profile of symptoms manifested during the initial clinical interview is then available for each patient. For each group in the relatives' typology a mean profile of symptoms as seen independently by psychiatrists and psychologists can be derived. Four of these patterns (mean profiles) are presented in Fig. 10.1.

The first question asked was whether the several types would be seen as manifesting different patterns of symptoms on the IMPS. The question of whether the patterns are different in shape can be answered through an application of the multivariate analysis of variance. An approximation of this procedure developed by

---

* The assignment of a patient to one of the types was accomplished by correlating (using the product-moment correlation) his profile with each of the six previously derived patient type patterns, and then assigning him to that category to which the profile-pattern correlation was highest. A patient was not assigned to a type category if the highest of the six profile-pattern correlations did not exceed the next highest by point-one.

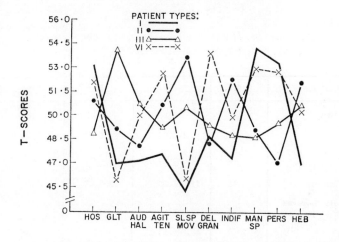

FACTORS: INPATIENT MULTIDIMENSIONAL PSYCHIATRIC SCALE

FIG. 10.1. Symptom patterns derived from psychiatric ratings of four patient types.

Greenhouse and Geisser (1959) was applied to the problem, and the results are presented in Table 10.4.

The interaction of patient types and measures will indicate whether the differences in profile shape are based on chance variation. The conservative test indicates that there is significant interaction beyond the 0.05 level of confidence. The profile shapes, in other words, are not parallel—i.e. the clinicians viewed the patterns of symptoms of the various groups, in the relative's typology, as different. In terms of whether the clinicians described the behavior of the types in ways similar to the relatives' descriptions, the answer is that for four of the types the corresponding descriptions are highly similar. Since the factors in the two rating scales, the Relative's Ratings and the Inpatient Multidimensional Psychiatric Scale, are different, this conclusion is necessarily based on a qualitative comparison of the factors and the items in the two inventories. But it is clear that the "well-integrated hyperactive, belligerent, paranoid" group described by the relatives (type I), are seen by the clinicians as prominent in "hostility, manic speech, and ideas of persecution", that the "withdrawn, periodically agitated type" (type II) is seen as predominantly "slower in speech and movement, and apathetic",

Table 10.4

Analysis of Variance of Psychiatric Symptom Ratings (IMPS Factors)
of Six Patient Types: Collaborative Study Sample

Source	d.f.	SS	MS	F
Scales (IMPS) [a]	9	8.55	.95	.01
Types	5	682.98	136.60	1.01
Individuals (within Types)	226	3,538.73	135.13	
Types X Scales	45	11,865.29	263.67	2.86[*] [b]
Individuals X Scales (within Types)	2034	187,750.73	92.31	
Total	2319	230,846.28		

[*] Significant at .05 level.

[a] The majority of items in three IMPS Factors, Disorientation, Delirium, and Memory Deficit, were rarely, if ever, used in describing this sample of patients. This resulted in extremely low scale scores for the large majority of the sample and minimal variability. The three scales were, therefore, deleted from the analysis.

[b] Using the conservative test the F ratio (Types X Scales) is significant at the .05 level. Degrees of freedom required adjustment to 5 and 226 because of the lack of independence of the scale variables. See Greenhouse and Geisser (1959) for rationale for statistical procedure.

and the "agitated, expansive, bizarre paranoid" group (type VI) is prominent on "delusions of grandeur, manic speech, and ideas of persecution". Two of the six types do not work out this well.

This then was one test of whether the types which were identified by relatives are generally observable to others. We have cross-validated these findings in a different population with very much the same results and feel that the associations are sufficiently clear.

With regard to question 2, a similar analysis was carried out using the set of measures derived from the nurses' ratings on the Ward Behavior Scale. The results of the analysis of variance, which are presented in Table 10.5, are similar to the results for the psychiatric ratings.

The interaction of types and measures is significant at the 0.01 level, indicating that the patterns presented by the types are not parallel, that they differ in shape. The patterns for the same four

Table 10.5

Analysis of Variance of Nurses' Ward Behavior Ratings (WBS Factors)
of Six Patient Types: Collaborative Study Sample

Source	d.f.	SS	MS	F
Scales	6	3.99	.67	.01
Types	5	1,817.79	363.56	1.82
Individuals (within Types)	222	44,278.99	199.46	
Types X Scales	30	9,698.22	323.27	4.16**
Individuals X Scales (within Types)	1332	103,623.05	77.80	
Total	1595	159,422.04		

** Conservative test (5 and 222 degrees of freedom) significant at .01 level.

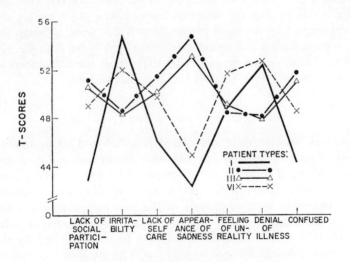

FACTORS: WARD BEHAVIOR RATING SCALE

FIG. 10.2. Behavioral patterns derived from nurses' ratings of
four patient types.

types are presented in Fig. 10.2. The prominent behavior for type I, the "agitated, belligerent, suspicious" group is "irritability" and "denial of illness". Type II, the "withdrawn, periodically agitated" patients are prominent on "appearance of sadness" and "confusion". What distinguishes these comparisons from those of the psychiatrists and relatives in Fig. 10.1, however, is the fact that the pattern for type III looks very much like that for type II, and the pattern for type VI, except for a general heightening of symptomatology, specifically in the social participation and confusion areas, is similar to that for type I. The patterns still make sense from the standpoint of translating from the relatives' to the ward nurses' descriptions—but the discreteness of the types is not as distinct on the Ward Behavior Scales results as on the IMPS. We would like to attribute this result in part to the fact that the factors which make up the Ward Behavior Scale are more global in nature, more experimental in quality, and not likely to be as sensitive to differences in patterns of behavior as the IMPS.

It might be expected, for example (after the fact), that since fewer factors are needed to account for the ward observers' ratings, that the observer and the scale are likely to be less discriminating in separating out types of behavior. Nevertheless, the results indicate that the finer differences among the types are not discriminated by the ward personnel with this scale, although the more pronounced differences among the types—for example, the socially obstreperous types (I and VI) versus the withdrawn or more depressed types (II and III), are discriminated.

PREDICTIVE VALIDITY OF THE TYPOLOGY

A final question to be considered here has to do with another kind of validity, one which has both theoretical and practical implications. The types are distinguished with regard to their varying patterns of manifest symptomatology and social behavior. If a treatment is administered to the patient group which has effects on certain kinds of behavior, then those patient types who manifest this kind of behavior ought to be more affected by the treatment than those types who do not. The question to be asked is whether the typology is predictive of response to treatment. It was tested in the context of the NIMH Collaborative Study. All patients in the study were randomly assigned to one of three phenothiazine (tranquilizing) drugs or placebo and treated for a period of six weeks. The treating psychiatrist, working under double blind conditions, was asked at the end of that time to indicate on a seven point scale the extent or lack of general improvement in the patient, i.e. from (1) "very much improved" through (4) "no change" to (7) "very much worse".

The data was subjected to a 5 (patient types) × 3 (drugs) analysis of variance which permitted a test of the significance of the differences among types with regard to response to drugs in general ("patient types" main effect) and possible differential

Table 10.6

Comparison of the Different Patient Types on Response to Drug Treatment

Patient Type	Mean Global Improvement [a]			Mean Across Three Drugs	Rank Order of Response
	Thioridazine	Fluphenazine	Chlorpromazine		
(N=19) Agitated, Belligerent, Suspicious	2.12	2.14	2.75	2.34	4
I (N=21) Withdrawn, Periodically Agitated	2.29	2.30	3.00	2.53	5
II (N=48) Acute Panic State	1.68	1.91	1.61	1.73	1
IV (N=19) Withdrawn, Helpless, Suspicious	3.00	1.88	2.00	2.29	3
I (N=24) Agitated, Expansive, Bizarre, Suspicious	1.83	2.00	2.08	1.97	2

Analysis of Variance [b]

Source	d.f.	F
Between Drugs	2	.764
Between Patient Types	4	3.099*
Interaction (Drugs x Types)	8	1.644
Error	116	
Total	130	

[a] Low score means more improvement.
[b] The method of unweighted means was used (Winer, 1962).
* Significant at .05 level.

reactions of the types to the several drugs (interaction of "types" and "drugs"). (Despite the large number of patients in the sample, it was necessary to exclude type V, because an insufficient number of patients were available in this category for the analysis. Further, since the interest in this analysis was in differential response to drugs, the placebo group was not included. In addition, the sample was reduced by a loss of some 8 per cent of the patients who for various reasons either did not complete the six weeks of treatment or for whom six week outcome data was not available.) The results of the analysis are presented in Table 10.6.

(1) The significant main effect for "patient types" indicates that the groups respond differently to drugs in general.

(2) The interaction of "patient types" and "drugs" is not significant, which indicates that there is no evidence as far as this general measure of improvement is concerned, that the "patient types" respond differentially to the several drugs.

The fact that the types do respond differently to the drugs as a group supports the contention of many clinicians in this field that the tranquilizing drugs are specific to certain symptom patterns rather than to schizophrenia in general. The difference is significant at the 0.05 level of confidence; the five types are ranked in order of therapeutic response in the last column of Table 10.6. The *"acute, panic state"* responds best; the *"withdrawn, periodically agitated"* group least to the drugs. Although not predicted before the experiment, the fact that the "acute, panic" group is most responsive to tranquilizing agents, is in agreement with what might have been expected from previous clinical theory and practice.

Multiple comparisons of pairs of "patient types" using the Newman–Keuls procedure (Winer, 1962), were carried out, and the difference in clinical response between these two types is found to be significant at the 0.05 level. The differences between the other pairs did not reach a statistically significant level.

So far it has been demonstrated that there is differential response to drugs among the five types; one type responds with significantly more improvement than another type.

Validation of the typology has taken two forms, then: First, a demonstration that behavioral patterns which identify the types are visible to others, which reassures us concerning their basic reality; second, an attempt to determine whether the system is pragmatically useful, whether it can predict response to treatment.

CONCLUDING COMMENT

In presenting this series of studies, we started by stressing the need for extending the descriptive-phenomenologic approach to psychopathology to the patient's behavior prior to his entrance into the hospital setting. In describing the method used, and the development of the typology, we thought it best to explore and to emphasize the relationships and the areas of overlap between findings in the two settings. It is important in the field of psychopathology to bring these bodies of information together because there is a basic need for straightforward, objective descriptive information about the overt behavior of schizophrenics.

At the same time, we are not satisfied that we fully comprehend the nature of these findings. In emphasizing the areas of overlap, there is the risk of not doing complete justice to the differences which obviously exist, both with regard to the several sets of dimensions which explain what is being observed in the different settings, and with regard to the potential that these several avenues of approach offer to our understanding of psychopathology.

There is no question that it will take some time to sort out the meaning of these various patterns of behavior in the community, which is why validity is such a central concern in these investigations.

Despite some differences in approach, the various patient classification systems which have arisen in this type of investigation, e.g. where the observers are lay people or professionals, appear to have a great deal in common, so that we ought to be getting closer to a basic descriptive framework. It is significant, for example, that the paranoid category, which accounts for one-half of all patients diagnosed as schizophrenic, has been separated into several specific behavioral types by more than one of the newer typologies.

We have not intended to imply, however, as we have indicated before (Katz and Cole, 1963), that classification at the descriptive level is some sort of ultimate goal in the field of psychopathology.

The main aims of this work are to extend information on what schizophrenic patients are like on a behavioral level, to classify them empirically along behavioral and symptomatic dimensions, and to determine whether the classification is predictive with regard to treatment response. A classification system at this level, if successful, should provide a more rational base for studies of uniformities in the genetic, historical, biochemical, and psycho-dynamic realms. To the extent that researchers in these areas can work with subtypes of schizophrenics who are behaviorally similar, the likelihood of finding uniformities and understanding dis-crepancies in these other spheres is that much greater. In order to have some impact on current thinking and clinical procedures, however, these new typologies require additional validation, both of a theoretical and a practical sort. The validation of "types", behavioral patterns, is more complicated than that of factors or of single variables, so that it is necessary to work out new approaches to problems of this sort as has been attempted in the present series of studies.

REFERENCES

BROVERMAN, D. M. Effects of score transformations in Q and R factor analysis techniques. *Psychological Review*, 1961, **68**, 68–80.

BURDOCK, E. I., HAKEREM, G., HARDESTY, A. S., and ZUBIN, J. *Ward Behavior Rating Scale.* New York Psychiatric Institute, 1959.

BURDOCK, E. I., HAKEREM, G., HARDESTY, A. S., and ZUBIN, J. A ward behavior rating scale for use with mental hospital patients. *Journal of Clinical Psychology*, 1960, **16**, 246–7.

BURT, C. Correlations between persons. *British Journal of Psychology*, 1937, **28**, 167–85.

CAFFEY, E. M., Jr., DIAMOND, L. S., FRANK, T. V., GRASBERGER, J. C., HERMAN, L., KLETT, C. J., and ROTHSTEIN, C. Discontinuation or reduction of chemotherapy in chronic schizophrenics. *Journal of Chronic Disease*, 1964, **17**, 347–58.

CATTELL, R. B. A note on correlation clusters and cluster search methods. *Psychometrika*, 1944, **9**, 169–84.

CATTELL, R. B. *The Description and Measurement of Personality.* New York: World Book, 1946.

CATTELL, R. B. The three basic factor-analytic designs—their inter-relations and derivatives. *Psychological Bulletin*, 1952, **49**, 499–520.

CATTELL, R. B. *Personality and Motivation Structure and Measurement.* New York: World Book Co., 1957.

CLYDE, D. J. *Manual for the Clyde Mood Scale.* Coral Gables: Biometric Laboratory, University of Miami, 1963.

COOLEY, W. W. and LOHNES, P. R. *Multivariate Procedures for the Behavioral Sciences.* New York, London: John Wiley, 1962.

CRONBACH, L. J. and GLESER, GOLDINE C. Assessing similarity between profiles. *Psychological Bulletin*, 1953, **50**, 456–73.

ELLSWORTH, R. B. and CLAYTON, W. H. Measurement of improvement in "mental illness". *Journal of Consulting Psychology*, 1959, **23**, 15–20.

EYSENCK, H. J. *The Scientific Study of Personality.* London: Routledge & Kegan Paul, 1952.

FISHER, R. A. The use of multiple measurements in taxonomic problems. *Annals of Eugenics*, 1936, **7**, 179–88.

FORGY, E. W. Detecting "natural" clusters of individuals. Paper read at Western Psychological Association meeting, Santa Monica, California, April 1963.

GILMOUR, J. S. L. A taxonomic problem. *Nature*, 1937, **139**, 1040–2.

GENGERELLI, J. A. A method for detecting subgroups in a population and specifying their membership. *Journal of Psychology*, 1963, **55**, 457–68.

GOLDBERG, S. C., COLE, J. O., and CLYDE, D. J. Factor analyses of ratings of schizophrenic behavior. *Psychopharmacology Service Center Bulletin*, 1963, **2**, 23–28.

GOLDBERG, S. C., KLERMAN, G. L., and COLE, J. O. Changes in schizophrenic psychopathology and ward behavior as a function of phenothiazine treatment. *British Journal of Psychiatry*, 1965, **111**, 120–33.

GREENHOUSE, S. W. and GEISSER, S. On methods in the analysis of profile data. *Psychometrika*, 1959, **24**, 95–112.

GUTTMAN, L. General theory and methods for matric factoring. *Psychometrika*, 1944, **9**, 1–16.

HARMAN, H. H. *Modern Factor Analysis*. Chicago: University of Chicago Press, 1960.

HARRIS, C. W. Characteristics of two measures of profile similarity. *Psychometrika*, 1955, **20**, 289–97.

HEINCKE, F. Naturgeschichte des herings. I die lokalformen und die wanderungen des herings in der Europaischen meeren. *Abhandlungen des Deutschen Seefischerei-Vereins*, 1898, **2**, 1–223.

HOLZINGER, K. J. and HARMAN, H. H. *Factor analysis*. Chicago: University of Chicago Press, 1941.

HOLTZMAN, W. H. Methodological issues in P technique. *Psychological Bulletin*, 1962, **59**, 248–56.

HONIGFELD, G., ROSENBLUM, M. P., BLUMENTHAL, I. J., LAMBERT, H. L., and ROBERTS, A. J. Behavioral improvement in the older schizophrenic patient: Drug and social therapies. *Journal of the American Geriatrics Society*, 1965, **13**, 57–71.

HONIGFELD, G. and KLETT, C. J. The nurses' observation scale for inpatient evaluation. *Journal of Clinical Psychology*, 1965, **21**, 65–71.

HORST, P. A simple method of rotating a centroid factor matrix to a simple structure hypothesis. *Journal of Experimental Education*, 1956, **24**, 231–7.

HORST, P. Multivariate models for evaluating change. In: Harris, C. W. (ed.). *Problems in Measuring Change*. Madison: University of Wisconsin Press, 1963.

KATZ, M. M. and COLE, J. O. A phenomenological approach to the classification of schizophrenic disorders. *Diseases of the Nervous System*, 1963, **24**, 147–54.

KATZ, M. M. and LYERLY, S. B. Methods of measuring adjustment and social behavior in the community: 1. Rationale, description, discriminative validity and scale development. *Psychological Reports*, 1963, **13**, 503–35.

LASKY, J. J., KLETT, C. J., CAFFEY, E. M., Jr., BENNETT, J. L., ROSENBLUM, M. P., and HOLLISTER, L. E. Drug treatment of schizophrenic patients: A comparative evaluation of chlorpromazine, chlorprothixene, fluphenazine, reserpine, thioridazine, and triflupromazine. *Diseases of the Nervous System*, 1962, **23**, 698–706.

LAZARSFELD, P. F. Chapters 10 and 11 in S. A. Stouffer *et al. Measurement and Prediction*. Princeton: Princeton University Press, 1950.

LINGOES, J. C. Multiple scalogram analysis: A set-theoretic model for analyzing dichotomous items. *Educational and Psychological Measurement*, 1963, **23**, 501–24.

LOEVINGER, JANE, GLESER, GOLDINE C. and DuBOIS, P. H. Maximizing the discriminating power of a multiple-score test. *Psychometrika*, 1953, **18**, 309–17.

LORR, M., O'CONNOR, J. P., and STAFFORD, J. W. The psychotic reaction profile. *Journal of Clinical Psychology*, 1960, **16**, 241–5.

LORR, M., McNAIR, D. M., KLETT, C. J., and LASKEY, J. J. Evidence of ten psychotic syndromes. *Journal of Consulting Psychology*, 1962, **26**, 185–9.

LORR, M. and O'CONNOR, J. P. Psychotic symptom patterns in a behavior inventory. *Educational and Psychological Measurement*, 1962, **22**, 139–46.

LORR, M., KLETT, C. J., McNAIR, D. M., and LASKY, J. J. *Inpatient Multidimensional Psychiatric Scale (Manual)*. Palo Alto: Consulting Psychologists Press, 1963.

LORR, M., KLETT, C. J., and McNAIR, D. M. *Syndromes of Psychosis*. New York: MacMillan, 1963.

LORR, M., KLETT, C. J., and McNAIR, D. M. Ward-observable psychotic behavior syndromes. *Educational and Psychological Measurement*, 1964, **24**, 291–300.

LORR, M. and KLETT, C. J. The constancy of the psychotic syndromes in men and women. *Journal of Consulting Psychology*, August 1965.

LUBIN, A. Linear and non-linear discriminating functions. *British Journal Psychology. Statistical Section*, 1950, **3**, 90–103.

LUNNENBORG, C. E., Jr. *Dimensional Analysis, Latent Structure and the Problem of Patterns*. Seattle: University of Washington, 1959.

McNAIR, D. M., LORR, M., and HEMINGWAY, P. Further evidence for syndrome-based psychotic types. *Archives General Psychiatry*, 1964, **11**, 368–76.

McQUITTY, L. L. Pattern analysis illustrated in classifying patients and normals. *Educational and Psychological Measurement*, 1954, **14**, 598–604.

McQUITTY, L. L. Elementary linkage analysis for isolating orthogonal and oblique types and typal relevancies. *Educational and Psychological Measurement*, 1957, **17**, 207–29.

McQUITTY, L. L. Hierarchical linkage analysis for the isolation of types. *Educational and Psychological Measurement*, 1960, **20**, 55–67.

McQUITTY, L. L. Hierarchical syndrome analysis. *Educational and Psychological Measurement*, 1960, **20**, 293–304.

McQUITTY, L. L. Typal analysis. *Educational and Psychological Measurement*, 1961, **21**, 677–96.

McQUITTY, L. L. Rank order typal analysis. *Educational and Psychological Measurement*, 1963, **23**, 55–61.

McQUITTY, L. L. Capabilities and improvements of linkage analysis as a clustering method. *Educational and Psychological Measurement*, 1964, **24**, 441–56.

MEEHL, P. E. Configural Scoring. *Journal of Consulting Psychology*, 1950, **14**, 165–71.

MEFFERD, R. B. Jr., MORAN, L. J., and KIMBLE, J.P., Jr. Use of a factor analytic technique in the analysis of long term repetitive measurements made upon a single schizophrenic patient. Paper presented at a symposium on multivariate analysis of repeated measurements on the same individual, American Psychological Association, Washington, D.C., September, 1958.

MOSELEY, E. C. Predicting response to phenothiazines—the right drug for the right patient. Paper read at the Tenth Annual VA Research Conference, Cooperative Studies in Psychiatry, New Orleans, March 1965.

NATIONAL INSTITUTE OF MENTAL HEALTH—PSYCHOPHARMACOLOGY SERVICE CENTER COLLABORATIVE STUDY GROUP. Phenothiazine treatment in acute schizophrenia, *Archives of General Psychiatry*, 1964, **10**, 246–61.

NEEDHAM, R. M. *The Theory of Clumps II*. Cambridge: Cambridge Language Research Unit, 1961.

NUNNALLY, J. The analysis of profile data. *Psychological Bulletin*, 1962, **59**, 311–19.

OVERALL, J. E. and HOLLISTER, L. E. Computer procedures for psychiatric classification. *Journal of American Medical Association*, 1964, **187**, 538–88.

OVERALL, J. E. and GORHAM, D. R. Factor space D^2 analysis applied to the study of changes in schizophrenic symptomatology during chemotherapy. *Journal of Clinical and Experimental Psychopathology and Quarterly Review of Psychiatry and Neurology*, 1960, **21**, 187–95.

OVERALL, J. E. and GORHAM, D. R. A pattern probability model for the classification of psychiatric patients. *Behavioral Science*, 1963, **8**, 108–16.

PARKER, RHODES, A. F. and NEEDHAM, R. M. *The Theory of Clumps*. Cambridge: Cambridge Language Research Unit, 1960.

PEARSON, K. On the coefficient of racial likeness. *Biometrika*, 1926, **18**, 105–17.

PENROSE, L. S. Distance, size and shape. *Annals of Eugenics*, 1954, **18**, 337–43.

PLATZ, A. Drug action in chronic schizophrenic subtypes. Paper read at the Tenth Annual VA Research Conference, Cooperative Studies in Psychiatry, New Orleans, March 1965.

RAO, C. R. and SLATER, P. Multivariate analysis applied to differences between neurotic groups. *British Journal of Psychology. Statistical Section*, 1949, **2**, 17.

RAO, C. R. *Advanced Statistical Methods in Biometric Research*. New York: John Wiley, 1952.

ROGERS, D. J. and TANIMOTO, T. T. A computer program for classifying plants. *Science*, 1960, **132**, 1115–18.

ROSS, J. The relation between test and person factors. *Psychological Review*, 1963, **70**, 432–43.

RUMKE, H. C. Contradictions in the concepts of schizophrenia. *Comprehensive Psychiatry*, 1960, **1**, 331–7.

RUMKE, C. L. Variability of results in differential cell counts in blood smears. *Triangle*, 1960, **4**, 154–8.

RYDER, R. G. Profile factor analysis and variable factor analysis. *Psychological Reports*, 1964, **15**, 119–27.

SAUNDERS, D. R. and SCHUCMAN, H. Syndrome analysis: An efficient procedure for isolating meaningful subgroups in a non-random sample of a population. Paper read at Third Annual Psychonomic Society Meeting, St. Louis, Missouri, September 1962.

SAWREY, W. L., KELLER, L., and CONGER, J. J. An objective method of grouping profiles by distance functions and its relation to factor analysis. *Educational and Psychological Measurement*, 1960, **20**, 651–73.

SLATER, P. The general relationship between test factors and person factors. *Nature*, 1958, **181**, 1225–6.

SOKAL, R. R. and SNEATH, P. H. A. *Principles of Numerical Taxonomy*. San Francisco: W. H. Freeman, 1963.

STEPHENSON, W. Some observations on Q technique. *Psychological Bulletin*, 1952, **49**, 483–98.

THORNDIKE, R. L. Who belongs in the family? *Psychometrika*, 1953, **18**, 267–71.

TRYON, B. *Cluster analysis*. Ann Arbor: Edwards Brothers, 1939.

TUCKER, L. R. Implications of factor analysis of three-way matrices for measurement of change. In: Harris, C. W. (ed.), *Problems in Measuring Change*, University of Wisconsin Press, Madison, Wis., 1963.

WINER, B. J. *Statistical Principles in Experimental Design*. New York: McGraw-Hill, 1962.

WITTENBORN, J. R. Symptom patterns in a group of mental hospital patients. *Journal of Consulting Psychology*, 1951, **15**, 290–302.

ZUBIN, J., FLEISS, J., and BURDOCK, E. I. A method for fractionating a population into homogeneous subgroups. Unpublished paper, 1963.

ZUBIN, J. Socio-biological types and methods for their isolation. *Psychiatry*, 1938, **1**, 237–47.

AUTHOR INDEX

238

SUBJECT INDEX